Six Plays

Luigi Pirandello

Translated by Felicity Firth,
Robert Rietti, John Wardle, Donald Watson
and Carlo Ardito

CALDER

CALDER PUBLICATIONS
an imprint of

ALMA BOOKS LTD
3 Castle Yard
Richmond
Surrey TW10 6TF
United Kingdom
www.calderpublications.com

The translations of 'Six Characters in Search of an Author', 'Henry IV'
(revised for the present edition), 'Caps and Bells', 'Honest as Can Be',
'The Vice' and 'A Dream – or Is It' first published in *Collected Plays* (Vols.
1–4) by John Calder (Publishers) Ltd, 1987–1996, and reprinted in *Plays*
Vol. 1 by Alma Classics (2011, repr. 2015).

This edition first published by Calder Publications in 2019

Translations © the relevant translators, 2019

Cover design by Will Dady

Printed in Great Britain by CPI Group (UK) Ltd, Croydon CR0 4YY

ISBN: 978-0-7145-4849-4

Contents

Six Plays

SIX CHARACTERS IN SEARCH OF AN AUTHOR

Sei personaggi in cerca d'autore (1921)

Translated by Felicity Firth

Author's Introduction

FOR A GREAT MANY YEARS NOW, though it seems no time at all, I have been assisted in my artistic labours by a sprightly young helpmate, whose work remains as fresh today as when she first entered my service.

Her name is Imagination.

There is something malicious and subversive about her, as her preference for dressing in black might suggest; indeed, her style is generally felt to be bizarre. What people are less ready to believe is that in everything she does there is a seriousness of purpose and an unvarying method. She delves into her pocket and brings out a jester's jingling cap, rams it onto her flaming coxcomb of a head and is gone. She is off to somewhere different every day. Her great delight is to search out the world's unhappiest people and to bring them home for me to turn into stories and novels and plays; men, women and children who have got themselves into every conceivable kind of fix, whose plans have miscarried and whose hopes have been betrayed; people, in fact, who are often very disturbing to deal with.

Well, some years ago, this assistant, this Imagination of mine, had the regrettable inspiration, or it could have been the ill-fated whim, to bring to my door an entire family; where or how she got hold of them I have no idea, but she reckoned that their story would furnish me with a subject for a magnificent novel.

I found myself confronted by a man of about fifty, wearing a dark jacket and light trousers, grim-visaged, with a look of irritability and humiliation in his eyes. With him was a poor woman in widow's weeds holding two children by the hand, a four-year-old girl on one side and a boy of not much more than ten on the other. Next came a rather loud and immodest young woman, also in black, which in her case contrived to look vulgarly dressy and suggestive. She was a-quiver with a brittle, biting anger, clearly directed against the mortified old man and against a youth of about twenty who stood detached from the others, wrapped up in himself, apparently contemptuous of the whole party. So here they were, the Six Characters, just as they appear on the stage at the beginning of the play. And they set about telling me the whole sad series of events, partly in turns, but often speaking all together, cutting in on each other, shouting each other down. They yelled their explanations at me, flung their unruly passions in my face, just as they do in the play with the luckless Producer.

Can any author ever explain how or why a character came to be born in his imagination? The mystery of artistic creation is the mystery of birth itself. A woman in love may desire to become a mother, but this desire by itself, however intense, will not make her one. One fine day she finds she is to be a mother, but she has no precise indication of when this came about. In the same way an artist, as he lives, takes into himself numerous germs of life, and he, too, is completely unable to say how or why at a given moment one of these vital germs gets lodged in his imagination to become in just the same way a living creature, though on a higher plane of life, above the vicissitudes of everyday existence.

I can only say that, having in no way searched them out, I found myself confronted by six living, palpable, audibly breathing human beings: the same six characters you now see upon the stage. They stood before me waiting, each one nursing his own particular torment, bound together by the mode of their birth and the intertwining of their fortunes, waiting for me to usher them into the world of art and make of their persons, their passions and their adventures a novel or drama, or at least a short story.

They had been born alive and they were asking to live.

Now I have to explain that for me as a writer it has never been enough to portray a man or a woman, however individual or exceptional, just for the sake of portraying them; happy or sad, I cannot just tell a story for the sake of telling it or describe a landscape simply as a creative exercise.

There are writers, quite a lot of writers, who like doing this. It satisfies them, and they ask no more. They are by nature what one might properly term historical writers.

But others go further. They feel a deep-seated inward urge to concern themselves only with persons, happenings or scenes which are permeated with what one might call a particular sense of life and so with some sort of universal significance. These, properly, are philosophical writers.

I have the misfortune to belong to this second category.

I detest the kind of symbolic art where all spontaneous movement is suppressed and where the representation is reduced to mechanistic allegory; it is self-defeating and misleading; once a work is given an allegorical slant you are as good as saying that it is only to be taken as a fairy tale; in itself it contains no factual or imaginative truth; it is simply there to demonstrate some sort of moral truth. This kind of allegorical symbolism will never answer the innermost need of the philosophical writer, apart from certain occasions where a fine irony is intended, as in Ariosto for instance. Allegorical symbolism springs from conceptual thought; it is concept, recreated as image, or striving to recreate itself as image. The philosophical writer, on the other hand, is looking for value and meaning in the image itself, while allowing the image to retain its independent validity and artistic wholeness.

Now, however hard I tried, I simply could not find this kind of meaning in the six characters. Consequently I decided there was no point in bringing them to life.

I kept thinking: I have given my readers enough trouble with all my hundreds of stories; why heap more trouble upon them with the sad story of this unhappy lot?

And so thinking I put them out of my mind. Or rather, I made every effort to do so.

But one does not give birth to a character for nothing.

Creatures of my mind, those six were already living a life which was their own and mine no longer, a life I was no longer in a position to refuse them.

And so it was that, while I went on grimly determined to expunge them from my consciousness, they, who by now had almost completely broken free of their narrative context, fictional characters magically transported outside the pages of a book, were carrying on with their own lives. They would pick on certain moments of my day to appear before me in the solitude of my study, and one by one, or two at a time, they would try to entice me, suggesting various scenes I might write or describe and how to get the best out of them, or pointing out unusual aspects of their story which people might find particularly novel or interesting, and so it went on.

Each time, for a moment, I would let myself be won over, and whenever I relented a little they would draw strength from my weakness and come back with fresh arguments and I would find myself near to being convinced. And so, as it became increasingly difficult for me to get rid of them, their task of tempting me became increasingly easy. There came a point where they had become a positive obsession. Then suddenly I hit on a way out.

Why not write a play, I thought, based on the unprecedented case of an author who refuses to allow a certain set of characters to live, and the plight of these characters who, being fully alive in his imagination, cannot reconcile themselves to being excluded from the world of art? They have already detached themselves from me; they have their own life; they have acquired speech and movement; by their own efforts, by struggling against me for their lives, they have emerged as fully-fledged dramatic characters, autonomous and articulate. They already see themselves as such; they have learnt to defend themselves against me; they are capable of defending themselves against anyone. Well then, why not let them go where dramatic characters usually go to live: put them on a stage. And see what happens.

And that is what I did. And what came out of it was an inevitable hotchpotch of tragedy, comedy, fantasy and realism in a completely original, and extraordinarily complex humoristic situation: that of a drama willing itself to be staged, determined at all costs to find a means of expression in the autonomous, living, speaking characters who embody it and suffer it in their inmost selves, and of the comedy resulting from the abortive effort at improvised theatrical realization. The surprise, first of all, on the part of the wretched company of actors, engaged in a daytime rehearsal of a play on a stage stripped bare of flats and scenery; surprise and blank incredulity on being faced by the six who introduce themselves as characters in search of an author and then this instinctive quickening of interest when the Mother in her black veil suddenly collapses in a faint and they get a glimpse of the drama encompassed by her and the other members of this extraordinary family, a dark ambiguous drama which comes crashing unannounced onto an empty stage in no way prepared to receive it and then the gradual intensification of their interest as the conflicting passions explode in turn, the Father's, then the Stepdaughter's, the Son's and the poor Mother's; passions, as I say, which vie to do each other down with a tragic lacerating fury.

And here it is, the universal meaning previously sought in vain in my six characters. They have found it; by going onto the stage by themselves they have uncovered it in themselves, in the frenzy of the desperate battle waged by each one against the others, and by all of them against the Producer and actors who do not understand them.

Unintentionally, inadvertently, each one of them, defending himself in a state of considerable mental agitation against the recriminations of the others, shows himself to be tormented by the same fierce sources of suffering that have racked my own spirit for years: the delusion of reciprocal understanding hopelessly based on the hollow abstraction of words; the multiple nature of every human personality, given all the possible ways of being inherent in each one of us; and finally the tragic built-in conflict between ever-moving, ever-changing life, and the immutability of form which fixes it.

The six characters give the impression of being on different planes, as if they were not all realized to the same degree. This is not just because some have leading roles and others have supporting ones; that would be a basic matter of the structural perspective proper to any narrative or dramatic work. Nor, given their purpose, can they be said to be incompletely formed. All six are at the same point of artistic realization; all six are on the same plane of reality, the imaginative plane on which my play is set. But the Father, the Stepdaughter and even the Son are realized as Mind or Spirit; the Mother is realized as Nature; and the last two are realized as "presences": the Boy who is an onlooker but for his single gesture, and the completely static Little Girl. This places the characters in a new perspective. An instinctive prompting had told me I must make some of them appear to be more fully realized artistically and others less so; others, again, were to be represented by the barest outline; there, simply, as part of what happens in the story. The most alive, the most fully realized, are the Father and the Stepdaughter; these two are the natural leaders who dominate the play, dragging along behind them the practically dead weight of the others: the demurring Son, the submissive, suffering Mother, and on either side of her the two children who consist of little more than their appearance and have to be led by the hand.

This was the point. They had to appear at the exact stage of development each had reached in the author's imagination at the moment when he decided to be rid of them.

Thinking back on it now, it seems little short of a miracle that I intuitively sensed the necessity for this, blindly hit on the solution with my new perspective, and actually made it work. And indeed the play was conceived quite literally in one of those flashes of imaginative illumination when all the elements of the spirit are miraculously in tune and work together in God-given concert.

It would be quite impossible for any human brain, coming at it cold, however strenuous its endeavours, to fathom and fulfil all the demands made by the form of this play. And this is why the following explanations of the play's sum and substance are not to be taken as an apologia for preconceived authorial intentions, dating from the outset of composition, but must be looked on as discoveries which I have been able to make since writing it, returning to it with a mind refreshed.

I wanted to show six characters who are looking for an author. The play cannot be performed because the author they are looking for is missing; so instead we have the comedy of their abortive search, with all the tragic overtones which stem from the fact of their having been rejected.

Can it be done? How do you represent a character you have rejected? Obviously you can only give him expression once he has taken shape in your imagination. And this is exactly how the six characters took shape. They were fully realized in my imagination as rejects: in search of another author.

I must make clear what it is that I have rejected: not the characters in themselves, obviously, but their drama, doubtless of paramount interest to them, but which did not interest me in the slightest, for the reasons I have already given.

But think what your drama means to you if you are a character.

If you are a creature of art or of the imagination, your drama is your means of existence. You exist as a character only in the context of, and by reason of, your drama. The drama is the character's *raison d'être*, his vital function; without it he would cease to be.

In dealing with the six characters, I accepted their being, while rejecting their reason for being. I isolated the organism and asked of it, not its original function but a different, more complex function, in which the original one was no more than one factor amongst others. This created a terrible and desperate situation, especially for the Father and the Stepdaughter, who crave life more intensely than the others, and have a fuller awareness of their status as characters, a status which gives them an absolute need of a drama, their own drama, of course, the only one they can imagine for themselves, but which they have seen rejected. It is an "impossible" situation, one which they feel they must escape from at all costs; their life or death depends on it. It is true that I provided them with another *raison d'être*, another function, the one offered by the "impossible" situation, the drama of being rejected characters in search of an author. But having had a life of their own already, the idea of this new *raison d'être* was way beyond their comprehension. Never could they imagine that this might now be their true essential function and the condition of their existence. If someone were to tell them this, they would simply not believe it. It is impossible to believe that our sole reason for living lies in a torment which we find both unjust and inexplicable.

In the light of all this I cannot imagine how my critics justify their objection to the character of the Father on the grounds that he oversteps the bounds of his function as a character and usurps, at times, the role of author. I have a gift for understanding those who do not understand me, and this tells me that the objection arises from the fact that the character expresses as his own a mental anguish which is recognizably mine. Which is a perfectly natural thing and of absolutely no significance. Quite apart from the fact that the Father's mental anguish springs from causes which are worlds away from the drama of my own personal circumstances, and is suffered and lived through for his reasons and not mine, a consideration which alone destroys the validity of the criticism, I would like to point out a distinction. There is a clear difference between my own inherent mental anguish which I can quite legitimately reflect in a character, as an organic part of him, and the activity engaged in by my mind in the creation of this work, the activity which has as its end product the drama of the six characters in search of an author. Now if the Father were collaborating in this activity, if he were actually helping to create this play about being an authorless character, then, and only then, would it be fair to say that he was usurping the author's role and open to criticism on those grounds. But the Father has not created his own status as "character in search of an author"; he suffers it. He suffers it as an inexplicable disaster and as a situation to be rebelled against and rectified with every resource he can muster. So this is what he is then, a "character in search of an author" purely and simply, even if he does claim my mental anguish as his own. If he were collaborating in the author's act of creation, he would have no problem in understanding the disaster which has befallen him; he would see himself as a viable character, conceived, certainly, as a rejected character, but the product of a poet's imagination like any other. He would then have no reason to agonize over his desperate search for someone to confirm and formulate his existence as a character. I mean, he would accept quite happily the reason for being his author has given him, and stop worrying about any he might give himself; he could snap his fingers at the Producer and his troupe instead of regarding them as a lifeline.

There is one character who is completely untroubled by this need simply to live, to live for the sake of living. It never occurs to her that she is not alive. It has never crossed her mind to wonder how she is alive, by what means or in what sense. She has no notion that she is a character because she is never, even momentarily, outside her "part". She does not know she has a "part".

Her unawareness is a natural part of her. Her role as Mother requires her to be close to nature; it does not demand any mental exertion; she does not exist as mind; she lives in a perpetual state of unresolved emotion which renders her incapable of realizing what she is, of knowing she is a character. But even so, she too is searching for an author in her own way and for her own reasons. At one point she seems glad to have been brought along to meet the Producer. Is it because she hopes he can give her life? No: it is because she hopes he will make her perform a scene with her son, into which she herself would put life, her own life, all that she can of it. But it is a scene which does not exist. It has never taken place and never could. Her hope of playing it shows how totally unaware she is that she is a character and of the limitations of the life available to her, fixed and predetermined in every moment, every gesture, every word.

She turns up on the stage with the other characters, but without any idea of what they are making her do. She obviously has her own view of the manic desire for life which possesses both her husband and her daughter and is the reason for her being here at all: as far as her tormenting and tormented spouse is concerned, this is just another of his unusual, weird and wonderful fixations; in her poor misguided daughter's case, she is filled with sheer horror at what she sees as fresh evidence of wantonness and rebellion. The Mother is completely passive. Everything about her circumstances, her life and what she thinks of it all is conveyed by the others; only once does she contradict them, and that is when her maternal instinct rises and rebels and she feels bound to explain that she never wanted to abandon either her son or her husband; her son was taken from her and her husband forced her to go. But she is simply setting the factual record straight; her knowledge and understanding are nil.

She is, in essence, Nature: Nature fixed and perceived as Mother.

This character did afford me one satisfaction which was new and must not be forgotten. Nearly all my critics, having in the past indiscriminately labelled my characters as peculiarly and irredeemably "inhuman", have had the goodness to say "with real pleasure" of this one, that here at last my imagination has produced a truly human figure. The reason for their compliment I think is this: that the poor old Mother, being all Nature, all Mother, and completely tied in her behaviour by her equation with this role, with no opportunity for the free exercise of the mind, emerges more or less as a chunk of flesh, fully alive in all her maternal functions: procreating; feeding, tending and loving her young, but with no need whatsoever to exercise her brain. And in this she is seen to be the realization of the true and perfect "human type". This must be so, since there appears to be no attribute of the human organism more superfluous than the mind.

But the critics, in spite of their nice compliment, have pretty well dismissed the Mother without exploring in any depth the complex of poetic values represented by this character in the play. I can grant that she is a very human figure because she is mindless and so is either quite unaware of being what she is or simply does not question it. But the fact that she does not know she is a character does not stop her being one. And in my play, this is her drama. And its most vital expression comes leaping out of her in her cry to the Producer when he is trying to make her realize that it has all happened already, and there is no cause now to shed any more tears, and she cries out: "No, it's happening now! It's happening all the time! My agony isn't made up! I am living my agony constantly, every moment; I am alive and it is alive and it keeps coming back, again and again, as fresh as the first time." She feels this, but she does not know that she feels it; it is experienced as something inexplicable, but felt in such a terrible way that it does not even occur to her that it is something that needs explaining, either to herself or to the others. She feels it, full stop. She feels it as pain and it comes straight out as pain in her cry. This is her way of giving utterance to the fixedness of life, which torments the Father and the Stepdaughter in quite a different way. These two are Mind where the Mother is Nature. Mind either rebels against fixity or seeks to exploit it; Nature, unless stirred up by sense, responds to it with tears.

The inherent conflict between the movement of life and the fixity of form is an inexorable condition not only of the spiritual order but of the physical order as well. Life can only come about by fixing itself in our corporeal form; it then proceeds to kill that form. Nature mourns this fixity in the irreversible and relentless process of the body's ageing. The Mother's mourning is similarly passive and perpetual. My device of giving this inherent human conflict three different faces in the play, of embodying it in three separate but simultaneous dramas, enables it to make its fullest impact. And what is more, the Mother's words are a declaration of the unparalleled power of artistic form – the only form which does not constrain or destroy life and which life does not destroy – in her cry to the Producer. If the Father and the Stepdaughter were to start all over again and re-enact their scene a hundred thousand times, her cry would still be uttered precisely at that point; it would ring out over and over again at the precise moment demanded by the life of the work of art: unchanging and unchangeable in its form, but not in any way a mechanical repetition or refrain, wrung from her by external pressure, but every time quite unexpected, bursting out afresh into new life, preserved for eternity in its imperishable living form. In just the same way, whenever we open the book, we shall always find the live Francesca confessing her sweet sin to Dante, and even if we go back again and again and read the passage a hundred thousand times, then, again and again, a hundred thousand times Francesca will speak her words, never in mechanical repetition, but every time as if for the first time, with such animated and unpremeditated passion that every time Dante will swoon in response. All living things, because they have life, have form, and for that reason must die: except the work of art, which lives in fact for ever, in that it is form itself.

The birth of a creature of the human imagination is the step across the threshold separating nothingness from eternity. This birth may sometimes be brought about quite suddenly, precipitated by necessity. While a play is gestating in the imagination, if a new character is needed to supply some necessary speech or action, he is born to order, exactly as required. This is the manner of Madame Pace's birth among the six characters, and it takes our breath away; it is like some convincing illusionist's trick. But it isn't a trick; it is a birth. The new character is alive, not because she was alive already, but because she has been successfully brought into being after the manner of her kind, as a "necessary" character. Theatrically the result is a break, a sudden change in the level of reality, because such a birth can only take place in the mind of a writer; it can't happen on the boards of a stage. Before anyone has realized what has happened, I have moved the scene: I have instantaneously shifted it back into my imagination without removing it from the spectators' gaze. I have set before them, not the stage now, but my own imagination in the guise of that stage, caught in the act of creation. This unforeseen and autonomous shifting of a given phenomenon from one plane of reality to another is a sort of miracle, rather like what happens when the statue of a saint starts to move; at that precise moment you cannot say that the statue is made of wood or stone. Mine of course is not an arbitrary miracle. The stage itself is fluid; in becoming the vehicle for the imaginative reality of the six characters it cannot exist as a fixed unalterable entity in its own right, just as, indeed, there is nothing established and preconceived anywhere in this play: everything here is in the making, shifting, experimental and unpremeditated. Even the place, the site of all this desperate transmutation backwards and forwards of formless, form-seeking life, has a shifting level of reality, and reaches a point where it changes organically.

When I first had the idea of making Madame Pace come into being before my eyes on the stage, I sensed that I could do it and I did it. If I had realized that her birth was going to have this effect of suddenly, silently, almost imperceptibly upsetting and recasting the scene's plane of reality, I surely would not have done it; the apparent illogicality of the idea would have restrained me. And the beauty of the work would have been lost. I was saved from delivering this deathblow by the sheer fervour of my inspiration, for contrary to all appearances and the misleading requirements of logic, the fantastic birth of Madame Pace is dictated by necessity and is intimately and mysteriously related to the whole life of the play.

The allegation that she does not quite come off because of the quasi-Romantic, unstructured and chaotic manner of her composition is to my mind absurd.

I understand what makes people say this. It is because the inner drama involving my six characters appears to be presented as a kind of free-for-all, without any co-ordinating pattern: there is no logical development, no sequential order to events. This is quite true. Had I searched until kingdom come I could not have found a method which was more harum-scarum, more weird, more arbitrary and complex, and indeed more Romantic, than the one I have used to present the inner drama of the six characters. All this is true, but I have not in fact presented that drama: the one I have presented is an entirely different one – need I repeat it – in which among other delights available to the discerning spectator is to be found a modest satire on Romantic procedures. This can be seen in the heated struggle engaged in by my characters to eclipse each other as they act out their roles in one drama, while all the time I have cast them in quite a different one of which they are oblivious; their tempestuous emotionalism which might stamp them as Romantic is thereby deprived of any solid basis and is placed on a humoristic footing. And the characters' own drama emerges in my work in the only way it can, not in the form it would have taken had I accepted it as a play in its own right, but as a rejected play, a bare "situation", developed spasmodically, in hints, in sudden rushes, in violent foreshortenings, in chaos and confusion: it is constantly interrupted, deflected, made to contradict itself; it is not even lived by two of its characters and is repudiated by another.

There is one character in fact, the Son, who repudiates the drama which makes him a "character", and derives his whole dramatic weight and significance not from his role in the inner play – in this he hardly appears at all – but from his role in the play which I have made about it. Indeed he is the only one who exists exclusively as a "character in search of an author"; the author he is looking for is not a playwright. This too was something which could not have been done in any other way. The character's attitude is absolutely basic to my conception of him, just as it is absolutely logical that he should add to the disorder and confusion of the situation by introducing yet another note of Romantic conflict.

It was this natural organic chaos that I had to put on the stage, and the staging of chaos does not mean at all the same thing as chaotic staging in the Romantic manner. My presentation is perfectly clear, straightforward and orderly; it can hardly be called confused when all the audiences of the world have had no difficulty whatever in grasping the work's plot, characters and differing levels of fantasy and reality, drama and comedy, and when its finer subtleties are readily perceived by those who look more closely.

Great must be the confusion of tongues among men if this kind of criticism can find utterance. But if the confusion of tongues outside is great, equally great is the perfect inward law which, followed to the letter, makes of my play a classic model in forbidding the use of words at its catastrophe. Just at the point when all have finally understood that life cannot be created through artifice, and that the six characters' drama cannot be played without an author to quicken it with spirit, the Producer, full of vulgar curiosity about how the story ends, gets the Son to give a blow-by-blow account of the sequence of events; the catastrophe explodes brutally and uselessly – it makes no sense and needs no human words – with the detonation of a firearm on the stage, cutting into and dissolving the sterile experiment of characters and actors, apparently without the aid of the poet.

The poet meanwhile, without their knowledge, has been biding his time, looking on as if from a distance throughout their tentative struggles, and waiting to make of these the very substance of a work of his own.

– *Luigi Pirandello*

The Characters

THE FATHER
THE MOTHER
THE STEPDAUGHTER
THE SON
THE BOY (*non-speaking*)
THE LITTLE GIRL (*non-speaking*)
MADAME PACE (*conjured into being in the course of the play*)

The Company

THE PRODUCER AND DIRECTOR OF THE COMPANY
THE LEADING ACTRESS
THE LEADING ACTOR
THE SECOND ACTRESS
THE YOUNG ACTRESS
THE YOUNG ACTOR
OTHER ACTORS AND ACTRESSES
THE STAGE MANAGER
THE PROMPTER
THE PROPERTY MAN
THE CHIEF STAGEHAND
THE PRODUCER'S SECRETARY
THE COMMISSIONAIRE
STAGEHANDS AND THEATRE STAFF

Daytime: the stage of a theatre.

N.B. *The play is not divided into acts and scenes. It will be interrupted twice: once, though without a curtain, when the* PRODUCER *and the* FATHER *withdraw to outline the scenario and the* ACTORS *leave the stage, and a second time when the* CHIEF STAGEHAND *lowers the curtain by mistake.*

The first sight that greets the audience on entering the theatre is the stage in its ordinary workaday guise. The curtain is up, the stage is empty, almost dark, and devoid of any items of scenery. This is to give us the impression, right from the start, that all we see is quite impromptu.

Two small flights of steps, one right and one left, link the stage to the auditorium.

On the stage the top of the prompter's box has been removed and lies shoved to one side.

On the other side, downstage, and facing away from the audience, are the working table and folding chair of the Producer-cum-Company Manager. Two other small tables of different sizes and various chairs are dotted about, available for the rehearsal if needed. There are chairs again right and left for the actors' use, and at the back somewhere, just visible, a piano.

As the house lights are lowered the CHIEF STAGEHAND *in blue overalls comes through a doorway onto the stage. He has a tool bag slung from his belt. He picks up some lengths of wood in a corner, brings them downstage and kneels to nail them together. The sound of his hammering brings the* STAGE MANAGER *running from the direction of the dressing rooms.*

STAGE MANAGER: What do you think you're doing?

CHIEF STAGEHAND: What does it look like? I'm banging this nail in.

STAGE MANAGER: Now? (*He looks at his watch*.) It's gone half-past ten. The producer will be here in a minute to rehearse.

CHIEF STAGEHAND: Yes, well. I've got a job to do an' all!

STAGE MANAGER: Maybe you have, mate, but not now.

CHIEF STAGEHAND: And when might you suggest?

STAGE MANAGER: Well, not just at the moment; a rehearsal's about to start. Come on, clear up all this clobber and let me get the set ready for Act Two of *The Rules of the Game*.

(*The* CHIEF STAGEHAND, *with much grumbling and muttering, collects up his wood and departs. In the meantime the members of the company,* ACTORS *and* ACTRESSES, *begin to assemble on the stage, wandering on in ones and twos. There are nine or ten of them, as required for today's rehearsal of Pirandello's The Rules of the Game. As they arrive they exchange "good mornings" with each other and with the* STAGE MANAGER. *Some go off to their dressing rooms: others, including the* PROMPTER, *with the rolled-up script tucked under his arm, stay chatting on the stage waiting for the* PRODUCER *to arrive and start the rehearsal. They sit or stand in groups, smoking, grumbling about their parts, reading out snippets from the odd theatre magazine.* ACTORS *as well as* ACTRESSES *should be dressed in cheerful clothes, light in tone, and this first improvised scene should be very lively and entirely natural. At one point one of them could sit at the piano and strum a dance tune to which the younger ones could dance.*)

STAGE MANAGER (*clapping his hands to call them to order*): Right! That's enough now! Come on! The Producer's here!

(*Song and dance are immediately broken off. The* ACTORS *turn to look into the auditorium as the* PRODUCER, *who is also the Director of the Company, enters from the back of the house and makes his way down the gangway. He wears a bowler hat, carries a stick under him arm, and has a fat cigar in his mouth. The actors acknowledge him as he advances down the auditorium and mounts the stage by way of one of the sets of steps. His* SECRETARY *hands him his post: the odd newspaper, a script.*)

PRODUCER: No letters?

SECRETARY: No letters. That's all there is.

PRODUCER (*handing him back the script*): Put that in my office. (*He looks round and addresses the* STAGE MANAGER:) I can hardly see what's going on. Get us a bit of light, will you?

STAGE MANAGER: Sure. (*He goes to see about it, and soon the right side of the stage where the* ACTORS *are is flooded with brilliant white light. Meanwhile, the* PROMPTER *has gone to his box, switched on his light and opened up his copy of the play.*)

PRODUCER (*clapping his hands together*): OK. Let's make a start. (*To the* STAGE MANAGER:) Who's missing?

STAGE MANAGER: Our leading lady.

PRODUCER: I might have known. (*He looks at his watch.*) We have lost ten minutes already. Put her name in the book, will you? She'll have to learn she can't be late for rehearsals. (*While he is speaking the* LEADING ACTRESS's *voice is heard from the back of the auditorium.*)

LEADING ACTRESS: No need for that, my dears! Here I am! I'm here! (*She is all in white and wears an enormous dressy hat. She carries a small lapdog in her arms. She comes running down the aisle and hurries up the steps.*)

PRODUCER: You do it on purpose, don't you – keep people waiting?

LEADING ACTRESS: I'm sorry. I had a ghastly time getting a taxi. I really meant to be on time. But I see you haven't started yet. And I'm not on at the beginning. (*She calls the* STAGE MANAGER *by name and hands over her dog.*) Be a dear, and pop him in my dressing room!

PRODUCER (*muttering under his breath*): Even the damned
dog! As if the place wasn't a bloody zoo already! (*He claps
his hands and turns to the* PROMPTER.) Right. We're off.
Act Two of *The Rules of the Game*. (*He sits down.*) Are
you with me, gentlemen? Who's on?

(*The* ACTORS *and* ACTRESSES *clear the front of the stage and
seat themselves on chairs at the side, except for the three who
are on stage to rehearse the scene, and the* LEADING ACTRESS
who, ignoring the PRODUCER'*s request, sits herself down at
one of the two small tables.*)

PRODUCER (*to* LEADING ACTRESS): Do I take it you're in
this scene?
LEADING ACTRESS: Me? No... why?
PRODUCER (*irritated*): Then get off for God's sake!

(*The* LEADING ACTRESS *gets up and goes and sits with the
others who are now well out of the way.*)

PROMPTER (*reading from the script*): "Leone Gala's house. An
unusual room which doubles as dining room and study."
PRODUCER (*to* STAGE MANAGER): We can use the red set.
STAGE MANAGER (*jotting it down*): The red set. Right.
PROMPTER (*still reading*): "A table laid for a meal. Desk with
books and papers. Bookcases and glass-fronted cabinets full
of good china and silver. A door, back, leading to Leone's
bedroom. Another door, left, leading to kitchen. The main
entrance is on the right."
PRODUCER (*standing and pointing*): Right, let's sort this out.
Main entrance over there. Kitchen, here. (*To the actor playing Socrates:*) You will use this door here. (*To the* STAGE
MANAGER:) Perhaps you can organize an inner door at
the back, there, and some curtains. (*He sits down again.*)
STAGE MANAGER (*making a note of it*): Right.

PROMPTER (*still reading*): "Scene I. Leone Gala, Guido Venanzi and Filippo, otherwise known as Socrates." (*To the* PRODUCER:) You want me to read the stage direction too?

PRODUCER: Yes, yes! That's what I said, isn't it?

PROMPTER (*reading*): "As the curtain rises, Leone Gala, in chef's hat and apron, is hard at work beating an egg in a bowl with a wooden spoon. Filippo, likewise dressed as a cook, is also beating an egg. Guido Venanzi is sitting listening to them."

LEADING ACTOR (*to the* PRODUCER): Look, do I really have to wear this thing on my head?

PRODUCER (*annoyed by this remark*): It would seem so! It's in the script! (*He makes a gesture to indicate the script.*)

LEADING ACTOR: Well I'm sorry, but I think it's ridiculous!

PRODUCER (*rising in fury*): Ridiculous, is it? You find it ridiculous! And what do you suggest? Can I help it if we can't get hold of good French plays any more so that now we're reduced to putting on plays by Pirandello? Nice stuff if you can understand it, but designed it would seem to get up the noses of actors... and critics... and audiences! (*The* ACTORS *laugh. The* PRODUCER *stands up, moves over to the* LEADING ACTOR *and yells at him.*) So it's "yes" to the chef's hat! And beat those eggs! And there's more to beating eggs than you might think! You're supposed to convey a sense of the very eggshells that they come from – so mind you do! (*More sotto voce laughter and ironic comment from the* ACTORS.) Quiet, please! I'd be obliged if you would listen! (*Again, addressing the* LEADING ACTOR:) I mean it, the very eggshells! The shell being the empty form of reason, devoid of its content of blind instinct. You, Leone Gala, are reason. Your wife is instinct. It's known as role-playing, right? And your role is to be a man who deliberately sets out to be his own puppet. Get the idea?

LEADING ACTOR (*with a hopeless gesture*): Frankly, no.

PRODUCER (*returning to his place*): Nor do I! Well, come on! Let's get started. Wait till you see how it ends... you'll like it! (*Confidentially to the* LEADING ACTOR:) Actually I think you should give us about three-quarters face. Otherwise, what with your mumbling and Pirandello's bumbling nobody is going to understand a thing! (*Clapping his hands together.*) Come on, then! Right, everybody? Let's start!

PROMPTER: Might I just ask – I'm so sorry – but may I put my lid back on? There's an awful draught!

PRODUCER: God, yes! Do what you like!

(*Meanwhile a uniformed* COMMISSIONAIRE *has approached the stage via the central aisle of the auditorium to tell the* PRODUCER *of the arrival of the* SIX CHARACTERS, *who have followed him in and now stand a little way behind him in a bewildered group, looking about them with a lost and puzzled air. Any stage production of the play must make absolutely clear the fundamental distinction between the* SIX CHARACTERS *and the* ACTORS *of the Company. The physical separation of the two groups, recommended in the stage directions once both are on the stage, should certainly help to make the distinction clear. Different-coloured lighting could also be used to reinforce it. But the most effective and apposite means I can suggest would be the use of special masks for the* CHARACTERS *of some material solid enough not to go limp with sweat, but light enough for the* ACTORS *to wear them comfortably, and so designed that the eyes, nostrils and mouth are left free. This device will elucidate the play's essential message. The* CHARACTERS *must not, in fact, seem to be phantasms; they must appear as figures of created reality, immutable constructs of the imagination: more real and more consistent, because of this, than the natural and volatile* ACTORS. *The masks will help convey the idea that these figures are the products of art, their faces immutably fixed so that each one expresses its basic motivation: the* FATHER's *face registering Remorse; the* STEPDAUGHTER's, *Revenge; the* SON's, *Contempt and the* MOTHER's *Sorrow. The* MOTHER *will have fixed wax tears in the dark hollows of her eyes and down her cheeks, like those seen on ecclesiastical images of*

the Mater Dolorosa. *Her dress, too, while simple, should be
of some special material and of an unusual design, with stiff
folds falling like those of a statue; it must not look like a shop
dress or be of a familiar pattern.*

The FATHER *is about fifty, balding slightly, his reddish hair
receding at the temples. A thick curly moustache fringes his still
youthful lips, which tend to part in a meaningless, uncertain
kind of smile. He has a wide forehead, outstandingly pale in
a pallid face; oval blue eyes, very bright and piercing; light
trousers and a dark jacket: his voice is sometimes mellifluous,
sometimes jerky and harsh.*

The MOTHER *gives the impression of someone appalled and
oppressed by an intolerable burden of shame and humiliation.
She is quietly dressed, in widow's black. When she lifts her
heavy crêpe veil she reveals a face which is more like wax than
ailing flesh. She keeps her eyes permanently downcast.*

The STEPDAUGHTER *is eighteen, arrogant and brash to the
point of insolence. Strikingly beautiful, she too is in mourning,
but in her case the clothes have a flashy stylishness. She is clearly
contemptuous of her shy, unhappy, bewildered younger brother, a
scruffy* BOY *of fourteen, also in black. She is warmly affectionate,
however, towards her little sister, a* LITTLE GIRL *of about four,
who wears a white frock tied at the waist with a black silk sash.*

The SON *is a tall young man of twenty-two. He bears himself
stiffly, as if grown rigid in the suppressed contempt he feels for
his* FATHER *and the sullen indifference he shows his* MOTHER.
*He wears a purple overcoat and has a long green scarf tied
round his neck.)*

COMMISSIONAIRE (*cap in hand*): Excuse me, sir.

PRODUCER (*snapping*): Well, what is it?

COMMISSIONAIRE (*hesitating*): There are some people here,
sir, asking for you.

PRODUCER (*again, very angry*): For Heaven's sake, man, I'm
rehearsing! It's your job to keep people out while rehearsals

are in progress! (*Peering into the auditorium.*) Who are you people? What do you want?

FATHER (*approaching the steps which lead up to the stage, followed by the others*): We are here in search of an author.

PRODUCER (*both angry and astonished*): An author? What author?

FATHER: Any author, sir.

PRODUCER: Well, there aren't any authors here. We're not rehearsing a new play.

STEPDAUGHTER (*rushing up the steps, with jubilant enthusiasm*): But that's even better! That's terrific! Have us! We can be your new play!

ONE OF THE ACTORS (*amid lively comment and laughter from the others*): Listen to her! How about that!

FATHER (*following the* STEPDAUGHTER *onto the stage*): Well, yes… but if there's no author… (*To the* PRODUCER:) Unless… would you like to be our author?…

(*The* MOTHER, *leading the* LITTLE GIRL *by the hand, starts up the steps. The* BOY *does so too, and halfway up they pause expectantly. The* SON *remains at the bottom, evidently sulking.*)

PRODUCER: Is this some kind of a joke?

FATHER: It's very far from being a joke, sir. What we bring you is a grievous and painful drama.

STEPDAUGHTER: We could make your fortune!

PRODUCER: Well, perhaps you would be so good as to remove yourselves! We really haven't time for all this nonsense!

FATHER (*hurt, using his "mellifluous" voice*): But I don't need to tell you, sir, I'm sure, that life is like that; it's made up of absurdities, things which don't make sense – and which, like it or not, don't need to be credible, because they are true.

PRODUCER: What the hell are you on about?

FATHER: I'm saying that it is actually more nonsensical to do the opposite, to force things into the mould of credibility to give them the appearance of truth. And might I point out, that, mad as it is, this is exactly what your profession tries to do.

(*Indignant reaction from the* ACTORS.)

PRODUCER (*getting up and looking the* FATHER *squarely in the face*): I see. You think our profession mad, is that it?

FATHER: Well, all this making untrue things seem true... pointlessly, as a kind of game... Your job is to make fictional characters seem true to life, am I right?

PRODUCER (*quickly, voicing the growing indignation of his* ACTORS): I really must insist on defending the dignity of the actor's calling. Today's playwrights, I grant you, may be turning out some pretty dull plays with some pretty dumb characters in them, but you know, we can claim to have given life, here on these boards, to some immortal masterpieces.

(*The* ACTORS, *mollified, give him a round of applause.*)

FATHER (*interrupting and pressing his point home passionately*): Right! That's exactly what I mean! You have created living beings! As much alive, or more so, as the kind who breathe and wear clothes! Not as real, possibly, but more true! So you see, we agree!

(*The* ACTORS, *impressed, exchange looks.*)

STAGE MANAGER: I don't get... First you said...

FATHER (*to the* PRODUCER): No, I'm sorry, that was meant for you, sir, when you barked at us that you had no time to waste on nonsense. Actually, in fact, who better than you should know that Nature's highest instrument in the creative process is the human imagination!

PRODUCER: All right, that's fine. But where does it get us?

FATHER: Nowhere. I'm simply trying to show you that there are a great many ways, and guises, in which one can be born: it might be as a tree or a stone, or water, or a butterfly... or a woman. It's also possible to be born as a character!

PRODUCER (*with ironic feigned amazement*): You mean you and your friends here have all been born as characters?

FATHER: Exactly so. And alive, just as you see us.

(*The* PRODUCER *and the* ACTORS *find this funny. They burst out laughing.*)

FATHER (*hurt*): I'm sorry you find it funny, because, as I said, we carry within us a painful drama, which I imagine you are capable of deducing from the sight of this lady here in her black veil. (*As he speaks he offers his hand to the* MOTHER *to help her up the remaining steps. Still holding her by the hand, he leads her with an air of tragic solemnity to the far side of the stage, which is suddenly bathed in an unearthly light. The* LITTLE GIRL *and the* BOY *follow the* MOTHER. *Then the* SON *crosses over, holding himself aloof and retiring to the background. Lastly comes the* STEPDAUGHTER, *who moves away from the others downstage, and stands leaning against the proscenium arch. The astonished* ACTORS *are momentarily silenced by this development, then applaud to show their appreciation of the little show that has just been staged.*)

PRODUCER (*amazed and then annoyed*): Stop that! Keep quiet! (*He turns to the* CHARACTERS.) I must ask you to leave! Will you kindly remove yourselves! (*To the* STAGE MANAGER:) Get them out of here for God's sake!

STAGE MANAGER (*approaches them and then stops as if restrained by a strange sense of awe*): Clear the stage, then, please! Come along!

FATHER (*to the* PRODUCER): But we can't, you see, we...

PRODUCER (*raising his voice*): Some of us have a job of work to do!

LEADING ACTOR: It shouldn't be allowed! They're making fools of us...

FATHER (*moving resolutely over to them*): I am amazed by your scepticism! Surely as actors and actresses you're quite accustomed to seeing fictional characters suddenly take on life before your eyes, here on this stage? What's the difficulty? Is it because (*pointing towards the* PROMPTER*'s box*) we're not in a script?

STEPDAUGHTER (*approaching the* PRODUCER *with an ingratiating smile*): You must believe we really are six characters, and fascinating ones at that!... Displaced, though... homeless.

FATHER (*edging her out of the way*): Displaced, yes, that is so... (*Quickly, to the* PRODUCER:) In the sense that the author who created us, who gave us our life, found later that he didn't want, or perhaps technically wasn't able, to bring us to birth in art. And this was criminal of him because you see, if you're lucky enough to be born as a character, you have nothing to fear from death. You don't die! Your creator dies, the writer, the instrument of your being, but you, the creature, can't die! Nor do you have to be particularly brilliant to achieve this kind of immortality; there's no need for you to do anything extraordinary. Who, after all, was Sancho Panza? Who was Mr Micawber? But they, you see, will live for ever, because as living germs they each took root in a fertile medium, an imagination able to nourish and develop them and ultimately give them immortality!

PRODUCER: Well, all that sounds very nice! But what do you want with us?

FATHER: We want to live, sir!

PRODUCER (*ironically*): So, it's immortal life you're after, is it?

FATHER: No. We want to live just for a moment. In them.

AN ACTOR: Oh, no! Come on!

LEADING ACTRESS: They want to live in us!

YOUNG ACTOR (*eyeing the* STEPDAUGHTER): It's OK by me! Do I get her?

FATHER: It's like this, you see: the play has yet to be made (*to the* PRODUCER), but if you're willing and your actors are willing, we can sort something out between us now, straight away!

PRODUCER (*annoyed*): Sort something out? Our job isn't to sort something out! We put on proper plays here by professional dramatists!

FATHER: Well, that's what we want! That's what we came here for!

PRODUCER: And where's the script?

FATHER: It's in us. (*The* ACTORS *laugh*.) The drama is in us; we are it! And we are desperate to get it out and put it on the stage. It's a compulsion, a passion!

STEPDAUGHTER (*with a sneer, and adopting a shameless attitude of mock seductiveness*): Passion, now! My passion! You don't know one half of it! My passion... for him! (*She is speaking of the* FATHER *and makes as if to embrace him, but instead bursts into strident laughter.*)

FATHER (*snapping at her fiercely*): You keep your place, miss! And you can take that laugh off your face for a start!

STEPDAUGHTER: No? Well, perhaps I may be allowed to show you my other talents! Ladies and gentlemen, in spite of my recent bereavement, I have pleasure in presenting to you my latest song-and-dance number! (*Vindictively she embarks on her song-and-dance act, the first verse of* Chu-Chin-Chow, *lyric by Dave Stamper, music* (*in foxtrot or slow one-step rhythm*) *by Francis Salabert:*)

In a fairy book a Chinese crook
Has won such wondrous fame
That nowadays he appears in plays
And Chu-Chin-Chow's his name.*

---

* These are the original words of the Dave Stamper song written for Ziegfeld Follies of 1917. A modern or more familiar alternative could be substituted.

(*The* ACTORS, *particularly the young ones, seem drawn towards her by some mysterious fascination. They crowd round as she performs, making as if to grab at her, but she eludes their clutches. Finally when they applaud her and the* PRODUCER *remonstrates with them, she stands looking abstracted as if lost in thought.*)

ACTORS AND ACTRESSES (*laughing and clapping*): Bravo! Encore!

PRODUCER (*angry*): That's enough! This isn't a bloody night-club! (*Confidentially and even anxiously to the* FATHER:) Is she a bit touched or something?

FATHER: Touched? No, it's worse than that!

STEPDAUGHTER (*running to the* PRODUCER, *cutting in quickly*): Worse! I'll say it's worse! It's worse, all right! Listen! Please! Let's act it now, our drama, then you'll see how at a certain point, I... when this sweet baby... (*She takes the* LITTLE GIRL's *hand and brings her from her* MOTHER's *side across to the* PRODUCER.) Have you ever seen such a pet? (*She picks her up and kisses her.*) Oh, my little love! (*She sets her down and speaks in great agitation, as if hardly aware of her words.*) Well, when this sweet baby here eventually gets taken from that poor Mother, and when this idiot here (*she roughly grabs the* BOY *by the sleeve and pushes him forward*) plays his rottenest trick of all, like the dumbhead he is (*shoving him back towards the* MOTHER), you won't see me for dust, I can tell you! I shall be off for good! And believe me, it can't come soon enough! Because after what... after what "took place" between him and me (*with a lurid wink in the* FATHER's *direction*), I can't stick the present company a moment longer; I can't bear to stand by and watch while this Mother eats her heart out over that poor sap. (*She indicates the* SON.) Look at him! Just look at him! Really cool, uninvolved, because he's legitimate, see, the legitimate son, much too good for the likes of me, or him there (*pointing to the* BOY) or this little thing here.

Because we are the bastards. Are you with me? Bastards.
(*She goes up to the* MOTHER *and puts her arms round her.*)
And this poor Mother, who is Mother to us all, he refuses to
acknowledge as his own. He treats her like dirt. To him she's
just the Mother of us three bastards. He is... vile! (*All this
is said rapidly in a state of extreme agitation. She reaches
a crescendo with her "three bastards" and then utters the
last word "vile" in a whisper, almost spitting the word out.*)

MOTHER (*in a tone of total anguish*): Please, sir, for the sake
of these two little ones, I beg you... (*She totters, unable to
go on.*) Oh my God...

FATHER (*rushing to support her; the astonished* ACTORS
in their consternation do so too): Get a chair, someone!
Quickly, a chair for this poor creature!

ACTORS (*coming forwards*): Is it real? Has she really fainted?

PRODUCER: Can we have a chair here, quickly!

(*One of the* ACTORS *brings a chair; the others crowd round
anxious to help. The* MOTHER *is now sitting. She tries to stop
the* FATHER *from removing the veil that hides her face.*)

FATHER: Take a look at her, sir! Just take a look at her!

MOTHER: Oh, don't! For God's sake, don't!

FATHER: Let them see you! (*He lifts up her veil.*)

MOTHER (*getting up and covering her face with her hands in
desperation*): Oh, sir, I beg you, stop this man from doing
the dreadful thing he has in mind! It's too horrible!

PRODUCER (*taken aback, bemused*): Can someone tell me
what the hell's happening round here! (*To the* FATHER:)
Is this lady your wife?

FATHER (*promptly*): Yes, she's my wife.

PRODUCER: Then how does she manage to be a widow, if
you're still alive?

(*The* ACTORS *release some of their tension in a noisy guffaw.*)

FATHER (*cut to the quick, with acrimony*): Don't laugh! Don't laugh like that! For pity's sake! This is the point, this is her drama! She had another man. Another man who should be here!

MOTHER (*with a shriek*): No! No!

STEPDAUGHTER: He's dead, and well out of it. I told you, he died two months ago. You can see, we are still in mourning for him.

FATHER: He's not here... but that's not because he is dead. He's not here because... well, one look at her should tell you. Hers isn't the drama of a woman torn between two men; I don't think she felt anything for them. She wasn't capable. Beyond, perhaps, a little gratitude. (Not for me! For him!) No, she isn't a woman; she's a mother! Her drama (and oh, yes, it's powerful stuff!) her whole drama is bound up in these four children, the children of the two men she had.

MOTHER: I had two men? You can stand there and say that I had two men, as if that was what I wanted? (*To the* PRODUCER:) He wanted it! He gave me the other man, he forced him on me! He made me, yes, he made me run away with him!

STEPDAUGHTER (*cutting in bitterly*): That's not true!

MOTHER (*startled*): What's not true?

STEPDAUGHTER: It just isn't true!

MOTHER: What do you know about it?

STEPDAUGHTER: It isn't true! (*To the* PRODUCER:) Don't you believe it! Do you know why she says that? She says it because of him! (*She points to the* SON.) She's tearing herself apart over the coldness of the son she abandoned when he was two years old. She's desperate to convince him that she only left him because she had to, because he (*pointing to the* FATHER) forced her to.

MOTHER: He forced me, all right! God knows he forced me! (*To the* PRODUCER:) Ask him if he didn't. Make him admit it! She (*she gestures towards the* STEPDAUGHTER) is not in a position to have an opinion.

STEPDAUGHTER: I just know that all the time you were with
my father, as long as he was alive, you were perfectly happy
and at peace. You can't deny it!

MOTHER: No, I don't deny it, I…

STEPDAUGHTER: He was so loving. He looked after you so
sweetly! (*To the* BOY, *angrily:*) Didn't he? Bear me out! Say
something, you fool!

MOTHER: Leave the poor boy alone! Why do you want to make
me out so ungrateful? I wouldn't dream of saying anything
against your father. I was simply answering his insinuation.
(*She is referring to the* FATHER.) When I walked out of his
house and left my son, it wasn't my fault! Nor was it for
my pleasure!

FATHER: She is perfectly right. It was my idea. (*A pause.*)

LEADING ACTOR (*to the others*): It wouldn't make a bad show!

LEADING ACTRESS: Nice to be the audience for once!

YOUNG ACTOR: It makes a change!

PRODUCER (*beginning to get really interested*): OK, let's listen!
Sh! Let's listen! (*As he says this he goes down the steps into
the auditorium where he stands facing the stage, as if to
get an audience's impression of the scene.*)

SON (*without moving and without raising his voice, which is
cold and ironic*): If you want to know what's coming next,
it's a slice of potted philosophy! He's about to tell you of
his evil genius, his Daemon of Experiment!

FATHER: You think you're so damn clever, but you're stupid!
That's typical! (*To the* PRODUCER:) He despises me, you
see, for this expression I have hit on to explain my behaviour.

SON (*scornfully*): Words!

FATHER: Well, yes! Words, words! As if we didn't all find them
a source of comfort! When we are desperately perplexed
or distressed, what do we do? We find some word which in
itself means nothing, but which offers us peace of mind!

STEPDAUGHTER: Super remedy for remorse, for instance!
Nothing like it!

FATHER: Remorse? That's not fair. I have used more than mere words to still my remorse.

STEPDAUGHTER: Oh... of course! What was it he wanted to offer me for my services? Oh yes, a hundred lire!

(There is a horrified reaction from the ACTORS.*)*

SON *(contemptuously to his stepsister)*: That was vile!

STEPDAUGHTER: Vile? But there it was, in a nice little pale-blue envelope on the mahogany table, round the back at Madame Pace's. *(To the* PRODUCER:*)* You know the kind of thing, sir! Smart boutique in the front, providing a cover for Madame's other little business, the "work rooms" at the back where she can employ girls from decent homes who need the cash.

SON: And now she's holding us all to ransom with the wretched hundred lire she was going to cost him. And bear in mind – as things turned out – he never had reason to pay it!

STEPDAUGHTER: Get it right, now! It was a very near thing! *(She bursts out laughing.)*

MOTHER *(getting up)*: Have you no shame!

STEPDAUGHTER *(quickly)*: Shame? This is revenge! I am at this moment trembling, trembling in every nerve to get at that scene and to live it! The room, now. There's a glass case displaying clothes, over here! Over there a sofa, doubling as a bed. A long mirror, here, and a screen. By the window we've got the famous mahogany table with the blue envelope on it with the money. I can see it! I could even pick it up! Perhaps you should all be looking the other way, as I've hardly got anything on! Not that it makes me blush. I can't blush any more. He's the one who is red in the face now. *(She indicates the* FATHER.*)* However, at the time I'm speaking of I can tell you he was pale! Very, very pale! *(To the* PRODUCER:*)* Of that I can assure you!

PRODUCER: I can't keep up with this!

FATHER: Of course you can't. Give the man a chance! (*To the* PRODUCER:) Can't you organize this a bit, sir?... let me explain things? You shouldn't really listen to this savage piece of character assassination without hearing what I've got to say!

STEPDAUGHTER: But it's not a story! You can't tell it like a story!

FATHER: I'm not telling a story – I just want to explain!

STEPDAUGHTER: Oh, yes, lovely! Explain it your way, you mean!

(*The* PRODUCER *climbs back onto the stage to try to restore order.*)

FATHER: But isn't this the whole trouble! It all comes back to words! We all carry round inside us a world made up of things as we see them; each one of us a whole world of his own! How can we ever hope to understand each other if I put into the words I use the meaning and value that things have for me in my interior world, while the person I'm talking to is bound to receive them with the meaning and value those words have for him, in a world that exists only inside him? We think we understand each other. In fact we never do. Look! The pity I felt for this poor woman (*he indicates the* MOTHER) – all my pity for her she took as cruelty!

MOTHER: But you sent me away!

FATHER: There, you see? She thinks I sent her away!

MOTHER: You're good at talking; I'm not... (*To the* PRODUCER:) But believe me, once he had married me... though goodness knows why he did!... I was a very simple person, no money or anything...

FATHER: But that's right! That's what I loved! You were simple, and I thought... (*She is clearly in disagreement, and he breaks off, shrugging desperately at the utter impossibility of making himself understood by her. He turns to the*

38

PRODUCER.) It's no good, you see? She won't see it! It is terrifying! Her mental deafness is absolutely terrifying! (*He taps his forehead.*) That's it, mental deafness! Plenty of heart, mind you, where her children are concerned. But in the head she's deaf! Dear sir, to the point of desperation!

STEPDAUGHTER (*to the* PRODUCER): You'd better get him to tell you just where all *his* intelligence has got us!

FATHER: If one only realized beforehand all the harm that can result from one's efforts to do good!

(*At this point the* LEADING ACTRESS, *distraught at the* LEADING ACTOR'*s attempts to flirt with the* STEPDAUGHTER, *comes up to speak to the* PRODUCER.)

LEADING ACTRESS: Is there going to be a rehearsal this morning?

PRODUCER: Yes, yes! But let me just hear this!

YOUNG ACTOR: It's new. I mean, it's not been done before!

YOUNG ACTRESS: It's fascinating!

LEADING ACTRESS: If you find that sort of thing fascinating! (*She darts a glance at the* LEADING ACTOR.)

PRODUCER (*to the* FATHER): Now, let's get this clear. (*He sits.*)

FATHER: Right. Well, look. I had this secretary. He was my junior, a rather downtrodden kind of fellow, utterly devoted… And he had this extraordinary understanding with my wife. They thought the same way about everything. Absolutely innocent, of course. He was as good and simple as she was. Both quite incapable of doing anything wrong… or even of thinking of it.

STEPDAUGHTER: So he did the thinking for them – and the doing!

FATHER: That's not true! I meant to do what was best for them – and for myself, I admit! It had got to the point, you see, where I couldn't say a word to either of them without their exchanging understanding looks. Their eyes kept meeting, looking for clues as to how to react to what I had said, how to keep me sweet! Well, you can imagine, this was enough in itself to keep me permanently on the simmer; I was in an unbearable state of constant exasperation!

PRODUCER: But... why didn't you sack the secretary?

FATHER: Exactly what I did! I sacked him, and then was left with the spectacle of this poor woman drifting round the house like a lost soul. She seemed not to belong, like a stray animal you keep out of kindness.

MOTHER: Is it any wonder!

FATHER (*quickly, turning to her, as if to get in first*): Ah, yes... our boy.

MOTHER: He had already taken the child from my arms, you realize!

FATHER: But not from cruelty! I did it so that he would grow up strong and healthy, close to nature!

STEPDAUGHTER (*pointing to the* SON, *ironically*): As you see!

FATHER (*quickly*): Is it my fault that he turned out like this? (*To the* PRODUCER:) I put him in the care of a foster mother, in the country, a peasant woman. My wife didn't seem strong enough, despite her humble origins. I was looking for the same kind of thing again, you see, that I looked for in marrying her. A fad, I suppose, but there you are. I have always been dogged by a hankering after a kind of sound moral wholesomeness. (*Here the* STEPDAUGHTER *again produces a guffaw of raucous laughter.*) Can't you stop her doing that? It's insufferable.

PRODUCER (*to the* STEPDAUGHTER): Stop it, for God's sake! Let me hear what he's saying!

(*At this remonstrance from the* PRODUCER *the* STEPDAUGHTER *immediately reassumes her lost far-away look as she is cut off in mid-laughter. The* PRODUCER *again takes up his position in the stalls to get the audience's view of the stage.*)

FATHER: I could no longer bear to have this woman in the house. Not so much because her presence was oppressive, which it was, really oppressive, but more, quite honestly, because of the pain – well, the anguish she was going through.

MOTHER: And he sent me away!

FATHER: Yes I did, I provided for her properly and sent her to that man – I gave her her freedom!

MOTHER: Your own freedom, more like!

FATHER: Well, yes, mine too, I admit it! And it all went horribly wrong! I thought I was doing the right thing! More for her than for me, I swear to that! (*He lays his hand on his heart, then turning quickly to the* MOTHER.) But I didn't lose sight of you, did I? I didn't lose sight of you... until the day when the damned fool carted you off to another town, overnight, without a word! He was idiot enough to resent the interest I took... which was perfectly innocent! There wasn't a thought in my head that wasn't entirely innocent! I got incredibly fond of this new little family that was growing up. I was interested. (*He points to the* STEPDAUGHTER.) She'll bear me out!

STEPDAUGHTER: You were interested all right! I was, you know, a real little girl. With pigtails down to my shoulders and my little knickers showing! About so high! I used to see him as I came out of the school gate. He came to see how I was growing up...

FATHER: That is a vile thing to say! That is disgusting!

STEPDAUGHTER: Have I got it wrong?

FATHER: This is quite outrageous! (*His tone suddenly changes to one of desperate self-explanation.*) The fact was, you see, once she had gone, my house seemed empty. She had filled it with the nightmare of her presence. Left on my own I almost went off my head. I used to wander blindly from room to room. He, you see (*indicating the* SON) had been in a foster home up till then. When he came home, somehow he didn't seem to be mine any more. With his mother no longer there to keep us together, he grew up in a world of his own. There was no relationship there, no feelings, no common interests. So then, it sounds odd, I know, but this is what happened – first I got curious, and then bit by bit I began to feel drawn towards her little family – I had created it in a way. The thought of it began to fill the emptiness of my life. I needed, I really needed to know she had found peace, to know she was completely taken up with the little tasks of daily life, safely and happily out of reach, where my complicated spiritual agonizings could no longer touch her. And to prove it to myself, I used to go and watch that little girl coming out of school.

STEPDAUGHTER: He did too! He used to follow me all the way home, smiling! And when we got there he used to wave, like this! And I'd glare at him, give him nasty looks. I didn't know who he was! I told my mum. She knew who it was all right. (*The* MOTHER *nods.*) At first she wanted to keep me off school, and I stayed at home for several days. When I started back at school, there he was again, waiting at the gate – he looked ridiculous – holding a big paper parcel! He came up and patted me and unwrapped a lovely big, real-straw hat with little rosebuds round the brim – for me!

PRODUCER: But this is a story not a play!

SON (*scornfully*): Fiction! Romantic fiction!

FATHER: Fiction? This isn't fiction! This is life! This is passion!

PRODUCER: That's as may be. It will never do on the stage!

FATHER: Now there you're right! This all happens before the play starts. I'm not suggesting we act this bit. I mean, you can see for yourself, she's hardly a little girl with pigtails any more...

STEPDAUGHTER: Nor can you see her little knickers!

FATHER: The drama is what comes next! An extraordinary, complicated story!

STEPDAUGHTER (*coming forwards, proud and menacing*): Once my father had died...

FATHER (*quickly to stop her saying any more*): ...they were faced with destitution! They came back here. I didn't know. She (*he points to the* MOTHER) was too stupid to tell me. She can hardly write, but she could have got her daughter or that boy to let me know they were in trouble.

MOTHER (*to the* PRODUCER): But how could I have known he felt like this!

FATHER: That was the wrong you did me – never guessing anything of how I felt!

MOTHER: Well, after all those years away, and everything that had happened...

FATHER: How could I help it if your fancy man went and carted you off like that? (*To the* PRODUCER:) I tell you, they disappeared overnight... He had got himself some kind of a job in another town. I never managed to trace them, and then, naturally over the years, my interest flagged. The drama erupted, unforeseen and cataclysmic, when they got back. Because I, Heaven help me, still suffering the misery of physical frustration... and misery is right! It is misery when a man lives alone, if he doesn't want some sordid affair, but he's not yet old enough to do without a woman nor young enough to go out and get one in a straightforward and acceptable fashion! Misery, did I say? Horror would be nearer the mark! Horror, because no woman can give him love any more... And once you've realized that, you should really do without... So! The fact is, we all clothe ourselves with a kind of outward dignity, for the benefit of other people. Inwardly, of course, one knows perfectly well the unconfessable intimate things that go on. One gives in, of course one does, to tempta-tion, but one scrambles up again very smartly afterwards in a great rush to re-establish the old dignity, set it upright whole and solid like a tombstone over a grave. That way we don't have to look at our shame; we have hidden and buried all trace of it and can forget it. We all do it, you

43

know! It's just that some things... well, one can't quite bring oneself to talk about them!

STEPDAUGHTER: Doing them's all right though, isn't it!

FATHER: Oh, people do these things! But in secret! That's why it takes more courage to talk about them. If you mention them, people say you are cynical. Which isn't true. You are only the same as everyone else – in fact a bit better, because you're not afraid to look rationally at the blushing face of human sexuality. There it is; it's part of our bestial nature, but we shut our eyes to it and refuse to see it. A woman... look... a woman... what does she do? She looks at us, all invitation, all enticement. So you grab her! And what happens? As soon as she's in your arms, she shuts her eyes – like that! It's her signal of surrender; she's saying: "Be blind, as I am blind."

STEPDAUGHTER: And what about when she gets past that stage? When she has grown out of the need to shut her eyes against her own blushes? When she can stare, quite unmoved, with wide dry eyes at the shame of the man in her arms, lying there, without love, his eyes closed against his lust! That's when it really makes you sick! That's when you can't stomach all this hair-splitting and high-flown philosophizing about man and his animal nature, all your excuses and justifications. I can't stand it, I tell you. Because if you are ever actually driven to live at that level, at the simple animal level, if you're ever forced to do without all the human "extras" like chastity, purity, idealism, duty, modesty, shame – you'll find nothing makes you more angry, nothing is more nauseating than bogus remorse: it's eyewash!

PRODUCER: Can we get to the point, do you think? All this is hardly relevant!

FATHER: Ah! Yes... well! A fact you see, on its own, is like an empty sack: it won't stand up! If you want it to stand up, you have to put something inside it, the motivation, the feelings that brought it about. I couldn't know, you see, that after the death of that chap when they all came back here without a bean, she tried to support her children by looking about for work as a seamstress... and in fact got taken on by Madame Pace!

STEPDAUGHTER: ...Who, I'd have you know, is a first-rate dressmaker. She serves a very distinguished clientele. It's a nice little arrangement. Her distinguished ladies come in very useful, as a cover for her other ladies, the not so distinguished ones!

MOTHER: And it goes without saying, I'm sure, that I hadn't the faintest suspicion that that monstrous creature gave me work because she had got her eye on my child...

STEPDAUGHTER: Poor Mum! And do you know what the old so-and-so did when I brought her the sewing my mother had done? She made me note down the amount of stuff she had ruined, and then she would deduct it, she'd deduct it from my pay! I was being made to pay, you see, while my poor old Mum thought she was making sacrifices on behalf of me and the other two. She used to sit up half the night doing Madame Pace's sewing!

(*The* ACTORS *register indignation.*)

PRODUCER (*anxious to get on*): And it was there that one day you met...

STEPDAUGHTER (*pointing to the* FATHER): Him! That's right! Him! Old-established client! You'll see what a good scene it makes! It's brilliant!

FATHER: When she bursts in in the middle, you see, the mother—

STEPDAUGHTER (*quickly, treacherously*): Almost in time!

FATHER (*shouting her down*): No! In time! In time! Because luckily, I recognize her in time! And then I take them all home with me! But just try and imagine how impossible things are between us now! She's, well, she's as you see her! But I can't even look her in the face!

STEPDAUGHTER: It's a laugh! There's no way – after that – that I can pass myself off as a nice well-brought-up young lady in keeping with his damnable notions of "sound moral wholesomeness".

FATHER: And this, for me, is the heart of the drama: I'm intensely aware, you see, that people are wrong to think of themselves as just one person. Each one of us is lots and lots of people. Any number, because of all the countless possibilities of being that exist within us. The person you are with me is quite different from the person you are with somebody else. But we go on thinking we're exactly the same person for everybody, the person we think we are in our own mind and in everything we do. But this isn't the case at all! It comes home to us best when by some ghastly mischance we are caught out in an untypical act. We suddenly find we are sort of dangling from a hook! I mean we can see that the act isn't "us", our whole self isn't in it. And it would be a savage injustice to judge us on that act alone, never to let us off the hook, to hold us to it, chain us up for life on the strength of it for all to see, as if that one action summed up our whole existence! So now do you see how treacherous this girl is being? She caught me out in an unrecognizable situation, in a place where for her I should never have been and doing something which in her eyes I should not have been able to do, and now she insists on seeing this undreamt-of contingency as my reality, identifying me with a single fleeting shaming moment of my life. This, sir, is what I feel most strongly of all. And you'll see that this is really what gives the play its power. And then of course there's the situation of the others. His, for instance (*he points to the* SON)…

SON (*with a contemptuous shrug*): You can leave me out of it! I don't come into it!

FATHER: What do you mean, you don't come into it?

SON: I don't come into it! I don't want to come into it! You know quite well I was never meant to be mixed up with you lot!

STEPDAUGHTER: He thinks we're dead common. He reckons he's got class. Though you'll notice perhaps that whenever I manage to wither him with a glance he always shifts his eyes away. He knows what he's done to me, all right.

SON (*hardly looking at her*): ...What *I've done*?

STEPDAUGHTER: Yes, you! You're the one who put me on the streets, matey! (*The* ACTORS *are shocked.*) Did you, or didn't you, oh, by your whole manner, make sure we never felt at home in your house? You didn't even treat us as guests! We were intruders, weren't we, invading your legitimate territory! (*To the* PRODUCER:) I'd like to show you certain little private scenes that took place between him and me! He says I took over the household. But can't you see? The way he was carrying on, I had to exploit my bit of advantage, my "cheap" advantage as he calls it, and make sure that when I walked into that house with my mother (who's his mother too!) I was going to be boss!

SON (*coming forwards slowly*): You see how it is. I'm fair game; they have an easy case against me. But try and see it my way. You are someone's son, quietly at home one day, and in marches a cheeky young woman who looks down her nose at you and says she has some sort of business with your father! Then back she comes, as if she owned the place, bringing that little girl with her, and proceeds to treat your father – God knows by what right – in a highly equivocal and offhand manner, asking him for money in a voice which suggests he has no choice but to give it her, that he's in no position to refuse.

FATHER: But that's right. I can't refuse. It's for your mother.

SON: Well, what do I know about that? When have I even seen my mother? When have I ever heard her mentioned?

For me she just turns up one day, with her, and that boy, and that little girl. They tell me, "Oh, didn't you know? She is your mother, too!" And then I get it. I pick it up from her manner (*he indicates the* STEPDAUGHTER) how it was they were suddenly able to come and live with us just like that... (*To the* PRODUCER:) What I feel, what I'm going through, I can't express and I don't want to. I can't even bring myself to think about it. So you see: no action can possibly be got out of me. Believe me, in dramatic terms, I'm an "unrealized" character. I'm just not one of them, I really don't belong! So leave me out, will you?

FATHER: How can we! Come on! Just because you're like that—

SON (*in violent exasperation*): How the hell do you know what I'm like! When have you ever bothered about me?

FATHER: I agree! I grant you that! But isn't this a dramatic situation in itself? This cutting yourself off is so cruel; I find it cruel and so does your mother. Think of her, coming home and meeting you for the first time, this fully grown stranger who she just knows is her son... (*He draws the* PRODUCER'S *attention to the* MOTHER.) Look at her now, she's crying.

STEPDAUGHTER (*angrily, stamping her foot*): She's so wet!

FATHER (*to the* PRODUCER, *with a quick gesture towards the* STEPDAUGHTER): And she can't stand him, you see! (*He points to the* SON.) He says he doesn't come into it, but in many ways he's the pivot of the action! Look at this young fellow clinging to his mother all the time. Do you see how abject and intimidated he is? Well, that's his fault! (*Indicating the* SON.) Perhaps the poor little chap is in the most hurtful situation of all: more than any of them he feels he doesn't belong. He finds it painfully humiliating to have been taken in – well, out of charity... (*Confidentially.*) He's exactly like his father. A dim sort of chap... never spoke.

PRODUCER: Can't really see it working, you know. Children are a damn nuisance on the stage.

FATHER: Don't worry, the nuisance removes itself pretty quickly! And so does the little girl. In fact she goes first...

PRODUCER: That's good. Well, then, yes! And I may say I am completely hooked, it is all deeply intriguing. Something tells me that we have the makings of a first-rate play here.

STEPDAUGHTER (*trying to butt in*): With a character like me you have!

FATHER (*pushing her out of the way in his anxiety to hear the* PRODUCER'*s decision*): Shut up, you!

PRODUCER (*not noticing the interruption*): It's certainly new...

FATHER: Oh yes, it's very new!

PRODUCER: I hand it to you for sheer nerve, though, coming in here and shoving the thing under my nose...

FATHER: You must understand, sir: born, as we are, for the stage...

PRODUCER: Are you an amateur company?

FATHER: Oh, no. I say "born for the stage" because...

PRODUCER: Come off it! You've had acting experience!

FATHER: None at all. Only the acting everybody does, in the parts we give ourselves in life or that other people give us. In my case I'd say the theatricality comes from passion itself. Strong feeling does that, gets a bit stagy, you know, when one gets worked up...

PRODUCER: Well, never mind! It doesn't matter. Now, look! You have to understand, I'm afraid, that without an author... I could put you in touch with someone...

FATHER: Oh, no! Don't do that! You be the author!

PRODUCER: Me? How could I?

FATHER: Yes, you! Why not?

PRODUCER: I've never written a play in my life!

FATHER: Well then, why not start now? There's nothing to it! Look at all the people who do! And your job is made that much easier for having us all here alive in front of you!

PRODUCER: There's more to it than that!

FATHER: Well, is there? I mean, seeing us actually live our play...

PRODUCER: OK! But you've still got to have somebody to write it!

FATHER: No, you haven't! All you need do is transcribe it, scene by scene, as it unfolds before you. All that's necessary at this point is to map out a very rough plan and then try it out!

PRODUCER (*climbing back onto the stage, tempted by the idea*): I'm almost tempted... ye-es, almost... for fun, maybe... Well, we could have a go...

FATHER: Oh yes, you must! You'll be amazed at the scenes which come out! I can give you a rough outline straight away!

PRODUCER: It's tempting... It's certainly tempting... OK. Let's give it a go. Come with me to my office. (*To the* ACTORS:) Take a break but don't go away. Be back here in a quarter of an hour or twenty minutes. (*To the* FATHER:) Come on then, let's see what we can do. You never know, it might result in something quite extraordinary...

FATHER: But it will! There's no doubt! They had better come too, don't you think? (*He refers to the other* CHARACTERS.)

PRODUCER: Oh yes, they'd better come. Come on! (*He turns to the* ACTORS *again before leaving the stage.*) Don't be late, then! A quarter of an hour! (*The* PRODUCER *and the six* CHARACTERS *cross the stage and disappear. The* ACTORS *remain on stage, exchanging baffled looks.*)

LEADING ACTOR: Can he be serious? What's he playing at?

YOUNG ACTOR: He's clean off his rocker!

A THIRD ACTOR: Does he expect us to improvise a whole play just on the spot?

YOUNG ACTOR: That's it! *Commedia dell'arte* type stuff!

LEADING ACTRESS: I hope he doesn't think I'm going to take part in such nonsense...

YOUNG ACTRESS: Well, I'm not going to!

A FOURTH ACTOR: I'd like to know just who those people are.

THE THIRD ACTOR: It's obvious! They're either loonies or crooks!

YOUNG ACTOR: I can't think what induced him to listen to them!

YOUNG ACTRESS: He fancies himself, perhaps. Sees himself as a playwright.

LEADING ACTOR: Well, it's preposterous! If this, my friends, is what the theatre's coming to…

A FIFTH ACTOR: I don't know, I think it's rather fun!

THE THIRD ACTOR: Oh, well! Let's see what comes of it!

(*Chatting amongst themselves, the* ACTORS *leave the stage, some through the small door at the back, some in the direction of the dressing rooms. The curtain stays up. There is an interval in the play of twenty minutes or so.*

Bells throughout the theatre warn the audience that the performance is about to start again.

The ACTORS, STAGE MANAGER, CHIEF STAGEHAND, PROMPTER *and* PROPERTY MAN *return to the stage from the dressing rooms, from the outside door and from the auditorium. At the same time the* PRODUCER *re-emerges from his office with the six* CHARACTERS. *The house lights go down and the stage is lit as before.*)

PRODUCER: All right, ladies and gentlemen! Are we all here? May I have your attention, please! Can we begin? (*He calls the* CHIEF STAGEHAND *by name.*)

CHIEF STAGEHAND: Yes! Here!

PRODUCER: Can you give us the small drawing room – three flats, one with a door, that's about it. As quick as you can!

(*The* STAGEHAND *at once goes off to carry out his instructions, and while the* PRODUCER *is making necessary arrangements with the* STAGE MANAGER, *the* PROPERTY MAN *and the* ACTORS, *the* SCENE-SHIFTERS *have organized a set as requested, a small parlour with pink-and-gold-striped wallpaper.*)

PRODUCER (*to the* PROPERTY MAN): Have a look and see if we've got a divan or a chaise longue.

PROPERTY MAN: Yes, we've got the green one.

STEPDAUGHTER: We can't have a green one! It was yellow plush with flowers on it. A great big thing, really comfortable.

PROPERTY MAN: We've got nothing like that!

PRODUCER: It doesn't matter! Give us the one we've got.

STEPDAUGHTER: How can you say it doesn't matter? Madame Pace's famous couch!

PRODUCER: It's only for a run-through! Please don't interfere. (*To the* STAGE MANAGER:) See if there's a display case, preferably long and low.

STEPDAUGHTER: And the table! The small mahogany table for the blue envelope!

STAGE MANAGER (*to the* PRODUCER): There's the small gilt one.

PRODUCER: That'll do fine.

FATHER: And a long mirror.

STEPDAUGHTER: And the screen! There has to be a screen. I can't possibly manage without that.

STAGE MANAGER: That's all right, miss, don't worry. We've got lots of screens.

PRODUCER (*to the* STEPDAUGHTER): Then some hat stands, right?

STEPDAUGHTER: Yes, a lot of those!

PRODUCER (*to the* STAGE MANAGER): Get them to bring whatever we've got.

STAGE MANAGER: No trouble, sir! Leave it to me! (*The* STAGE MANAGER *hurries off to do as he is told, then returns and arranges as he thinks best the props brought on by the scene-shifters, while the* PRODUCER *carries on talking to the* PROMPTER, *the* CHARACTERS *and the* ACTORS.)

PRODUCER (*to the* PROMPTER): You could be getting yourself ready. Look, here's an outline of the scenes divided up into acts. (*He hands him several sheets of paper.*) You'll have your work cut out, you know.

PROMPTER: Do you want it in shorthand?

PRODUCER (*pleasantly surprised*): What? You can do shorthand?

PROMPTER: I may not be much of a prompter, but shorthand, now...

PRODUCER: Better and better. (*To a* STAGEHAND:) Go and get some paper from my office – get plenty, as much as you can find! (*The* STAGEHAND *hurries off and returns almost at once with a thick wad of paper which he hands to the* PROMPTER.)

PRODUCER (*to the* PROMPTER): Just follow the scenes as we do them and try to get down the lines, well, the main ones anyway! (*To the* ACTORS:) Right, clear the stage, please! Can you all come over onto this side (*he points to stage left*) and let's have your full attention!

LEADING ACTRESS: But, look here, we...

PRODUCER (*cutting in*): Keep calm, nobody's asking you to improvise!

LEADING ACTOR: What do we have to do, then?

PRODUCER: Nothing! Just keep your eyes and ears open for the present. Then later, you'll all have proper scripted parts. Right now we're going to have a rehearsal, of a sort. They (*he indicates the* CHARACTERS) are going to be doing it.

FATHER (*as if roused from a reverie, suddenly aware of the confusion all around him*): You mean us? But what do you mean, a rehearsal?

PRODUCER: You're going to rehearse, rehearse for my actors!

FATHER: But if we *are* the characters...

PRODUCER: OK. So you're the characters. But my dear good sir, we don't have characters acting here. The actors do the acting. The characters belong in the script (*he gestures towards the* PROMPTER)... when there is a script!

FATHER: Exactly! But since there isn't one and you good people are lucky enough to have the characters here in person...

PRODUCER: Bloody marvellous! You're proposing to do the whole thing on your own, then! Be your own actors, your own producers, everything!

FATHER: Of course, just as we are.

PRODUCER: Well, my word, that would be some show, I can tell you!

LEADING ACTOR: And what would that leave for us to do?

PRODUCER: You don't for one moment imagine you can act, do you? This has got to be a joke! (*The* ACTORS *are in fact laughing.*) Look, there you are, they're laughing! (*Recollecting himself:*) Anyway, where were we! Now, to cast this thing! Well, it's easy: the parts pretty well cast themselves. (*To the* SECOND ACTRESS:) You will be the mother. (*To the* FATHER:) We shall have to find a name for her.

FATHER: Her name's Amalia.

PRODUCER: No, that's your wife's name. We shan't want to use her real name.

FATHER: Why ever not? If that's her name... But of course, if this lady here has got to do it... (*He waves bleakly in the direction of the* SECOND ACTRESS.) I see her (*referring to the* MOTHER) as Amalia. But it's up to you... (*He gets more and more confused.*) I don't really know what to say... I'm beginning to feel... well, as if my own words are ringing false, and are no longer really mine, somehow.

PRODUCER: Don't let that worry you! Don't let that worry you at all! We'll see we get the tone right! As for the name, if you want Amalia, then Amalia it shall be, or whatever you like. For the moment let's not use names. Let's simply say that you (*to the* YOUNG ACTOR) are the Son; (*to the* LEADING ACTRESS:) that you, of course, are the Stepdaughter...

STEPDAUGHTER (*galvanized*): What? What? That woman there? (*She bursts out laughing.*)

PRODUCER (*angrily*): What's so funny?

LEADING ACTRESS (*indignantly*): I'm not having this! No one has ever laughed at me! If I can't be treated with respect, I'm off!

STEPDAUGHTER: Well, no, I'm sorry. It's not you I'm laughing at.

PRODUCER (*to the* STEPDAUGHTER): You should feel honoured at being played by...

LEADING ACTRESS (*promptly and furiously*): ..."That woman there"!

STEPDAUGHTER: It really wasn't you I was thinking of! It was me! I just don't see myself in you at all! That's it. I don't know, you're not... you're not in the least bit like me!

FATHER: That's just it. (*To the* PRODUCER:) Look! What we want to express...

PRODUCER: What you want to express! Do you think, then, that you can provide your own means of expression? You couldn't begin!

FATHER: What? Are you saying we haven't got it in us to express ourselves?

PRODUCER: Of course you haven't! In this theatre anything you express becomes material for my actors to work on. They give it body and shape, voice and gesture. And they have usually tackled far more ambitious material than yours, which, let's face it, is pretty trivial stuff. If it works as a play, it will be entirely thanks to them, no doubt about it.

FATHER: Well, I daren't contradict you. But may I say that for us this is an extremely painful process. This is what we look like! You can see *these* are our bodies, *these* are our faces...

PRODUCER (*cutting him short, losing patience*): That's no problem! Faces are no problem! Make-up will fix all that!

FATHER: All right. But what about voices, gestures...

PRODUCER: Look, the fact is... There's no place here for you, as yourself. Here you just don't exist. An actor represents you, and that's it!

FATHER: I understand. And I think I'm beginning to get a glimmering of why our author decided not to write us into a play. He saw us as we are, alive... I'm not casting aspersions on your actions, I wouldn't dream of doing that! But the idea now of seeing myself acted by someone else, by some actor...

LEADING ACTOR (*pompously rising and coming over with his entourage of giggling young* ACTRESSES): By me, if you have no objection.

FATHER (*with honeyed deference*): I am deeply honoured. (*He bows. To the* PRODUCER:) The fact is, I think, that however hard our friend here tries, with all the will in the world and with all his professional skill, to absorb my being... (*He gets confused.*)

LEADING ACTOR: Go on, go on. (*The* ACTRESSES *laugh.*)

FATHER: Well, I mean, his rendering of me, even with the help of make-up... well, with his build... (*There is laughter from the* ACTORS.) ...it will hardly be me, I'm thinking, as I really am. It will be more – quite apart from the face – it will be more of a personal interpretation of what I'm like, an impression of what I'm like – if indeed he has one. It won't be me, as I feel myself to be inside here. And this is something that needs to be taken into account by anybody forming an opinion of us.

PRODUCER: Is it the thought of the critics that's worrying you? Here was I, thinking you had something to say! The critics can say what they like. Our job is to get on with putting this play together, if we can! (*Breaking away and looking round.*) Right! Now – is the set ready? (*To the* ACTORS *and* CHARACTERS:) Out of the way, please, everyone! Let's have a look! (*He climbs down off the stage.*) Don't let's waste any more time! (*To the* STEPDAUGHTER:) Will the set do, do you think?

STEPDAUGHTER: Frankly, no! I don't recognize it at all!

PRODUCER: Oh, for Christ's sake! You can't expect us to reproduce for you *in toto* an exact replica of Madame Pace's back room as you knew it! (*To the* FATHER:) A small parlour, you said, with flowered wallpaper?

FATHER: Yes. White flowered wallpaper.

PRODUCER: Well, it's not white. It's striped. So what! I think the furniture is just about OK. Can we have that small table forwards a few inches please! (*The* STAGEHANDS *move it. To the* PROPERTY MAN:) Bring an envelope, too, would you? Blue, if possible. And give it to the Father.

PROPERTY MAN: An ordinary envelope?

PRODUCER: ⎫
FATHER: ⎬ Yes, an ordinary envelope!

PROPERTY MAN: Ordinary envelope coming up! (*Exit.*)

PRODUCER: Right! Let's get going! We want the young lady on first. (*The* LEADING ACTRESS *steps forwards.*) Hold on a minute! Not you! This young lady! (*He indicates the* STEPDAUGHTER.) You're supposed to watch...

STEPDAUGHTER (*chipping in quickly*): ...How I live it!

LEADING ACTRESS (*huffily*): Don't worry, I shall live it all right, once I get a look in!

PRODUCER (*with his hands to his head*): Ladies and gentlemen, can we please cut the cackle! Now: Scene I, the Young Lady and Madame Pace. Oh! (*He looks round momentarily flummoxed, then climbs back on stage.*) What about Madame Pace?

FATHER: She isn't with us.

PRODUCER: So what do we do?

FATHER: But she is alive! She's just as alive as we are!

PRODUCER: Fine! Can you tell us where?

FATHER: Look, let me try something. (*To the* ACTRESSES:) Would you ladies be good enough to let me have your hats a moment?

ACTRESSES (*surprised and amused, all speaking at once*): What? Our hats? What does he want? Whatever for? Whatever next!

PRODUCER: Whatever are you going to do with those? (*The* ACTORS *laugh.*)

FATHER: Nothing much. Just hang them up here a moment on these pegs. Perhaps some of you would be good enough to let me have your coats as well...

ACTORS (*all at once, again surprised and amused*): Coats too? Now what happens? I reckon he's bonkers.

ACTRESSES: What do you want them for? Just our coats?

FATHER: I just want to hang them up here a moment... I'd be awfully grateful... I hope you don't mind...

ACTRESSES (*taking off their hats and some their coats, and hanging them up amid a good deal of laughter*): Well, why not? There we are, then! It's a laugh, but he really means it, I reckon! Is it a fashion show?

FATHER: That is exactly what it is! There! A fashion show!

PRODUCER: May one ask what all this is in aid of?

FATHER: Indeed you may! If we prepare the scene a little more authentically, who knows but what she may not be drawn towards the implements of her trade and appear among us! (*He invites them to look towards the door at the back of the set.*) Now watch! Watch!

(*The door opens and* MADAME PACE *emerges and advances a few paces onto the stage. She is a hideous old harridan, enormously fat, with a garish carrot-coloured woollen wig perched above her raddled face and a scarlet rose stuck over one ear, à l'espagnole. She wears a tasteless but modish gown of gaudy red silk, and carries a fan made of feathers in one hand while flourishing a lit cigarette between two fingers of the other. At her appearance the* ACTORS *and* PRODUCER *back away with horrified gasps and slip hastily down the steps into the auditorium as if making for the central aisle and main exit. The* STEPDAUGHTER, *however, runs up to* MADAME PACE *with all the deference befitting an employee.*)

STEPDAUGHTER (*as she runs up to her*): Here she is! Here she is!

FATHER (*glowing with pleasure*): It's Madame Pace. Didn't I tell you! Here she is!

PRODUCER (*controlling his initial amazement, indignantly*): What the hell are you playing at?

LEADING ACTOR: Can someone tell me what's going on?

YOUNG ACTOR: Where has she sprung from?

YOUNG ACTRESS: She must have been there all the time!

LEADING ACTRESS: They do it with mirrors, darling!

FATHER (*raising his voice above theirs*): Let me speak! Why do you have to be so small-minded and pick everything to pieces! You're destroying the miracle, for that's what it is! Reality itself kindled into life, conjured up, brought into being by the scene itself and drawn towards it, with more right to life in this place than you have. She has more truth than you have! Which of you actresses is going to be Madame Pace? Well: here is Madame Pace! You've got to admit that whoever takes the part will be less true than she is, for she actually is Madame Pace in person! Look! My daughter recognized her and ran straight up to her! Now watch, just watch this scene!

(*With some hesitation, the* PRODUCER *and* ACTORS *return to the stage. The* STEPDAUGHTER *and* MADAME PACE *have by now been engaged in their scene together for some time, throughout the* ACTORS' *protestations and the* FATHER's *reply. Their low whispered conversation is naturalistic, held at a pitch totally unsuited to the stage. So when the* ACTORS' *attention is drawn to the scene by the* FATHER *and they turn to watch it, they see* MADAME PACE, *her hand under the* STEPDAUGHTER's *chin, gabbling away unintelligibly into the girl's raised face. For a moment they strain to hear what is being said, but give up almost at once.*)

PRODUCER: Well?

LEADING ACTOR: What's she saying?

LEADING ACTRESS: I can't hear a word!

YOUNG ACTOR: Speak up! Speak up!

STEPDAUGHTER (*leaving* MADAME PACE *smiling – an indescribable smile – while she comes towards the group of* ACTORS): Speak up? How can we speak up? These aren't

things that can be said out loud! Oh, I could say them out
loud to put *him* down! (*She is referring to the* FATHER.)
That was just revenge! But with Madame it's a very different matter. She could go to prison!

PRODUCER: Well, well, well. Is that so? My dear child, in the
theatre you have to make yourself heard! Do you realize we
can't hear you even up here on this stage? What the devil's it
going to be like when there's an audience? And anyway you
can perfectly well speak out loud to each other; we shan't
be here when the time comes. You've got to imagine the
two of you are on your own in that back room and there's
no one to hear you.

(*The* STEPDAUGHTER *with a winning gesture wags her finger
several times to disagree. There is a touch of malice in her smile.*)

PRODUCER: Why not?

STEPDAUGHTER (*in a knowing whisper*): Because there's
someone who will hear us if she says it all out loud!

PRODUCER (*in consternation*): You haven't got somebody else
about to jump out at us? (*The* ACTORS *make as if to leave
the stage again.*)

FATHER: Oh, no, no! She means me. I would be there you
see, on the other side of that door, waiting. And Madame
knows this. In fact, you must excuse me. I must go so as to
be ready for my cue. (*He makes as if to go.*)

PRODUCER (*stopping him*): No, wait a moment! This is theatre!
You've got to consider the requirements of the medium!
Look, before you're ready to come on…

STEPDAUGHTER (*interrupting*): Let's get on! Let's do it now!
I'm dying to live that scene, I'm mad to live that scene! If he's
ready to do it straight away, I'm ready too! More than ready!

PRODUCER (*shouting her down*): But first we've got to get
that first scene straight, the one with you and Madame!
Can you not take that in?

STEPDAUGHTER: For Heaven's sake, she has only told me what you already know: that once again my mother has done her sewing badly; that the stuff's ruined; and that I must be patient if I want her to go on helping us out of our financial difficulties.

MADAME PACE (*advancing with an air of great importance*): It is so, *señor; porque* never would I try to profit myself, to advantage myself...

PRODUCER (*flabbergasted*): Is that how she speaks?

(*The* ACTORS *burst into fits of laughter.*)

STEPDAUGHTER (*laughing too*): That's how she speaks! Half in Spanish, half in English; it's really funny!

MADAME PACE: It does not seem to me *buena crianza*, how you say – good manners, that you laugh of me. I try to *hablar* your language *como puedo, señor!*

PRODUCER: But it's terrific! Leave it in! Don't change it! This will get them! In fact it is just what it needs to lighten the crudity a bit. You speak exactly like that, dear! It will be great!

STEPDAUGHTER: It will be great all right! You bet it will! It will be great for me, too, won't it, listening to my special instructions in that language. It ought to be a right good laugh! Hilarious, wouldn't you say, hearing that there's a *viejo señor* who wants to amuse himself *con migo!* Wouldn't you agree, Madame?

MADAME PACE: Not "*viejo*", *linda*, "*viejito*", a little bit old! But *mejor para ti*, all the better! If you don't like him, at least he will have *prudencia*.

MOTHER (*She rises from her seat, to the astonishment and consternation of the* ACTORS, *who have taken no notice of her until now. They rush to hold her back and burst out laughing as she tears the wig from Madame Pace's head and flings it to the ground*): You devil! You devil! You monster! Oh my child!

STEPDAUGHTER (*trying to hold her back*): No, Mum, no! No, please!

FATHER (*at the same time ditto*): Come on, just be calm. Sit down, now.

MOTHER: Get her out of my sight!

STEPDAUGHTER (*to the* PRODUCER *who has also hurried over*): We can't have my mother here, we just can't!

FATHER (*also to the* PRODUCER): They can't be in the same place! That's the reason why she wasn't with us when we first arrived. If you put them together it all happens too soon.

PRODUCER: Never mind! Don't let's worry! This is just a sort of rough sketch. It's all useful, even if it's a bit of a muddle. It gives me a chance to piece together the various strands. (*He turns to the* MOTHER *and takes her back to her chair.*) There we are, take it easy, now. Sit yourself down.

(*Meanwhile the* STEPDAUGHTER, *back on the stage, takes up her scene with* MADAME PACE *again.*)

STEPDAUGHTER: Come on then, Madame.

MADAME PACE (*offended*): Oh, no! *Gracias*, no! I, here, do not do *nada* if there is your Mother.

STEPDAUGHTER: Come on, show in the *viejo señor*, who wants to amuse himself *con migo*. (*She turns to all assembled and announces in dictatorial tones.*) This scene, now, it has to be done! So let's get going! (*To* MADAME PACE:) You can go!

MADAME PACE: I go! I go! Most *seguramente* I go! (*She leaves in high dudgeon, picking up her wig on the way and glaring at the* ACTORS *who snigger and clap.*)

STEPDAUGHTER (*to the* FATHER): Make your entrance! No, don't bother to go off again! Come here! Let's say you're on already! Right! Now I'm standing here, all modest, with my head down like this! OK then! Nice and loud. Sort of fresh-sounding, like someone coming in from outside: "Good afternoon, my dear..."

PRODUCER (*back in the auditorium*): Hold on! Who's directing this show, you or me? (*To the* FATHER, *who looks rather hesitant and perplexed:*) Carry on, go right ahead! Go to the back. Don't exit. Just come forward again.

(*The* FATHER *does this in something of a daze. He is very pale. Wholly engrossed now in the reality of his created life, he smiles as he moves downstage, as if not yet touched by the drama which is about to burst upon him. The* ACTORS *are suddenly attentive as the scene begins.*)

PRODUCER (*in a hasty whisper to the* PROMPTER): Be sure to get all this down, won't you!

THE SCENE

FATHER (*as he approaches, a new note in his voice*): Good afternoon, my dear.

STEPDAUGHTER (*her head bowed, barely controlling her disgust*): Good afternoon.

FATHER (*he eyes her tentatively, peering under the hat which almost hides her face. When he sees how very young she is, he exclaims, as if to himself, half-delighted and half-fearful of landing himself in a risky situation*): Ah! Er... it won't be the first time, will it?... I mean, it won't be your first time here?

STEPDAUGHTER (*her head still bowed*): No.

FATHER: You've been here before? (*The* STEPDAUGHTER *nods.*) More than once? (*He waits for her answer, peers again at her face, smiles and then speaks.*) Well, then... you oughtn't to be so... Would you let me take your hat off?

STEPDAUGHTER (*quickly, to stop him, her disgust now all too evident*): No, no. I'll take it off myself. (*She quickly does so, trembling. The* MOTHER *watches all this in a state of extreme agitation. She sits with the* SON *and the younger children who cling to her closely all the time, on the opposite side of the stage from the* ACTORS. *As she follows the scene between the* FATHER *and the* STEPDAUGHTER *her face registers pain, outrage, anxiety and horror. From time to time she hides her face or utters a moan.*)

MOTHER: Oh God! Oh, my God!

FATHER (*he seems momentarily stunned by this sob from the* MOTHER; *after a pause he resumes his earlier tone*): Here, give it to me. I'll put it down. (*He takes the hat from her hands.*) But a pretty little head like yours needs something a bit more special, I think. Why don't you come over here and help me choose you one of Madame Pace's confections?... No?

YOUNG ACTRESS: Hey! Those are our hats you've got there!

PRODUCER (*quickly and angrily*): Shut up, can't you! For God's sake don't try and be funny! This is the big scene! (*To the* STEPDAUGHTER:) Carry on then, please!

STEPDAUGHTER (*to the* FATHER): No, really, I couldn't.

FATHER: Don't say you refuse! You must accept! I should be so disappointed... Look, they really are extremely pretty. Madame Pace would be so pleased. She puts them out specially, you know!

STEPDAUGHTER: Oh no, sir. You see... I shouldn't be able to wear it.

FATHER: What's the trouble? Are you worried about what they will think at home when you turn up in a new hat? Well! Shall I tell you? Shall I tell you what to say?

STEPDAUGHTER (*desperate, finding all this unbearable*): No, that's not it! I shouldn't be able to wear it, because I'm... well, look: you might have noticed! (*She shows him her black dress.*)

FATHER: You're in mourning! My dear, I'm sorry. Of course, I see now. I really beg your pardon. Believe me, I'm most desperately sorry.

STEPDAUGHTER (*mustering all her strength in an effort to conquer her abhorrence and disgust*): All right, all right, it doesn't matter! I should be thanking you, really! There's absolutely no call for you to go apologizing and getting upset. Please don't think any more about what I told you. As for me, well, obviously (*she forces herself to smile*), I've really got to stop thinking about it, these clothes I mean.

PRODUCER (*breaking in, addressing the* PROMPTER *and coming back up onto the stage*): Hold on! Stop a minute! Don't write that down. Omit that last bit! (*To the* FATHER *and the* STEPDAUGHTER:) You're doing fine! Absolutely fine! (*To the* FATHER:) Go straight on with the next bit as we said! (*To the* ACTORS:) That hat scene was ravishing, don't you think?

STEPDAUGHTER: But the best bit's just coming now! Can't we go on?

PRODUCER: Hold your horses a moment! (*To the* ACTORS:) Obviously it has all got to be treated rather lightly...

LEADING ACTOR (*nodding in agreement*): Nice and zippy!

LEADING ACTRESS: It shouldn't present any problems. (*To the* LEADING ACTOR:) We could try it now, couldn't we?

LEADING ACTOR: Fine by me!... I'll make my entrance! (*He goes off ready to come in again through the door at the back.*)

PRODUCER (*to* LEADING ACTRESS): All right, then. Now, you've just finished your scene with Madame Pace. I'll take care of writing that up. You will be over here... Hey, where are you off to?

LEADING ACTRESS: Wait a sec, let me put my hat back on... (*She goes to get her own hat from the hat stand.*)

PRODUCER: That's lovely. Right. You stand here, with your head bowed...

STEPDAUGHTER (*amused*): But she's not wearing black!

LEADING ACTRESS: I shall be, don't worry, and with more success than you, duckie!

65

PRODUCER (*to the* STEPDAUGHTER): Keep out of this, will you? Just watch! You might learn something. (*He claps his hands.*) OK. Let's have your entrance!

(*He climbs down again to get the audience's view. The door at the back opens and the* LEADING ACTOR *comes on. He has the breezy over-familiarity of a seasoned ladies' man. Performed by the* ACTORS, *the scene comes over as completely different. In no way, however, must it smack of parody. It is clearly supposed to be the new improved version, with embellishments. When the* STEPDAUGHTER *and* FATHER *hear their own words uttered by the* ACTOR *and* ACTRESS, *they obviously completely fail to recognize themselves. During the scene which follows they express their surprise, amazement and distress in various ways, in gesture, laughter and downright protest. The* PROMPTER'*s voice can be clearly heard throughout.*)

LEADING ACTOR: "Good afternoon, my dear."
FATHER (*butting in, unable to restrain himself*): No!

(*The* STEPDAUGHTER'*s response to this entrance of the* LEADING ACTOR *is to burst out laughing.*)

PRODUCER (*furiously to them both*): Shut up! And stop laughing for Christ's sake! How the hell do you expect us to get anything done!
STEPDAUGHTER (*turning towards him*): I'm sorry! But how can I help it? Your actress manages to stand in her place without moving, but Heavens, if it were me and I heard someone say "good afternoon" to me in that voice, I'd burst out laughing, as in fact I did.
FATHER (*also approaching the* PRODUCER): She's quite right... it's the manner, and the tone of voice...
PRODUCER: Well, stuff the manner and the tone of voice! Just get out of the way, will you, and let me watch this rehearsal!

LEADING ACTOR (*coming downstage*): Look, I'm supposed to be an old bloke in a brothel, right?

PRODUCER: Yes, of course, take absolutely no notice. Start again! You're doing fine! Start again! (*He waits for the* ACTOR *to continue.*) Right then...

LEADING ACTOR: "Good afternoon, my dear."

LEADING ACTRESS: "Good afternoon."

LEADING ACTOR (*going through the same motions as the* FATHER *peering under the girl's hat, but then expressing very distinctly satisfaction followed by apprehensiveness*): "Ah!... but, I say, this won't be the first time, I hope..."

FATHER (*who can't help correcting him*): Not "I hope". "Will it?" "Will it?"

PRODUCER: He says it should be "Will it?" – question.

LEADING ACTOR (*with reference to the* PROMPTER): I heard him say "I hope".

PRODUCER: Don't worry! It's the same thing! "Will it", "I hope" – nothing in it! Just carry on! Come on! A bit lighter, maybe. Look, let me show you. Look, like this! (*He mounts the stage and plays the scene through from the* FATHER's *entrance.*) "Good afternoon, my dear."

LEADING ACTRESS: "Good afternoon."

PRODUCER: "Ah! but, I say..." (*He turns to the* LEADING ACTOR *to ensure that he has taken in his gesture of peering under the brim of the girl's hat.*) See? Surprise, and anxiety, and satisfaction, all at once. (*Back in the role, to the* LEADING ACTRESS:) "...it won't be the first time, will it? The first time you've been here?" (*Turning back to the* LEADING ACTOR.) See what I mean? (*To the* LEADING ACTRESS:) Then you say "No, sir." (*To the* ACTOR *again:*) A little more... how shall I put it... *souplesse*! (*He returns to the stalls.*)

LEADING ACTRESS: "No, sir."

LEADING ACTOR: "You've been here before? More than once?"

PRODUCER: No, hold on! Let her nod first. "You've been here before?" (*The* LEADING ACTRESS *raises her head, her eyes* half-closed in a show of pained disgust. At a word from the PRODUCER she nods violently twice.)

STEPDAUGHTER (involuntarily): Oh, my God! (She claps a hand to her mouth to muffle her laughter.)

PRODUCER (turning): What now?

STEPDAUGHTER (quickly): Nothing, nothing!

PRODUCER (to LEADING ACTOR): Come on, it's you now!

LEADING ACTOR: "More than once? Well, then... you oughtn't to be so... Would you let me take your hat off?" (The LEADING ACTOR's voice and gestures as he utters this last line cause the STEPDAUGHTER, whose hand is still held over her mouth, to burst out into a noisy guffaw through her fingers, in spite of her real effort to restrain herself.)

LEADING ACTRESS (furious, returning to her chair): I'm damned if I'm going to stay here to be laughed at by her!

LEADING ACTOR: I agree! I've had enough!

PRODUCER (shouting at the STEPDAUGHTER): Stop that noise! Don't you dare do that again!

STEPDAUGHTER: Yes, of course. I'm sorry. I'm sorry.

PRODUCER: Your behaviour is quite appalling! Appalling! I don't know how you dare!

FATHER (trying to intervene): Yes, sir, I know, you are perfectly right! But don't be too hard on her!

PRODUCER (remounting the stage): Why shouldn't I be hard on her! She's a disgrace!

FATHER: You're right of course, but you know it really is such a very strange sensation...

PRODUCER: What's a strange sensation? What's strange? What's strange about it?

FATHER: I admire your actors, I really admire them. This gentleman, and this lady here. But there's no doubt about it – they're not us!

PRODUCER: Well, of course they're not! How could they be? They are actors!

FATHER: That's it! Actors! And they both do a very nice job playing our parts. But you've got to see that to us it looks quite different. It's supposed to be the same, and it just isn't!

PRODUCER: How isn't it the same? What's different about it?

FATHER: It has turned into something... which belongs to them now; it's not ours any more.

PRODUCER: Well, that stands to reason! I've been over all this already!

FATHER: Yes, I do understand. I do.

PRODUCER: Well, then. That's it then, isn't it? (*He turns to the* ACTORS.) This really means we'll have to do the rehearsing on our own in the normal way. I have always found it impossible to rehearse with authors present! Nothing is ever right! (*He turns again to the* FATHER *and the* STEPDAUGHTER.) Come on, we'll give it another go with you two. If you can manage not to laugh.

STEPDAUGHTER: Oh, I shan't laugh now, I shan't laugh now. My good bit is coming now, don't you worry!

PRODUCER: All right, then! Now when she says "Please don't think any more about what I told you"... and then "I've obviously got to stop thinking about these clothes" and so on, well at that point (*turning to the* FATHER) you've got to come in quickly and say "Oh yes, I understand, I understand!" and then immediately afterwards you've got to ask her...

STEPDAUGHTER (*interrupting*): What! What does he ask?

PRODUCER: He's got to ask the reason why you're in mourning!

STEPDAUGHTER: But he didn't! You're so wrong! Look, when I said to him to take no notice of my dress, do you know what he said? He said, "Right! Well, let's take this little dress off, then, shall we, as quickly as we can!"

PRODUCER: Oh, that would go down a bomb! My dear girl, you'd bring the whole theatre about my ears!

STEPDAUGHTER: But it's true!

PRODUCER: But for Heaven's sake, truth doesn't come into it! This place is a theatre. Truth's all right, but only up to a point!

STEPDAUGHTER: How do you want to do it, then?

PRODUCER: You'll see! Just let me carry on for the moment!

STEPDAUGHTER: Oh, no, you don't! You want to use my feelings of disgust, you want to use all the cruel and humiliating stages by which I became the thing I am, to concoct a sentimental little romantic sob story; you want him to ask me why I'm in mourning and me to tell him that my daddy died two months ago. Well, we are not having it! Not on your life! He has got to say to me exactly what he did say! "Let's take this little dress off, then, shall we, as quickly as we can!" And I, still sick at heart and grieving for my father, I went over there, do you see?... behind that screen. And with fingers trembling with embarrassment and loathing, I unhooked the top half of my dress...

PRODUCER (*tearing his fingers through his hair*): Good God, girl! What are you saying!

STEPDAUGHTER (*her voice raised in frenzy*): The truth! Only the truth!

PRODUCER: Well, I don't deny this may well be the truth... and I understand, I understand how horrifying all this must have been for you, but I urge you to see that it's just not possible to put this stuff on the stage!

STEPDAUGHTER: Not possible? Well! In that case... thank you very much... you can count me out!

PRODUCER: No, wait... look!

STEPDAUGHTER: You can count me right out. You've decided between you what's possible on the stage; you've fixed it together in that room! Thanks a lot! I know exactly what's happened! I know what he's after! He wants a chance to flaunt his spiritual agonies. Well, I want to put on my drama! The drama of what has happened to me!

PRODUCER (*with a fierce shrug of annoyance*): Your drama, is it? I see! But it isn't just your drama, is it? What about everybody else's! What about his! (*He points to the* FATHER.) What about your mother's! One character can't be allowed to go hogging the stage like that and upstaging all the others! They have all got to come together in an evenly balanced picture. We can only represent the representable. I know as well as anybody else that everyone's got a rich inner life they want to lay bare. But this is precisely the problem: how to expose just the right amount to keep a proper balance with the rest of the cast; just enough to give an indication of all that inner life you've got tucked away! I mean, can you imagine, if each character were given a full-scale monologue... why not a lecture?... in which he could stand up before the audience and dollop out publicly the rich mix that's stewing away inside him! (*In a kindly, conciliatory tone:*) You'll have to exercise self-restraint, I'm afraid. In fact it will be in your own interest. Let me warn you, that it might not go down at all well, all these ferocious outbursts and protestations of disgust, when you yourself have admitted, if I may say so, that you had already been with other men before him, and more than once, in that establishment of Madame Pace's.

STEPDAUGHTER (*She pauses to recollect herself, then in a low voice, her head bowed*): That's true. But can't you see that for me, those other men are all him!

PRODUCER (*not understanding*): All him? What is that supposed to mean?

STEPDAUGHTER: When somebody goes wrong, isn't it always the responsibility of the person who set the whole thing going in the first place? All the blame goes back to him, before I was born even. I mean, look at him! You can see it's true!

PRODUCER: All right, then! That's quite a packet he's got on his conscience! Give him the chance to act it out!

STEPDAUGHTER: What? How can he? How can he present himself as a man of conscience, tormented by fine moral scruples, if you're going to let him off the other bit?... if you're going to skip the horror: the moment when he realizes that the woman in his arms, the prostitute, whom he's just asked if she will kindly remove her black dress – is the little girl... right?... the little girl he used to go and watch coming out of school? (*These last words have been spoken in a voice shaking with emotion. The* MOTHER, *hearing them, is overcome by an access of irrepressible anguish, which finds expression first in a kind of stifled moaning and then erupts in a paroxysm of tears. Her emotion silences everyone and there is a long pause.*)

STEPDAUGHTER (*as soon as her* MOTHER's *sobs allow, in a sombre resolute tone*): So far this is all just between us. We haven't been seen by the public. And tomorrow you will make your own play out of us, and you'll put it all together in whatever way you fancy. But do you want to see it really, our drama? Shall we let it explode for you, as it really happened?

PRODUCER: What could be better? Then I can pick out whatever I can use.

STEPDAUGHTER: All right, then. Get that Mother on stage.

MOTHER (*her tears giving place to a high scream*): No, no! Don't let them do it! Don't let them do it!

PRODUCER: It's only to have a look, my dear!

MOTHER: I can't! I can't!

PRODUCER: But why not, if it has all happened already? Why should it matter now?

MOTHER: No, it's happening now! It's happening all the time! My agony isn't made up! I am living my agony constantly, every moment; I'm alive and it's alive and it keeps coming back again and again, as fresh as the first time. Those two children there, have you heard them speak? They can't speak, not now. Their business is to cling to me, all the time, to keep the pain alive. For themselves, they don't exist, they don't exist any more! And my elder girl here has run away; she had made off and left me, and now she's lost... lost...

If I see her standing here before me now, it's the same thing,
it's for the same reason, to keep the agony fresh, to keep
it going, all the agony I have suffered through her as well!
FATHER (*solemnly*): The eternal moment! I told you about it.
She's here to catch me, to string me up before the public,
fixed, hooked, chained for ever to the pillory of that one
shaming fleeting moment of my life. It is what she has to
do. And you, sir, cannot really let me off it.
PRODUCER: Oh, I don't say I'm not going to show it: it will be
the focal point of the whole first act, making a great climax
when she (*he indicates the* MOTHER) discovers you...
FATHER: That's right. That's the moment that seals my fate;
that final scream of hers that marks the culmination of all
our suffering.
STEPDAUGHTER: I can still hear it now! That scream sent me out
of my mind! Oh, you can do what you like with my part, I
don't care! Have me in my clothes, if you like. As long as my
arms are bare, just the arms. They have got to be bare because,
you see, standing like this... (*She goes up to the* FATHER *and
places her head against his breast*.) ...with my head here like
this, and my arms like this round his neck, I could see a vein
throbbing, just here in my arm. And then, as if that single pal-
pitating vein filled me with revulsion, I screwed up my eyes like
this... like this... and buried my head in his chest! (*Turning
towards the* MOTHER:) Scream, Mum, scream! (*She buries
her head in the* FATHER*'s breast again, and with her shoulders
tensed as if to protect herself from the scream, she adds in
tones of muffled anguish:*) Scream like you screamed then!
MOTHER (*flinging herself upon them to separate them*): No!
Oh my child! My child! (*She tears the* STEPDAUGHTER
away.) Oh you brute, you dirty brute! It's my daughter!
Can't you see it's my daughter!
PRODUCER (*moving back, at the scream, to the edge of the
stage, while the* ACTORS *appear flabbergasted*): Splendid!
Absolutely splendid! And then curtain, curtain!

FATHER (*hurrying over, distraught*): That's it, you see! That's exactly how it happened!

PRODUCER (*enthusiastically, entirely won over*): Yes, we'll cut it right there! Curtain! Curtain!

(*At the* PRODUCER*'s repeated cries of "Curtain!" the* STAGE MANAGER *lowers the curtain, leaving only the* FATHER *and the* PRODUCER *in front of it.*)

PRODUCER (*looking up and raising his hands*): Good God! When I say "Curtain" I mean, "That's where we'll have a curtain", so they go and lower the bloody thing! (*He lifts up the curtain to enable the two of them to return to the stage.*) But what a curtain! It's absolutely stunning! Can't fail! I'd stake my shirt on that first act!

(*The* PRODUCER *and the* FATHER *return through the curtain to the stage.*

When the curtain goes up we find the first set dismantled and in its place a small garden fountain.

The ACTORS *are sitting on one side of the stage and the* CHARACTERS *on the other. The* PRODUCER *is standing lost in thought, chin in hand, in the centre of the stage.*)

PRODUCER (*shaking himself out of his reverie, after a pause*): Well, then. Let's move on to Act Two. Best to leave it all to me, I think, as we agreed. Everything will be just fine!

STEPDAUGHTER: It's the bit where we go to live with *him* (*she indicates the* FATHER) much to his disgust over there! (*She is referring to the* SON.)

PRODUCER (*out of patience*): All right. But leave it to me, will you?

STEPDAUGHTER: As long as you make it clear how much he loathed us coming!

MOTHER (*shaking her head in her corner*): Not that it did us any good!

STEPDAUGHTER (*turning on her, sharply*): That's not the point! The worse it was for us, the guiltier he felt about it!

PRODUCER (*still impatient*): I've got the picture, don't worry! I'll keep it all in mind. Specially at the beginning.

MOTHER (*in beseeching tones*): But please... make me easy in my mind... please make sure people realize that I tried every means I could think of—

STEPDAUGHTER (*interrupting bitterly*): ...Of squaring me! Oh yes, of getting me to give up the fight! (*To the* PRODUCER:) Go on, let her have her way! It's perfectly true. She did try. I get quite a kick out of it in fact because, well, you'll see: the more abject she gets, and the more she makes up to him – the more he holds himself aloof. He just... is... not... there. Serves her right!

PRODUCER: Are we going to get on with it then, this Act Two?

STEPDAUGHTER: I'll shut up! But your idea of putting the whole thing in the garden isn't going to work!

PRODUCER: Why not?

STEPDAUGHTER: Because of him! (*She points to the* SON.) He spends the whole time shut up in his room, on his own! And anyway, my little brother's bit all happens in the house. I told you. Poor little soul!

PRODUCER: All right, then. But we can't keep switching about all the time changing scenes. You can't put up little signs saying "House", "Garden", "House" three or four times in one act!

LEADING ACTOR: They used to...

PRODUCER: Yes, in the days when audiences were about as sophisticated as that little girl!

LEADING ACTRESS: They were better at accepting the illusion!

FATHER (*jumping up suddenly*): Illusion? I would ask you not to speak of illusion! I would beg you not to use that word. For us it has a particularly cruel ring!

75

PRODUCER (*astonished*): For Heaven's sake, why?

FATHER: Oh, yes, cruel, cruel! You really ought to understand.

PRODUCER: What are we supposed to say? Illusion is our stock-in-trade... the illusion we have to create...

LEADING ACTOR: ...With our acting...

PRODUCER: ...To make the play live for the audience!

FATHER: I understand. But maybe you are incapable of understanding us. I'm sorry, but the fact is, you see, for you and your actors all this is – quite rightly – a kind of game...

LEADING ACTRESS (*taking offence and interrupting*): A game! This isn't kids' stuff! This is serious acting!

FATHER: I'm not saying it isn't. And let me say, I entirely understand how you play it! As artists – as your producer says – you have to create a perfect illusion of reality.

PRODUCER: That's right.

FATHER: But what if you stop to consider that we, the six of us (*he gestures briefly to indicate the six*) have no other reality; that we don't exist outside this illusion!

PRODUCER (*floored by this and looking round at the blank puzzled faces of his* ACTORS): How exactly do you mean?

FATHER (*he stands and looks at them a moment, then, with a bleak smile*): Can't you see? What other reality could we have? What for you is an illusion, that has got to be created, for us is our only reality. (*He pauses briefly, then walks over to the* PRODUCER *and continues.*) And we're not the only ones, you see. Just you think about it! (*Looking him straight in the eyes:*) Can you tell me who you are? (*He stands, pointing his finger at him.*)

PRODUCER (*disturbed, with a half-smile*): Tell you who I am? I'm me!

FATHER: And if I suggested that you were not you, that you were me?

PRODUCER: I'd tell you you were mad! (*The* ACTORS *laugh.*)

FATHER: You're quite right to laugh. Of course everything here is a game! (*To the* PRODUCER:) That's how you can argue that your actor there, the man himself, will only be playing at being me, the person I am. Do you see I've caught you out?

PRODUCER (*annoyed*): But you have *said* this before! Have we got to have it all again?

FATHER: No, that wasn't in fact the point I was trying to make. I am actually asking you to set aside your game a moment (*he glances apprehensively at the* LEADING ACTRESS *and corrects himself*)... your art, the art you practise here with your actors, and consider my question, my serious question which I repeat: who are you?

PRODUCER (*in amazement and exasperation to the* ACTORS): My God, the man's got a nerve! Calls himself a "character" and has the gall actually to ask me who I am.

FATHER (*with quiet dignity*): A character, my dear sir, may always ask a man who he is. Because a character really does have a life of his own, stamped with his own characteristics which ensure that he is always who he is. While a man – I don't mean you in particular, but a man in general, can very easily be "no one".

PRODUCER: Right! Well, perhaps I'd better get it into your head that I'm the producer of this play and the director of this company!

FATHER (*continuing softly, his tone mellifluous and deferential*): I'm trying to find out, sir, how your present self sees your past self, how the man you are today sees the man you were once upon a time. Think of yourself as once you were, sir, and the illusions that you had, the way you saw the world around you and inside you! That was the world for you, in those days, sir! Now, thinking back on those lost illusions, on all that vanished-seeming world which once was the world for you, don't you feel something give way beneath your feet, not just these boards but the very ground of your existence? Knowing that in just the same way the "you" of today, which feels like reality here and now, is destined to seem an illusion tomorrow?

PRODUCER (*who has not really understood, but is dazed by the speciousness of the argument*): Well, where does that get you?

FATHER: Oh, nowhere, I just wanted to show you that if we (*he refers to himself and the other* CHARACTERS) have no reality outside illusion, then perhaps you ought not to place too much faith in your reality, either, the solid flesh and blood you have today – on the grounds that like yesterday's reality, today's too will surely turn out to be illusion by tomorrow.

PRODUCER (*determined to make light of all this*): That's good! Now tell me that you and this play of yours are more real and true than I am!

FATHER (*with the utmost seriousness*): Of that there can be no doubt at all.

PRODUCER: Is that so?

FATHER: I thought you had understood that all along.

PRODUCER: You are more real than me?

FATHER: If your reality can change from one day to the next…

PRODUCER: Of course it does! That's obvious! It's always changing. Everybody's is.

FATHER (*raising his voice to a shout*): But not ours! Not ours, do you see? That's the difference! It doesn't change, it can't change, it can never be any different, ever, because it's fixed, as it is, once and for all. We are stuck with it, sir, and therein lies the horror; stuck with an immutable reality. You should find our presence chilling.

PRODUCER (*suddenly facing him squarely, struck by an idea which has just occurred to him*): What I'd like to know, though, is: who has ever heard of a character stepping out of his part and holding forth about it like you do, expounding it and explaining it. Who has ever heard of such a thing? Tell me that! I'm sure I haven't!

FATHER: No, you've never heard of such a thing because on the whole authors keep quiet about the birth pangs they endure producing their creations. Once an author's characters come to life and stand before him as living beings, they decide what to say and do, and he simply follows their suggestions. If he doesn't like the way they are, that's just too bad! A character, once born, takes on such a degree of independence from his author that one can imagine all sorts of situations for him that have never occurred to the author. He can take on a completely new meaning sometimes that the author never dreamt of.

PRODUCER: Yes, well, I know that!

FATHER: Well, then, what's so amazing about us? If you can imagine the disaster it is for a character to go through what I've described, to be born in the imagination of an author who then turns round and refuses him life – can you then say that such a character, abandoned like that, alive but denied life, is wrong to go and do what we are doing? Aren't we right to come and beg of all of you the thing we begged of him, time and time again, beseeching him, urging him, appearing before him one after the other... I would go... or she would go (*indicating the* STEPDAUGHTER) or sometimes this poor Mother...

STEPDAUGHTER (*moving downstage in a kind of trance*): Yes, it's true, I did. I used to go, to tempt him, time after time... in that cheerless study where he did his writing, just as it was getting dark. He would be sitting there, sunk in his armchair, not even bothering to turn on the light. The room would get darker and darker and the darkness would be teeming with our presence. We went there to tempt him. (*She seems to be back in the study she is describing. The* ACTORS' *presence appears to irritate her.*) Go away, can't you? Can't you leave us be? Mum's there, with that "son"... I'm there with the little one... that kid always on his own... and then, me with *him* (*she nods almost imperceptibly in the* FATHER's *direction*)... and then me alone, alone in the dark again! (*She gives a sudden start as if anxious to grasp hold of the vision she has of herself, glowing with life in that darkness.*) Oh, my life! What scenes, what scenes we used to suggest to him! And I was the one who tempted him most of all!

FATHER: You did. But maybe that was it! Perhaps it was your fault; you tried too hard, you overdid it!

STEPDAUGHTER: Rubbish! He made me like this, didn't he? (*She approaches the* PRODUCER *and adopts a confidential tone.*) I think the real reason was discouragement with the theatre, or disgust with it – the way it lets itself be dictated to by public taste...

PRODUCER: Let's get on! Let's get on, for Heaven's sake! Let's get to what in fact happened!

STEPDAUGHTER: It seems to me you're going to have an awful lot to choose from, once we get inside that house! Especially as you said we couldn't keep changing the scene or putting up notices every five minutes.

PRODUCER: Too right! We have to take the facts, knock them into shape and compress them into a close-knit plot. It can't be done your way; you want to see your little brother coming home from school and wandering round the rooms like a lost soul, hiding behind doors and hatching his plot, the plot you spoke of as... what was it you said?

STEPDAUGHTER: It drained him, sir, it drained the life out of him!

PRODUCER: Yes... odd way of putting it... Still, we see the plot "looming larger and larger in his eyes", was that it?

STEPDAUGHTER: That's right, sir. You have only to look at him! (*She points to where he stands beside his* MOTHER.)

PRODUCER: Fine! And then, at the same time, you want us to show the little girl playing away, all unawares, in the garden. One in the house, one in the garden... you really think we can do that?

STEPDAUGHTER: Oh yes, having a lovely time in the sunshine! That is my one compensation, to see her so happy, so thrilled with that garden; coming after the misery and squalor of that horrible bedroom where the four of us all slept together. She and I shared a bed – think of it! Me with my horrible contaminated body next to hers! She used to hold me ever so tight in her loving, innocent little arms! And whenever she saw me in the garden she used to come running up to me to hold my hand. She had no time for the big flowers; she was only interested in finding the "ickle baby ones", and how she used to love showing them to me! She'd get so excited! (*At this point she breaks off, overwhelmed by the memory, and gives way to a long and desperate fit of crying. She is sitting at a small table where she lets her head fall onto her arms. Her emotion silences every one. The* PRODUCER *approaches her in a fatherly manner, and says to comfort her:*)

PRODUCER: We'll have the garden, don't worry, we'll have the garden! We'll make it all right for you, you'll see! We'll put the whole action in the garden. (*He calls a* STAGEHAND *by name.*) Send down a tree or two, will you? Couple of small cypresses here in front of the fountain! (*Two cypresses are lowered and hammered hastily in place by the* CHIEF STAGEHAND.) That's roughly it for now, just to give us an idea. (*He calls out to the* STAGEHAND *again.*) Hey! Can we have a sky-cloth?

STAGEHAND (*from the flies*): What?

PRODUCER: A sky-cloth! A backcloth! Here, behind the fountain! (*A white cloth is dropped from the flies.*) Not white, you idiot! I said sky, didn't I? Never mind! Leave it now! I'll manage. (*He calls the* ELECTRICIAN.) Lights! Switch off, will you, and let's have a bit of atmosphere. Moonlight, please! The blues in the batten and a blue spot on the cloth! Good! That's fine! (*A mysterious moonlit scene appears as ordered; the atmosphere of a garden at evening under the moon affects the way the* ACTORS *move and speak.*)

PRODUCER (*to the* STEPDAUGHTER): How's this then? Instead of wandering about the house and hiding behind doors, the boy can do his wandering about here in the garden and hide behind the trees. But you realize it may be a bit tricky finding a child actress to do the little girl's scene with you, the bit where she shows you the flowers. (*To the* BOY:) Anyway you come on out here! Let's see if we can work this one out! (*The* BOY *does not move.*) Come on! Come on! (*He drags him forwards and tries to make him hold his head up. Each time the boy's head sags forwards.*) Good God, he's a total disaster! What's wrong with the lad? He has surely got to speak sometime! (*He puts a hand on his shoulder and guides him behind the trees.*) Now, come on! Let's see what you can do! Just hide here... that's the idea... Try peering out a bit, sort of on the lookout... (*He stands back to see the effect. As the* BOY *follows his instructions the* ACTORS *show signs of disquiet. They are very much impressed.*) Ah, that's splendid... splendid... (*He turns again to the* STEPDAUGHTER.) How would it be if the little girl were to come upon him peering out like that? Then she could run over to him and that would surely make him say something?

STEPDAUGHTER: It's no good hoping he will say anything as long as *he's* around! (*She indicates the* SON.) You would have to get rid of him, first.

SON (*firmly making his way towards one of the sets of steps leading off the stage*): Only too ready to oblige! My pleasure! What could be better?

PRODUCER (*rushing to hold him back*): No! Where are you off to? Wait!

(*The* MOTHER *gets up, horrified, deeply distressed at the thought of his going. She instinctively reaches out her arms to stop him, but without leaving her place.*)

SON (*at the footlights, to the* PRODUCER *who is holding on to him*): I've really got nothing to do with all this. Will you please let me go! Let me go, will you?

PRODUCER: What do you mean, you've got nothing to do with it?

STEPDAUGHTER (*in a cool, unruffled tone, tinged with irony*): Don't stop him! He won't go away!

FATHER: He has to play the dreadful scene in the garden with his Mother.

SON (*quickly, with fierce resolution*): I'm not acting in any play! I have said that right from the start! (*To the* PRODUCER:) Let me go!

STEPDAUGHTER (*running over to the* PRODUCER): Allow me, will you? (*She frees the* SON *from the* PRODUCER*'s grasp.*) Let go of him! (*She turns to the* SON *as soon as he is freed.*) All right then, off you go! (*The* SON *stands, his arms outstretched towards the steps, but he is held back as if by some mysterious force so that he cannot go down them. Then to the astonishment and perturbation of the* ACTORS, *he moves slowly across the footlights towards the other set of steps, where he stands at the top in the same attitude, posed for descent but unable to move. The* STEPDAUGHTER, *who has followed his movements as though challenging him to go, bursts out laughing.*) He can't, you see? He can't get away! He has got to stay here. He is tied and chained by a bond that's quite indissoluble. But if I'm still here – and I do get away in the end when everything happens as it must and at last I get out because I hate him so much and can't bear the sight of him – I say if I'm still here and can put up with seeing him and having him here, do you think he would stay here a moment if he could go? No, he can't budge! He has got to stay here with that marvellous father of his, and that mother, and be their only child again... (*Turning to the* MOTHER.) Come on then, Mummy! Let's have it! (*Explaining the* MOTHER*'s movements to the* PRODUCER:) Look, you see, she had got up already. She had got up to try and stop him going. (*To the* MOTHER, *as if exercising some kind of magic power:*) Come along, that's the way... (*To* *the* PRODUCER:) Imagine what it's costing her to show her feelings like this in front of your actors, but she's so desperate to get near him that – look! See? She's even willing to go through that scene again!

(*The* MOTHER *has indeed crept up to the* SON, *and the moment her daughter finishes speaking she stretches out her arms towards him to indicate her readiness to play the scene.*)

SON (*quickly*): Oh, no! Not me! Not me! If I can't leave, then I'll stay here, but, for the umpteenth time, I'm not acting in any play!

FATHER (*seething with fury, to the* PRODUCER): Make him, can't you?

SON: No one can make me!

FATHER: Well then I will!

STEPDAUGHTER: Wait a minute! Wait! First we've got to get the little one over to the fountain! (*She runs to get the* LITTLE GIRL, *falls to her knees in front of her, and takes her little face between her hands.*) Oh, my poor darling, and such a lost look in those lovely big eyes; whatever do you make of this place! It's a stage, my pet! What's a stage? Well, look, it's a place where people play at being serious. They act plays there. And we're going to act a play. Yes, seriously, that's right! You, too... (*She puts her arms round her, hugging her close and rocking gently to and fro.*) Oh, my little love, my little love, what a horrid play it's going to be for you! What a horrible thing they have thought up for you! The garden... the fountain... Yes, of course, it's a pretend fountain! That's the trouble, my pet, that everything here is pretend! And perhaps for you a pretend fountain is more fun than a real one, because you can play in it, can't you? But no... it's only for the others that it's a game; not for you, my poor pet, you're all too real! You are really playing in a real pond, a lovely big green one with reeds growing

84

in it to make shade and reflections, and lots of baby ducks swimming about and making ripples in the shady surface. Then you want to catch one of the baby ducks… (*She gives a shriek which fills everyone with horror.*) No, Rosetta my love, no! Your mummy's not looking after you, because of that swine of a son! I am half out of my mind with distress… and that boy there… (*She leaves the* LITTLE GIRL *and turns with her usual impatience to the* BOY.) What do you think you're doing out here, skulking around like a little tramp? The way you carry on, it will be your fault too if that poor little thing gets drowned: you don't have to look like that – I have paid for you all to be here, haven't I? (*She seizes him by the arm to try and drag his hand out of his pocket.*) What have you got there? What are you hiding? Let's see your hand, come on! (*She wrenches the hand out of the pocket and, to everyone's horror, reveals that he is grasping a revolver. She registers satisfaction as she looks at it and then adds darkly.*) Ah! And where did you get that gun? (*The* BOY, *his eyes vacantly staring, seems stunned and does not answer.*) You stupid idiot! In your place I shouldn't have killed myself; I'd have killed one of those two, or both of them, father and son together! (*She pushes him back into his hiding place behind the cypress; then she takes the* LITTLE GIRL *and lifts her into the fountain and lays her gently down inside it out of sight. She then sinks wearily down beside the fountain, and leans against it, her face hidden in her arms.*)

PRODUCER: That's terrific! (*He turns to the* SON.) Meanwhile…
SON (*peevishly*): Meanwhile nothing! It's a lie! There never was a scene between her and me! (*He is referring to the* MOTHER.) Go on, get her to tell you! She'll tell you what happened! (*While he speaks the* SECOND ACTRESS *and the* YOUNG ACTOR *have detached themselves from the* ACTORS' *group and are now standing carefully observing the* MOTHER *and* SON *with a view to recreating their parts.*)

MOTHER: Oh yes, it's true all right. I had gone to his room.

SON: To my room! Right? Not the garden at all!

PRODUCER: It doesn't matter where it was! We've got to rear-range the action. I explained that.

SON (*suddenly aware of the* YOUNG ACTOR*'s scrutiny*): What the hell do you want?

YOUNG ACTOR: Nothing. I'm just watching.

SON (*looking round and seeing the* SECOND ACTRESS): And here's another one! I suppose you're doing her part?

PRODUCER: Of course she is! Of course! And you should be damn grateful they're taking so much trouble!

SON: Yes, well! Thanks very much! But haven't you realized yet that you're not going to be able to do this play? You haven't got us inside you! Your actors can only look at us from the outside! How can you expect anybody to live their life in front of a kind of distorting mirror, which doesn't just freeze our expression in a reflected image, but twists it into a total travesty which we don't even recognize?

FATHER: He's right! He's quite right! He really is, you know!

PRODUCER (*to the* YOUNG ACTOR *and the* SECOND ACTRESS): All right, then, you two take yourselves off!

SON: It's all useless, anyway. I'm staying out of it.

PRODUCER: Just shut up a moment, will you? I want to hear what your Mother has to say! (*To the* MOTHER:) So – you had gone in?

MOTHER: Yes, I had gone to his room. I couldn't bear it any longer. I was sick with anxiety. I had to get it off my chest. But as soon as he saw me come in…

SON: I didn't want a scene! I went out of the room. I went because I didn't want a scene. I never have gone in for scenes. Do you understand?

MOTHER: It's true. Everything he says is true!

PRODUCER: But all the same we've got to do it now, this scene between you two! It's the key to the whole thing.

MOTHER: I'm here. I'll do it. Oh, if only you could find some way for me to speak to him a moment! If only I could pour out my heart to him!

FATHER (*violently, coming threateningly close to the* SON): You're going to do this scene, son! You're going to do it for your mother's sake!

SON (*more determined than ever*): I'm not doing anything!

FATHER (*seizing hold of his coat and shaking him*): Oh, yes you are, by God! I'll see to that! Can't you hear what she's saying to you? Haven't you any natural feelings?

SON (*grabbing in turn at his* FATHER): I won't! I won't! That's all there is to it!

(*There is general agitation. The* MOTHER, *horrified, tries to come between them and separate them.*)

MOTHER: Don't fight! For pity's sake don't fight!

FATHER (*not letting go*): You'll do as you're told! You'll do as you're told!

SON (*struggling with him and finally throwing him to the ground near the steps, much to everybody's shock*): But what the hell's got into you? Aren't you ashamed to go flaunting your disgrace – our disgrace – in front of people? I'm keeping out of it! I'm keeping out! That's what *he* wanted, isn't it! Our author who wouldn't put us on a stage!

PRODUCER: But you came and found yourselves a stage.

SON (*indicating the* FATHER): He did! I didn't!

PRODUCER: Are you saying you're not here?

SON: He's the one who wanted to come. He dragged us along here! And he's the one who went in there with you to dream up not just what happened, but, for Heaven's sake, a whole lot of stuff that never happened at all!

PRODUCER: Go on then, you say what happened! Tell me! You left your room… did you say anything?

SON (*after a moment's hesitation*): Nothing. Because, I told you, I didn't want to make a scene!

PRODUCER (*egging him on*): Right, and then what? What did you do next?

SON (*everyone watches uneasily as he walks a few steps across the stage*): Nothing. I went across the garden… (*He breaks off, lost in dark thoughts.*)

PRODUCER (*made uneasy by his reticence, urging him to say more*): Well? What happened when you went across the garden?

SON (*at the end of his endurance, holding up an arm to hide his face*): Why must you make me talk about it? It's horrible!

(*The MOTHER is shaking all over. A stifled moaning sound comes from her as she looks towards the fountain.*)

PRODUCER (*softly, taking in her look, and turning to the SON with rising apprehension*): The little girl?

SON (*staring straight in front of him, towards the audience*): There, in the fountain…

FATHER (*on the floor still, pointing towards the MOTHER, his voice full of pity*): She followed him out there, you see.

PRODUCER (*to the son, anxiously*): What did you do then?

SON (*slowly, still staring straight out in front*): I ran to the fountain. I rushed over to fish her out… but suddenly I stopped, because behind those trees I saw a sight which made my blood run cold: it was the boy. He was standing there stock still and staring like a mad thing at the drowned body of his little sister in the fountain. (*The STEPDAUGHTER is still huddled up against the fountain so that the child's body is hidden from view. Her uncontrollable sobs reach us like an echo from the depths. There is a pause.*) I went up to him, and then… (*A revolver shot rings out from behind the trees where the BOY has been hiding.*)

MOTHER (*with a harrowing cry, as she comes running with the SON and all the ACTORS amid general confusion*): My son!

my son! (*And then amid all the hubbub and shouting can be heard her cry:*) Help! Help!

PRODUCER (*his voice distinguishable among the cries of the others as he cuts a path through them all, while the* BOY *is carried out, and taken behind the white cloth*): Is he hurt? Is he really hurt? (*All except the* PRODUCER *and the* FATHER, *who is still on the floor over by the steps, have disappeared behind the white sky-cloth and stay there awhile murmuring in subdued and anxious voices. Then the* ACTORS *return to the stage, emerging from either side of the cloth.*)

LEADING ACTRESS (*returning from the right, very upset*): He's dead! Poor boy! He's dead! Oh, how ghastly!

LEADING ACTOR (*returning from the left, laughing*): Some corpse! He's pretending! It's a fake! Don't you believe it!

OTHER ACTORS (*from the right*): It's not a fake! It's true! He's really dead!

OTHER ACTORS (*from the left*): Rubbish! It's a fake! He's pretending!

FATHER (*standing up and shouting them all down*): There's no pretence! It's the truth; it's real! That, ladies and gentleman, is reality! (*And he too disappears, in despair, behind the cloth.*)

PRODUCER (*who can stand it no longer*): Pretence! Reality! What the hell! I've had enough! Lights! Lights! Lights! (*Suddenly the stage and auditorium are flooded with brilliant light. The* PRODUCER *heaves a great sigh as if released from a nightmare. Baffled and bemused looks are exchanged all round.*) Dear God! What a crazy setup! They have made me lose a whole day's work! (*He looks at his watch.*) You can go! You can go! There's not time to do anything now. It's too late to start rehearsing again. I'll see you all tonight! (*As soon as the* ACTORS *have said goodbye and left, he calls to the man on the lights.*) Hey! (*He calls his name.*) Switch off, will you!

(*The whole theatre is immediately plunged into total darkness.*) Good God! You might have left me a light or two to get out by!

(*The next moment a green floodlight comes on behind the backcloth. It seems a mistake. Four enormous clear-cut shadows of the* CHARACTERS *(less the* BOY *and the* LITTLE GIRL*) are projected against the cloth. The* PRODUCER *takes one look and rushes in terror from the stage. As he does so the green light at the back goes off and is replaced by the earlier blue moonlit effect on the front of the stage. Slowly the* CHARACTERS *emerge from behind the cloth. First the* SON *comes forwards, from the right side, followed by the* MOTHER, *her arms outstretched towards him. Then the* FATHER *advances from the left. They come to a halt halfway down the stage and stand there like figures in a trance. Lastly the* STEPDAUGHTER *emerges from the left and runs towards one of the stairways. She stops at the top step for a moment to look back at the other three. She lets out a piercing squeal of laughter and hurls herself down the steps. She runs up the central aisle to the back of the auditorium where she stops again, turns and gives another burst of laughter at the sight of the three left on the stage. She disappears from the auditorium and as she runs out through the foyer, her laughter is heard growing fainter and fainter. There is a short pause, and then the…*)

CURTAIN

HENRY IV

Enrico IV (1922)

Translated by Robert Rietti and John Wardle
(Revised for the present edition
by Alessandro Gallenzi)

Characters

HENRY IV
MARCHESA MATILDE SPINA (DONNA MATILDE)
The MARCHIONESS FRIDA, *her daughter*
The YOUNG MARQUIS CARLO DI NOLLI
BARON TITO BELCREDI
DOCTOR DIONISIO GENONI
LANDOLF (*Lolo*), HAROLD (*Franco*), ORDULF (*Momo*),
    BERTOLD (*Pino*), FOUR YOUNG MEN *employed to pose*
    as the Emperor's "Counsellors"
GIOVANNI, *an old butler*
TWO MENSERVANTS *dressed in eleventh-century costume*

The action of the play occurs in an isolated country house in
    Umbria during the 1920s.
ACT ONE: *The throne room.*
ACT TWO: *Another room in the house.*
ACT THREE: *The throne room.*

There is a short passage, enclosed by square brackets, towards
the end of Act One (p. 127), which Pirandello suggested could
be omitted in performance, in order not to hold up the action.

Act One

The large hall of the house. It has been furnished and decorated with great care, in order to suggest a hall that could be the throne room of HENRY IV *in the imperial palace at Goslar. But conspicuous amongst so many antiques are two life-size modern oil portraits. They hang at the back of the room, just above a ledge of carved wood, which runs the whole length of the back wall. The ledge is wide and protrudes so that people can sit on it, as on a long bench. The portraits are on either side of the throne, which is in the middle of the wall. The portraits represent a man and a woman, both young and in fancy dress – the man is* HENRY IV, *the woman is* MATILDE OF TUSCANY. *There are two doors on the right and one on the left.*

When the curtain rises, the TWO MENSERVANTS, *as if startled, jump up from the ledge, on which they have been sprawling full length, and, picking up their halberds, post themselves at the foot of the throne, to right and left, afterwards standing there like a couple of statues. After a few seconds* HAROLD, LANDOLF, ORDULF *and* BERTOLD *come in by the second door on the right. They are young men who are paid by the* MARQUIS CARLO DI NOLLI *to pretend to be "Privy Counsellors" – that is, vassals of the sovereign who belong to the lower echelons of the aristocracy at* HENRY'S *Court. They are accordingly dressed like German knights of the eleventh century.* BERTOLD, *whose real name is* FINO, *is just starting on the job. The other three, although showing him the ropes, are amusing themselves at his expense. The whole of this opening scene should be acted with ingenious vivacity.*

LANDOLF (*to* BERTOLD, *as if continuing an explanation*):
   And this is the throne room.

HAROLD: At Goslar.

ORDULF: Or, if you like, at the Harzburg Castle.

HAROLD: Or at Worms.

LANDOLF: Follow our lead and jump from one place to the
   next, according to the particular historical scene we're
   playing.

ORDULF: Might be Saxony.

HAROLD: Lombardy.

LANDOLF: On the Rhine.

1ST MANSERVANT (*remaining still, moving only his lips*):
   Psst! Psst!

HAROLD: Yes?

1ST MANSERVANT (*rigid as ever, and sotto voce, referring
   to* HENRY IV): Is he coming or not?

ORDULF: He's asleep. Take it easy.

(*Both* MENSERVANTS *relax. The second, after letting out a
sigh of relief, stretches himself out on the ledge again.*)

2ND MANSERVANT: You might have said so!

1ST MANSERVANT (*going down to* HAROLD): Give me a
   light, will you?

LANDOLF: A-ha! No pipes in here!

1ST MANSERVANT: Don't worry, it's only a cigarette.

(HAROLD *produces his lighter.* 1ST MANSERVANT *lights his
cigarette and goes to sprawl on the ledge.*)

BERTOLD (*he has been taking things in, half in admiration,
   half in bewilderment*): But… this room… these clothes…
   I don't understand. He is Henry the Fourth of France,
   isn't he?

(*The others laugh at this.*)

LANDOLF (*egging his companions on to make fun of* BERTOLD): Henry of France! Listen to him!

ORDULF (*as above*): He thought it was Henry the Fourth of France!

HAROLD: Henry the Fourth of Germany, my dear chap. Salic Dynasty and all that.

ORDULF: The great and tragic emperor.

LANDOLF: Henry the Fourth of Canossa. We wage a terrible war here... between State and Church, day after day.

ORDULF: Empire against Papacy.

HAROLD: Antipopes against popes.

LANDOLF: Kings against anti-kings.

ORDULF: War against the Saxons.

HAROLD: And all the rebel princes.

LANDOLF: Even the Emperor's own sons.

BERTOLD (*holding his head as if to shield it from this flood of information*): Of course, of course! I see it now. No wonder I couldn't understand when I found myself in this costume and saw this room. I was right, wasn't I? No one wore anything like this in the sixteenth century.

HAROLD: Sixteenth?

ORDULF: We're bang in the middle of the eleventh!

LANDOLF: Work it out for yourself. If we're outside Canossa, on the 25th of January 1071, then...

BERTOLD (*more and more bewildered*): Good Lord... then it's a disaster!

ORDULF: It certainly is if you still think you are at the French Court!

BERTOLD: But then, I've studied the wrong history!

LANDOLF: My dear fellow, we are four hundred years ahead of you. You aren't even born yet.

BERTOLD (*flaring up*): They should have told me it was Henry the Fourth of Germany, not of France. They gave me a fortnight to swot up on all the facts. God knows how many books I've been leafed through… and all for nothing.

HAROLD: But didn't you know that poor old Tito was going to play Adalbert of Bremen?

BERTOLD: Adalbert of where? I didn't know a thing!

LANDOLF: Well, you see, when Tito died, the young Marquis di Nolli…

BERTOLD: That's right. *He's* the chap who engaged me. Why didn't he tell me?…

HAROLD: Maybe he thought you knew.

LANDOLF: He didn't want to take on anyone else in Tito's place. He thought the three of us who were left would be enough. But he started shouting: "They've driven Adalbert away from me!" You see, he didn't realize poor Tito was dead, and as he thought of him as Bishop Adalbert, the old man assumed he'd been driven away from Court by his rivals, the Bishops of Cologne and Mainz.

BERTOLD (*holding his head with both hands*): I don't know anything about that story!

ORDULF: Now, that's a big problem, my friend!

HAROLD: The worst of it is we don't know who you're supposed to be, either.

BERTOLD: Not even you? You don't know who I'm to play?

ORDULF: Well… Bertold, I suppose.

BERTOLD: Bertold who? And why Bertold?

LANDOLF: Because he started shouting: "They've driven Adalbert away from me, so now I must have Bertold. I want Bertold!"

HAROLD: We didn't know what he was talking about. We'd never heard of Bertold.

ORDULF: But now you are here… so Bertold you are!

LANDOLF: You'll be fine in the part.

BERTOLD (*concerned, making for the door*): Oh no, thank you very much! I'm off. I'm off!

(*The others laugh while* HAROLD *and* ORDULF *pull him away from the door.*)

HAROLD: Calm down, calm down!

ORDULF: You're not Bertoldo, the character of that fairy tale, are you?

LANDOLF: And if it's any comfort to you, we don't know who we are, either. He's Harold, he's Ordulf, I'm Landolf. These are the names he's given us, and we're used to it now. But who knows who we really are – just names from that period! Yours must be a name from that time too: Bertold. Poor old Tito was the only one among us who had a specific role, based on historical details: he was the Bishop of Bremen. He looked like one too. He was magnificent, poor Tito!

HAROLD: Of course – he was able to read about it in the history books!

LANDOLF: And the way he used to dominate His Imperial Majesty too! Took him in hand, guided, advised him like a tutor or counsellor. If it comes to that, we're counsellors as well – "Privy Counsellors" – but that's only because it's down in the history books that Henry the Fourth was hated by his great nobles because he surrounded himself at Court with young men belonging to the petty aristocracy.

ORDULF: Which is us.

LANDOLF: Exactly. Royal small fry! Devoted enough – a bit dissolute, cheerful…

BERTOLD: Have I got to be cheerful?

HAROLD: Well, of course… like us.

ORDULF: It's not always easy, believe me!

LANDOLF: It's a pity really, because, as you can see, everything's here. With these costumes we could mount a lovely production of some historical play – the kind of thing that goes down so well in the theatre these days. And the story of Henry the Fourth has enough material for not just one, but a dozen plays. Well! All four of us and those two clowns there (*indicating the* MENSERVANTS), standing to attention at the foot of the throne – we're all here with nothing to do, no one to direct us, to give us a few scenes to play... The form – how can I put it? – the form is there, but there is no content! We're worse off than the actual Privy Counsellors of the real Henry the Fourth, because, well, no one gave them parts to play either, but at least they didn't know they were supposed to be acting! What they did they just did. It wasn't acting – it was simply their life, you know? They looked after their own interests and didn't care about the others; they sold investitures and Heaven knows what. Whereas we... here we are, all dressed up in this fine throne room – to do what? Nothing. Like six puppets hanging on the wall, waiting for someone to take us down, give us our moves and tell us what to say.

HAROLD: Oh, come off it. Don't exaggerate! At least we have to know how to answer him correctly! Don't we? If he says something to you and you aren't quick on your cue with the right answer... God help you!

LANDOLF: Well yes, I admit that.

BERTOLD: Well, that's no small thing! And how am I to know the right answers when I've been swotting up Henry the Fourth of France and suddenly I'm supposed to know all about Henry the Fourth of Germany?

(*The others laugh again.*)

HAROLD: You must make up for lost time pretty quickly!

ORDULF: Don't worry, we'll help you.

HAROLD: There are plenty of books next door. All you need to begin with is a little brush-up.

ORDULF: You must know a few things in general...

HAROLD: Look! (*He spins* BERTOLD *round to show him the portrait of* MARCHESA MATILDE *on the back wall*.) Who is she, for instance?

BERTOLD (*gazing at the picture*): That woman? Well, if you ask me, she seems out of place here. Two modern paintings among all these antiques!

HAROLD: You're quite right. As a matter of fact, there weren't any pictures here at first. There are two niches behind them. They were supposed to house statues in the style of that period. Since they remained empty, the two paintings were placed there to cover them up.

LANDOLF (*interrupting*): They certainly would be out of place if they were just paintings.

BERTOLD: What are they then? Aren't they portraits?

LANDOLF: Yes – if you go and touch them, you'd say they *are* paintings. But to *him* (*with a mysterious gesture towards the right, indicating* HENRY IV), who never touches them...

BERTOLD: Well, what are they to him?

LANDOLF: They're... mind you, this is only my own interpretation, but I don't think I'm far out. They're images. Images like... well, reflections in a mirror... does that make sense? This one (*pointing to the portrait of* HENRY IV) shows him alive as he is today in this throne room, which is in the style of the eleventh century. Why do you look surprised? If you were put in front of a mirror now, it would still be the real, living you of today dressed up in period costume that you'd see, wouldn't it? Well then, it's as though there were two mirrors right there, reflecting back at us living images – here, in a world that... oh, don't you worry, you'll see, you'll see. While you're with us it'll all come to life.

BERTOLD: Look, I don't want to go mad here...

HAROLD: Go mad? You'll have fun!

BERTOLD: But how did you get to learn all this?

LANDOLF: My dear fellow, you don't go back eight hundred years in history without bringing a bit of experience with you.

HAROLD: Come on, come on... You'll see – you'll soak it up in no time.

ORDULF: You'll learn everything too, in our school.

BERTOLD: Well, for God's sake, start teaching me at once. At least give me the main details.

HAROLD: Leave it with us... Something from me, something from him...

LANDOLF: We'll tie up all your loose ends and get you in good shape, as a perfect, well-mannered puppet. Now, let's get on with it (*taking him by the arm to lead him out*).

BERTOLD (*resisting and looking at the woman's portrait*): No, wait a moment. You haven't told me who she is. Is she the Emperor's wife?

HAROLD: No. The Emperor's wife is Bertha of Susa, sister of Amadeus II of Savoy.

ORDULF: And the Emperor can't stand her. He wants to be with us and behave like a young man, so he's thinking of divorcing her.

LANDOLF: She's his bitterest enemy – Matilde, Marchesa of Tuscany.

BERTOLD: Oh, I know! The one who played host to the Pope...

LANDOLF: That's the one. At Canossa.

ORDULF: Pope Gregory the Seventh.

HAROLD: Yes, our bugbear. Come on, let's go.

(*All four are making for the door on the right by which they came in, when the door on the left opens and* GIOVANNI, *the old butler, enters, wearing a tailcoat.*)

GIOVANNI (*in a hurry, very agitated*): Here... psst! Franco! Lolo!

HAROLD (*stopping and turning*): What do you want?

BERTOLD (*surprised to see* GIOVANNI *come into the throne room in a tailcoat*): But what... What's he doing here?

LANDOLF: A man from the twentieth century! Go away!

(*He and the other two run towards him threateningly to drive him away, as a joke.*)

ORDULF: He's an emissary of Gregory the Seventh. Get out!

HAROLD: Out! Out!

GIOVANNI (*defending himself, very annoyed*): Now stop it, will you?

ORDULF: No. You can't come in here.

HAROLD Get out! Out!

LANDOLF (*to* BERTOLD): It's all sorcery, you know? This is some demon conjured up by the Wizard of Rome. Come on, draw your sword! (*He makes as if to draw his own.*)

GIOVANNI (*shouting*): Will you stop fooling! The Marquis has just arrived, with a group of people.

LANDOLF (*rubbing his hands*): Oh good! Any women?

ORDULF: Old? Young?

GIOVANNI: There are two gentlemen...

HAROLD: Yes, but what about the women? Who are they?

GIOVANNI: The Marchesa Spina and her daughter.

LANDOLF (*incredulously*): What?

ORDULF (*as above*): The Marchesa, you said?

GIOVANNI: Yes, yes, the Marchesa!

HAROLD: And who are the men?

GIOVANNI: I don't know.

HAROLD (*to* BERTOLD): They'll be giving us some material, you see?

ORDULF: All of them envoys from Gregory the Seventh. We'll
have fun!

GIOVANNI: Will you let me finish?

HAROLD: Sure, sure.

GIOVANNI: I think one of the two gentlemen is a doctor.

LANDOLF: Oh, I see, another doctor!

HAROLD: Bravo, Bertold, you've brought us luck.

LANDOLF: We'll show this doctor what's what!

BERTOLD: It looks to me as if I've landed right in it!

GIOVANNI: Will you listen? They want to come in here, in
this room!

LANDOLF (*astonished and appalled*): What? Her? The
Marchesa in here?

HAROLD: Then we'll get some real material!

LANDOLF: I'd say this is where the real tragedy begins!

BERTOLD (*curious*): Tragedy? Why?

ORDULF (*pointing at the portrait*): Because she is that woman
– don't you understand?

LANDOLF: Her daughter is engaged to the Marquis.

HAROLD: What are they doing here? Can someone tell us?

ORDULF: If *he* sees her, there'll be hell to pay.

LANDOLF: Perhaps he won't recognize her any more.

GIOVANNI: If he wakes up, you'd better keep him busy next
door.

ORDULF: Oh yes? Are you joking? How?

HAROLD: You know how hard it is!

GIOVANNI: Damn it, by force if necessary! Those are the
orders I was given! Off with you – go!

HAROLD: Yes, yes – perhaps he's already woken up by this time!

ORDULF: Right, we're going, we're going!

LANDOLF (*to* GIOVANNI, *as he goes off with the rest*): You
will have to explain everything!

GIOVANNI (*calling after them*): Lock the door after you and
hide the key! (*Pointing to the door on the right:*) And that
door too!

(LANDOLF, HAROLD, ORDULF *and* BERTOLD *go out by the second door on the right.*)

GIOVANNI (*to the* TWO MENSERVANTS): You two as well. Out! That way (*pointing to the first door on the right.*) Lock the door and take the key.

(*The* TWO MENSERVANTS *go out as directed.* GIOVANNI *goes to the door on the left and opens it to admit the* MARQUIS DI NOLLI.)

DI NOLLI: Have you given everyone their orders?
GIOVANNI: Yes, my lord! It's all under control.

(DI NOLLI *goes out again for a moment to ask the others to join him. The first to enter are* BARON TITO BELCREDI *and* DOCTOR DIONISIO GENONI, *then* DONNA MATILDE SPINA *and the* MARCHIONESS FRIDA. GIOVANNI *bows and goes out.* DONNA MATILDE *is about forty-five, still beautiful and shapely, although it is all too evident that she tries to mend the inevitable ravages of time. The effect of this strong yet expert make-up is to make her look something like a fierce Valkyrie. The make-up is all the more pronounced and deeply unsettling on her mouth, which is sad and extremely beautiful. She has been a widow for many years, and is on intimate terms with* BARON TITO BELCREDI, *whom neither she nor anyone else ever takes seriously, it would seem. What* TITO BELCREDI *really means to her he alone knows, so he can afford to laugh if she has to feign ignorance about it herself. He even manages to smile when others are amused by her jokes at his expense. Slim, prematurely grey, though a little younger than the* MARCHESA, *he has a curiously bird-like head. He would be extremely lively if his supple agility (which makes him a formidable swordsman) were not, as it were, sheathed in a kind of sleepy, Arab-like languor, which betrays itself in his strange nasal and drawling voice.* FRIDA, *the* MARCHESA's *daughter, is nineteen. Overshadowed by her imperious and rather-too-showy mother, she lacks vitality, and in her obscurity she resents the gossip caused by her mother's behaviour – which is more detrimental to her than to her mother. Luckily,* FRIDA *is engaged to the* MARQUIS CARLO DI NOLLI, *a stiff young man who is very tolerant of others, but won't go beyond the limited sense of his own worth – which he is perhaps himself unsure about. In any case, he is discomfited by the various responsibilities he feels are weighing him down. It is as if others – lucky them – may gossip and amuse themselves, but not he – not because he wouldn't like to, but simply because he can't. He is dressed in strict mourning for the recent death of his mother.* DOCTOR DIONISIO GENONI *has the rubicund and shameless face of a satyr, with protruding eyes and a little pointed beard, which shimmers like silver; he has good manners and is nearly bald. They enter showing discomfort, almost fear, all (except* DI NOLLI) *looking around with curiosity. At first they speak in low tones.*)

BELCREDI: Ah, magnificent! Magnificent!

DOCTOR: Most interesting. His mania is consistent, even to the extent of surrounding himself with the right things. Magnificent, yes, indeed – magnificent.

DONNA MATILDE (*who, after looking around for her portrait, sees it and moves towards it*): Ah, there it is! (*She gazes at it from a good distance, experiencing mixed feelings.*) Yes, yes... Oh, look... My goodness... (*calling her daughter*) Frida, Frida! Look.

FRIDA: Ah... your portrait.

DONNA MATILDE: No! Look! It isn't me! It's you!

DI NOLLI: Yes, you're right. Didn't I tell you?

DONNA MATILDE: I would never have believed it. (*She rouses herself, as if from a shiver.*) God, how weird! (*Looking at her daughter:*) But how, Frida? (*She puts an arm round* FRIDA'*s waist and draws her close.*) Come here. Don't you see yourself in me, there?

FRIDA: Well, to tell you the truth...

DONNA MATILDE: You don't think so? How can it be? (*Turning to* BELCREDI:) Tito, look. You tell us!

BELCREDI: No, thank you. I refuse to look, on principle!

DONNA MATILDE: What a fool! He thinks he's paying me a compliment. (*Turning to the* DOCTOR:) Doctor, you tell us.

(*The* DOCTOR *walks towards the picture.*)

BELCREDI (*turning his back and pretending to call him secretly*): Psst! No, Doctor! For God's sake, don't do it!

DOCTOR (*puzzled but smiling*): Why shouldn't I do it?

DONNA MATILDE: Pay no attention to him. Come here. He's insufferable.

FRIDA: He's a full-time fool – didn't you know?

BELCREDI (*to the* DOCTOR, *as he resumes his approach*): Watch your feet, watch your feet, Doctor! Your feet!

DOCTOR: My feet? Why?

BELCREDI: You've got iron boots.

DOCTOR: Who, me?

BELCREDI: Yessir! Mind you don't crush those... four tiny glass slippers.

DOCTOR (*laughing*): Rubbish! After all, there's nothing strange in a daughter resembling her mother.

BELCREDI: Crash! Now you've done it!

DONNA MATILDE (*with exaggerated anger, moving towards* BELCREDI): Why "crash"? What is it? What did he say?

DOCTOR (*candidly*): Isn't it true?

BELCREDI (*answering* DONNA MATILDE): He said there was nothing strange, and you seemed thunderstruck! Well then, why, if it's such a natural thing?

DONNA MATILDE (*even more annoyed*): What a fool, what a fool you are! It's just because it *is* so natural. Because that (*pointing at the portrait*) isn't my daughter at all. It's a picture of me! And what took me aback was to see my daughter rather than myself. And my surprise was genuine – don't you dare doubt it!

(*After this outburst, an embarrassed silence.*)

FRIDA (*quietly, annoyed*): Oh God! It's always the same. Must we always argue over every trifle?

BELCREDI (*also quietly, but almost sheepishly and apologetically*): I haven't raised any doubts. But I noticed that you, unlike your mother, were not surprised at all, from the very beginning – or if there was something you were surprised about, it was that she thought you looked so much like that portrait.

DONNA MATILDE: Well, of course! Because she can't see how I was at her age, whereas I can easily recognize myself in her as she is today.

DOCTOR: Very true. Because a portrait catches a moment and fixes it for ever; for the young lady this is a remote moment with no memories of it, whereas for the Marchesa it must recall a host of things that are not in the painting – gestures, motions, glances, smiles...

DONNA MATILDE: Exactly!

DOCTOR (*addressed to her*): Naturally you can see all these things again now in your daughter.

DONNA MATILDE: He always has to spoil any genuine emotion I feel – just to infuriate me.

DOCTOR (*dazzled by the light of his own explanation, he turns to* BELCREDI *and proceeds in a professional tone*):

Resemblance, my dear Baron, often comes from things we can't explain. And this accounts for the fact that—

BELCREDI (*cutting the lecture short*): —that someone might even see a resemblance between you and me, my dear Professor.

DI NOLLI: Please, please... enough of that! (*He points to the two doors on the right to warn that someone may overhear them.*) It's been such great fun coming here...

FRIDA: Of course. When he's around... (*She indicates* BELCREDI.)

DONNA MATILDE (*quickly*): That's just why I didn't want him to come.

BELCREDI: When I give you so much cause for amusement behind my back! There's ingratitude for you!

DI NOLLI: Tito, please! Enough! You know the doctor is here on serious business, and how anxious I am about the whole thing.

DOCTOR: Quite, quite. Now, first let us get one or two points clear. Donna Matilde, may I ask how this portrait comes to be here? Did you give it to him?

DONNA MATILDE: Certainly not. On what basis could I have done that? I was Frida's age... and not even engaged. No, I gave it away three or four years after the accident. Her mother (*gesturing to* DI NOLLI) begged me to.

DOCTOR: And she was *his* sister? (*He nods his head towards the doors on the right, indicating* HENRY IV.)

DI NOLLI: Yes, Doctor. And this visit of ours today is to discharge a debt – a debt I owe my mother, who died a month ago. Otherwise Frida and I would be travelling now.

DOCTOR: And occupied with other things altogether, I understand.

DI NOLLI: Well... She died in the firm belief that her brother – she adored him, you know – was close to recovery.

DOCTOR: And, if you don't mind me asking, what made her believe that?

DI NOLLI: Some strange words he said to her just before she died, apparently.

DOCTOR: Strange words, you say? Well, well… it would be very helpful to know what they were.

DI NOLLI: Well, I don't know. All I can tell you is that she came home terribly upset after her last visit to him. Apparently he had been unusually affectionate towards her, as if he sensed that she would soon die. On her deathbed she made me promise never to neglect him, to have him checked, examined…

DOCTOR: I see. Good. Now, now let's see… Often, you know, the merest trifles… So, this portrait—

DONNA MATILDE: Really, Doctor, I don't think we ought to attach too much importance to that. The only reason I was struck by it was that I hadn't seen it in years.

DOCTOR: But please, please… listen…

DI NOLLI: It's true. That painting has been there a good fifteen years—

DONNA MATILDE: Longer. It must be more than eighteen years.

DOCTOR: Do excuse me, but neither of you knows yet what I want to ask. I think these two portraits are very, very significant. They were painted, I take it, before the famous… the most unfortunate… cavalcade. Am I right?

DONNA MATILDE: Yes, of course.

DOCTOR: What I meant was… when he was perfectly in his mind, right? Was it his suggestion that you should have your portrait painted?

DONNA MATILDE: Oh no, Doctor. Most of us who took part in the pageant had one done – just as a souvenir.

BELCREDI: Yes, I had mine done too… as Charles of Anjou.

DONNA MATILDE: As soon as our costumes were ready.

BELCREDI: Because, you see, at first the idea was to hang them all together, in the hall of the house where the pageant was being held, as a memento. But then everyone wanted to keep their own.

DONNA MATILDE: And, as I told you, I handed over mine – without too much regret – because his mother... (*She indicates* DI NOLLI *again.*)

DOCTOR: Do you know whether it was he who requested it?

DONNA MATILDE: I don't know. Possibly... Or maybe it was his sister – she was very fond of him.

DOCTOR: Another thing... another thing: was the pageant his idea?

BELCREDI (*quickly*): No Doctor, it was mine. It was mine.

DOCTOR: Will you please...

DONNA MATILDE: Don't listen to him! It was poor Belassi's.

BELCREDI: Belassi's!

DONNA MATILDE (*to the* DOCTOR): Yes, Belassi. He died two or three months later, poor man.

BELCREDI: But Belassi wasn't even there when...

DI NOLLI (*annoyed at the prospect of another argument*): For Heaven's sake, Doctor, do we really have to establish whose idea it was?

DOCTOR: Well, it would certainly help me to...

BELCREDI: It was mine – mine, I tell you! This is funny! Not that it's not something to be proud of, seeing the results. Listen, Doctor, it came about like this – I remember it perfectly. I was at the club, one evening early in November, looking through a German illustrated magazine – just for the pictures, mind you, because I don't know any German. There was a picture showing the Kaiser in some university town where he was a student.

DOCTOR: Bonn... it was Bonn.

BELCREDI: All right, Bonn. He was on horseback and dressed up in one of those queer outfits that German students wore in medieval times. Behind him, also on horseback and in costume, was a bunch of other students – noblemen, of course. It was that picture which gave me the idea. You see, at the club we were already thinking of organizing some big masquerade for the next carnival. So I suggested this historical pageant – well, historical... it was a bit of a mishmash. Each of us was to represent a historical personage, from any century – king, emperor, prince – and ride next to his lady, queen or empress... And the horses would be in armour, of course, according to the style of the period. Well, the proposal was accepted.

DONNA MATILDE: My invitation came from Belassi.

BELCREDI: If he said it was his idea, he was lying. I tell you, he wasn't even in the club that night, when I made the suggestion. For that matter, neither was *he*! (*He indicates* HENRY IV.)

DOCTOR: And I suppose he chose to represent Henry the Fourth?

DONNA MATILDE: Yes, because I had said, without giving it too much thought, that I wanted to be the Marchioness Matilde of Tuscany, which I chose because of my name.

DOCTOR: I... er... don't quite see the connection...

DONNA MATILDE: Oh well. Neither did I at first, when he said that in that case he would be at my feet like Henry the Fourth at Canossa. Well, I had heard about Canossa, but the truth is I remembered the story only vaguely. So when I looked it up afterwards in order to get ready for my role, I found it a bit weird that I was supposed to be a most faithful and zealous friend of Pope Gregory the Seventh, taking part in a fierce struggle against the German Empire. Then I understood why he wanted to ride next to me in the pageant as Henry the Fourth... because I'd chosen to represent his deadly enemy!

DOCTOR: Oh, I see... and would that be because...

BELCREDI: Good Lord, Doctor, because he was assiduously paying court to her, and she (*indicating* DONNA MATILDE), naturally...

DONNA MATILDE (*piqued, in a fierce tone*): Yes, yes, naturally indeed! Naturally! All the more "naturally" then!

BELCREDI (*with a gesture towards* DONNA MATILDE): She just couldn't stand him.

DONNA MATILDE: Oh, that's not true! I didn't dislike him. Quite the contrary. But you see, as soon as a man wants me to take him seriously...

BELCREDI (*finishing her sentence*): He gives you striking proof of what a fool he is.

DONNA MATILDE: No, my dear. Not in his case. He wasn't nearly such a fool as you are.

BELCREDI: But I've never asked to be taken seriously.

DONNA MATILDE: You're telling me! But he wasn't someone to be trifled with. (*To the* DOCTOR, *in a different tone:*) One of the misfortunes of being a woman, my dear doctor, is to find, every so often, a pair of eyes staring at you with a restrained, intense promise of eternal love! (*She laughs rather shrilly.*) There's nothing more ridiculous. If only men could see that "for ever" look in their eyes! It's always sent me into fits of laughter. And even more at the time! But I must confess – and I can now, after more than twenty years – when I laughed at him, it was partly for fear. Because I could tell he meant that promise! And that would have been very dangerous for me.

DOCTOR (*attentively, showing great interest*): Ah, this is it. That's something I'd be most interested to know about. Why "very dangerous"?

DONNA MATILDE (*light-heartedly*): Because he wasn't like the rest. And because I was always – well, to be honest, I still am – how shall I put it?... (*looking for a simple word*) impatient – that's it – impatient of anything that is staid and overly stuffy. But then I was too young, you see. And a woman. I had to grin and bear it. I should have been braver, but I felt I didn't have enough courage.

So I laughed at him too. Afterwards I regretted it. I even hated myself for it, because I seemed to be laughing at him in exactly the same way as all those stupid people who made fun of him.

BELCREDI: Like they do at me, more or less.

DONNA MATILDE: People laugh at you, my dear, because you pretend to be humble! It was the opposite with him. And then people laugh at you in your face.

BELCREDI: Well, better than behind my back.

DOCTOR: Please, please, let's get back to the point. From what you tell me, I gather he already was a bit excitable, wasn't he?

BELCREDI: Yes, Doctor, he was, but in a curious way.

DOCTOR: How?

BELCREDI: Well, at first impression—

DONNA MATILDE: At first impression! He was like that, Doctor – certainly a bit unconventional, but only because he was exuberant, eccentric…

BELCREDI: I am not saying he faked his excitement. On the contrary: he was often genuinely excited. But I bet, Doctor, he himself immediately realized that he was overexcited. This accompanied, I think, every spontaneous outburst. And I'm sure he suffered for this. Sometimes he would get comically angry with himself!

DONNA MATILDE: That's true.

BELCREDI (*to* DONNA MATILDE): And I'll tell you why. (*To the* DOCTOR:) Because, I think, that flash of lucid perception would instantly detach him from his own personal feeling, which would then seem to him… not affected, because it was sincere, but something which he felt he had at once to… how can I put it?… to "intellectualize", in order to compensate for the real heartfelt warmth he thought he lacked. And so he improvised, exaggerated, let himself go, as it were, to… to bring on a self-obscuring daze. This made him look fickle, erratic and... yes, I must admit: even ridiculous at times.

DOCTOR: And, perhaps, unsociable?

BELCREDI: Not in the least! He was great at organizing tableaux vivants, dances, charity shows – just for the fun of it, you know. And he was a damn good actor, I can tell you.

DI NOLLI: And since his madness he's become quite brilliant. Terrifying.

BELCREDI: He always was. Since that accident when his horse threw him...

DOCTOR: He knocked the back of his head, I believe?

DONNA MATILDE: It was horrible! He was right next to me. The horse reared, and there he was on the ground, with the horse about to trample on him—

BELCREDI: But at first we didn't think he was seriously hurt. Of course, it stopped the procession and things got a bit chaotic – everyone trying to make out what had happened – but by then he'd been carried into the house.

DONNA MATILDE: You couldn't tell he was hurt. Not a scratch or a drop of blood.

BELCREDI: Everyone thought he'd just fainted.

DONNA MATILDE: And about two hours later he...

BELCREDI: Ah, yes, he turned up again in the hall of the house – that's what I was about to say.

DONNA MATILDE: His face didn't look right. That's what I noticed at once.

BELCREDI: No, that's not true. No one realized anything, Doctor, I swear.

DONNA MATILDE: Well, of course! You were all behaving like lunatics.

BELCREDI: Because we were all acting out our roles, for fun. It was bedlam!

DONNA MATILDE: So you can imagine how terrified we were when it dawned on us that he wasn't acting – that he was in earnest.

DOCTOR: Ah... you mean that he too...

BELCREDI: Oh yes, he came and joined us. We thought he'd recovered and had started to play his part too, like the rest of us – or rather, better than us, because, as I was saying, he was a very good actor. In short, we thought he was joking!

DONNA MATILDE: They began to lash at him with their whips...

BELCREDI: And then he, being armed like a king, unsheathed his sword and hurled himself at two or three people. In that moment, everyone was terrified.

DONNA MATILDE: I shall never forget that scene. Our masked faces, flustered and distorted... and that awful mask of his, which wasn't a mask any longer, but madness itself!

BELCREDI: Yes, Henry the Fourth himself! Henry the Fourth in person, and in a fit of fury.

DONNA MATILDE: The obsessive thought of that masquerade, Doctor, which had been haunting him for over a month, must have contributed to it. This obsession was always apparent in everything he did.

BELCREDI: The research he put into it! Down to the smallest details... the minutiae...

DOCTOR: That explains it. The fall and concussion that affected his brain turned what was a momentary fixation into something permanent – permanent and long-lasting. Such accidents can make one unbalanced, or even go mad.

BELCREDI (*to* FRIDA *and* DI NOLLI): You see, my dears, what tricks life can play on us? (*To* DI NOLLI:) You were four or five when it happened. (*To* FRIDA:) And your mother thinks you have taken her place in that picture – although it was painted before she even dreamt of bringing you into the world... I've already turned grey, and as for him (*pointing to the picture of* HENRY IV),

a blow on the back of the head, and bang! He's Henry
the Fourth for ever.

DOCTOR (*rousing himself from his thoughts, he spreads
his fingers wide in front of his face, as if to claim
attention, preparing to launch into a scientific explanation*): Now then, ladies and gentlemen, it is exactly
this... (*He is interrupted by* BERTOLD, *who bursts in
from the first door on the right – the one nearer to
the proscenium. He has a perturbed, exasperated look
about him.*)

BERTOLD: I'm sorry, I didn't mean to... (*He stops all at once,
seeing the confusion caused by his sudden appearance.*)

FRIDA (*shrieking, trying to take refuge*): Oh God, he's here!

DONNA MATILDE (*drawing back in alarm and holding one
hand in front of her eyes so as not to see him*): Is it him?
Is it him?

DI NOLLI (*quickly*): No, no, calm down.

DOCTOR (*bewildered*): Well, who is he?

BELCREDI: Someone who's sneaked out of our masquerade.

DI NOLLI: He's one of the four young men we keep here to
humour him in his delusion.

BERTOLD: I'm sorry, sir.

DI NOLLI: Sorry my foot! I gave orders that the doors were
to be locked and that no one was to come in here.

BERTOLD: Yes, sir, but I couldn't stand it any longer... Please
allow me to leave!

DI NOLLI: Oh. You're the new one? You came this morning?

BERTOLD: That's right, sir, and I can't stand it – on my word.

DONNA MATILDE (*to* DI NOLLI *apprehensively*): What does
this mean? I thought you said he was perfectly calm now.

BERTOLD (*quickly*): Oh, it's not *him*, your ladyship. It's those
other three. Here to "humour him" you said, sir? A fat
lot of humouring they do! If you ask me, they're the ones
who are bonkers. I arrive here this morning, and instead
of helping me, sir, they...

(LANDOLF *and* HAROLD *now appear in the same doorway. They seem hurried and upset, but they stop on the threshold to ask permission to enter.*)

LANDOLF: May we come in, please?

HAROLD: May we, sir?...

DI NOLLI: Oh, come in, come in, for Heaven's sake! What's all this? What's going on?

FRIDA: I'm getting out of here. I'm out. I'm frightened.

(*She makes a step towards the door on the left.*)

DI NOLLI (*restraining her*): Frida, please.

LANDOLF (*pointing to* BERTOLD): Sir, this idiot...

BERTOLD (*remonstrating*): Thanks very much, my friends, but I'm not having this – not having this!

LANDOLF: What's that supposed to mean?

HAROLD: He's ruined it all, sir, running away like this!

LANDOLF: It's sent him into a rage. We can't hold him back any more in the other room. He has ordered us to arrest him, and wants to pass his sentence on him from the throne, at once. What shall we do?

DI NOLLI: Go and lock that door! Lock it! Now!

(LANDOLF *locks the door.*)

HAROLD: Ordulf can't possibly hold him there on his own...

LANDOLF: We could, at least, announce immediately that you've arrived, sir? It might distract him. That is, if it's settled how we are to present you...

DI NOLLI: Yes, yes, that's all arranged. (*To the* DOCTOR:) Doctor, do you think you could examine him at once?

FRIDA: I'm not doing this, Carlo! I'm going! Mother, will you come with me, please? Please!

DOCTOR: Well, he's not armed, is he?

DI NOLLI: Of course not, Doctor! (*To* FRIDA:) Come on, Frida, don't be so childish. After all, it was you who decided to come.

FRIDA: I didn't, if you don't mind. It was Mother.

DONNA MATILDE (*firmly*): And I'm staying. So, what are we going to do?

BELCREDI: Excuse me, but is it really necessary for us to dress up like this?

LANDOLF: Absolutely! Absolutely, sir! Unfortunately, as you can see... (*indicating his own costume*) if he saw you all in modern dress, it would be a disaster.

HAROLD: He would think of some diabolical disguisement.

DI NOLLI: Just as they look dressed up to you, so he'd think we were masquerading in these clothes.

LANDOLF: Perhaps that would be nothing, sir. The truth is, he'd think it was all the work of his mortal enemy.

BELCREDI: Pope Gregory the Seventh!

LANDOLF: Yes. He says he's a "pagan".

BELCREDI: The Pope? That's a good one.

LANDOLF: Yes, sir. He says he conjures up the dead – accuses him of practising black magic. He's scared stiff of him.

DOCTOR: Persecutory delusions...

HAROLD: He'd fly into a rage.

DI NOLLI (*to* BELCREDI): But you don't have to be there, you know? We will go next door. What matters is that the doctor sees him.

DOCTOR: You mean... on my own?

DI NOLLI: You'll be with them (*indicating the three young men*).

DOCTOR: No, no... I meant, what about you, madam?...

DONNA MATILDE: Of course. I want to be there too. I want to be there. I want to see him again.

FRIDA: But why, Mother? Oh, please do come with us!

DONNA MATILDE (*haughtily*): Allow me to do as I please. I tell you, this is why I have come. (*To* LANDOLF:) I shall be Adelaide, his mother-in-law.

LANDOLF: Good, excellent. The Empress Bertha's mother. Excellent... As long, madam, as you wear the ducal crown and a cloak to hide everything else. (*To* HAROLD:) Go, go!

HAROLD: Wait a minute. What about this gentleman? (*He indicates the* DOCTOR.)

DOCTOR: Oh, yes. Didn't we say I should be a Bishop... Bishop Hugo of Cluny?

HAROLD: Abbot, I think you mean, sir. Abbot Hugo of Cluny.

LANDOLF: But Hugo's been here many times.

DOCTOR (*surprise*): What do you mean "he's been here"?

LANDOLF: Don't worry. All I meant was that since it's a quick disguise—

HAROLD: —we've used it before.

DOCTOR: But—

LANDOLF: There's no danger he'll remember. He's more interested in the clothes than the people wearing them.

DONNA MATILDE: That's just as well for me too, then.

DI NOLLI: Come, Frida, we'll go. Come, Tito, you come with us.

BELCREDI: Well, no... if she stays, I stay.

DONNA MATILDE: But I don't need you, really.

BELCREDI: I know I won't be of much use, but I'd like to see him too. Am I allowed?

LANDOLF: Well, yes, I think three might be better than two.

HAROLD: How are we going to dress him, then?

BELCREDI: Well, can't you find a quick disguise for me too?

LANDOLF (*to* HAROLD): I know: a Cluniac monk.

BELCREDI: A Cluniac monk? How does that look?

LANDOLF: The Benedictine habit they wear in the Abbey of Cluny. You'll be a monk in attendance on Monsignore. (*To* HAROLD:) Go, go! (*To* BERTOLD:) And you too, and make yourself scarce for the rest of the day. (*As*

HENRY IV

they are about to leave:) No, wait! (*To* BERTOLD:)
Bring here the clothes he'll give you. (*To* HAROLD:)
And you, go and announce at once the arrival of the
Duchess Adelaide and Monsignore Hugo of Cluny.
Got it?

(HAROLD *and* BERTOLD *go out by the first door on the right.*)

DI NOLLI: We'll go, then.

(*He and* FRIDA *go out by the door on the left.*)

DOCTOR (*to* LANDOLF): I trust I will be well received as
   Hugo of Cluny?
LANDOLF: Absolutely. Don't worry. The Monsignore has
   always been welcomed here with the greatest courtesy.
   And there's nothing to worry about for you either, madam.
   He's never forgotten the time he was kept waiting in
   the snow for two days, frozen stiff, and that it was only
   thanks to you two that he was admitted to the Castle of
   Canossa and the presence of Gregory the Seventh, who
   had refused to receive him.
BELCREDI: And what about me, if you don't mind my
   asking?
LANDOLF: I think you should stay respectfully out of the way.
DONNA MATILDE (*in nervous irritation*): Go away altogether,
   you mean?
BELCREDI (*quietly, but angrily*): You've got yourself into
   a state!
DONNA MATILDE: I am what I am! Leave me alone!

(BERTOLD *returns with their costumes.*)

LANDOLF (*seeing him enter the hall*): Ah, here are your
   costumes. This is your cloak, madam.

DONNA MATILDE: One moment. Let me take my hat off.

(*She does so and holds it out for* BERTOLD *to take.*)

LANDOLF: All right, take it away. (*Then, offering to fit the crown on* DONNA MATILDE:) May I?

DONNA MATILDE: Good Heavens, isn't there a mirror in here?

LANDOLF (*pointing to the door on the left*): There are some next door. Perhaps you'd rather put it on yourself?

DONNA MATILDE: I would prefer to. Give it here. I won't be a minute.

(*She takes back her hat from* BERTOLD *and goes out with him. He takes the crown and the cloak. Meanwhile, the* DOCTOR *and* BELCREDI *get into their Benedictine garb as best they can.*)

BELCREDI: I must say I never thought I'd turn into a Benedictine monk. This madness of his must be costing a fortune!

DOCTOR: Well, all forms of madness are expensive!

BELCREDI: When you've a fortune to go with it!

LANDOLF: Yes, sir, we have a whole wardrobe next door – all costumes of the period, copied to perfection from actual dresses of the day. It's my special responsibility: I go to all the best theatrical costumiers. We spend quite a lot.

(DONNA MATILDE *re-enters, wearing the cloak and crown.*)

BELCREDI (*admiringly*): Oh, magnificent! Truly regal.

DONNA MATILDE (*bursts out laughing at the sight of him*): My goodness, hide away! You are grotesque! You look like an ostrich dressed up as a monk!

BELCREDI: What about the doctor?

DOCTOR: Well, well... what can we do?

DONNA MATILDE: The doctor doesn't look so bad – but you really look ridiculous.

DOCTOR (*to* LANDOLF): Do you often get visitors up here?

LANDOLF: It depends. Sometimes he'll command that a certain person he brought to see him. Then we have to find someone who's willing to act the part. Ladies too...

DONNA MATILDE (*displeased, but wishing to hide it*): Really? Ladies too?

LANDOLF: Well, initially, yes... quite a few.

BELCREDI (*laughing*): Oh really? Dressed up too? (*Indicating the* MARCHESA:) Like this?

LANDOLF: Well, you see, the kind of ladies who...

BELCREDI: Who lend their favours... I see. (*To* DONNA MATILDE, *maliciously:*) Be careful... he could be dangerous for you...

(*The second door on the right opens and* HAROLD *enters. He first makes a gesture, secretly warning the others to stop talking, then he announces solemnly:*)

HAROLD: His Majesty the Emperor.

(*Enter first the* TWO MENSERVANTS, *who take up their posts one each side of the throne. Then comes* HENRY IV, *followed by* ORDULF *and* HAROLD, *who walk respectfully behind him.* HENRY IV *is nearly fifty, extremely pale. His hair is grey on the back, but fair around the forehead and temples, where he has obviously used a dye, which is almost childish. In contrast to his tragic pallor is a doll-like dab of colour on each cheek – also very obvious. Over his royal robes he wears a penitent's sackcloth, as at Canossa. His eyes have a spasmodic, frightening vacancy about them.*)

This look is at odds with his general bearing, which is that of one who wishes to display humble repentance almost too obviously, as though he wanted people to realize the humiliation is far from deserved. ORDULF *holds in his hands the imperial crown.* HAROLD *carries the sceptre with the eagle and the orb with its cross.*)

HENRY IV (*bowing first to* DONNA MATILDE *and then to the* DOCTOR): Your Ladyship... Monsignore. (*He sees* BELCREDI *and is about to bow to him too, but turns to* LANDOLF *and asks warily, in an undertone:*) Who is that? Peter Damian?

LANDOLF: No, sire, he is a monk from Cluny who came in attendance on the abbot.

HENRY IV (*He scrutinizes* BELCREDI *again with growing mistrust; then, noticing that* BELCREDI *is looking irresolutely, awkwardly, from* DONNA MATILDE *to the* DOCTOR, *as if looking for a clue, he draws himself up and shouts*): It is Peter Damian! No need for you to look at the Duchess, Father! (*He turns quickly to* DONNA MATILDE, *as if to fend off some danger.*) I swear to you – I swear to you, my lady, that my heart has changed towards your daughter. I confess that if he (*indicating* BELCREDI) had not come to forbid me in the name of Pope Alexander, I would have repudiated her. Oh yes, there were some who were ready to support me in the divorce: the Bishop of Mainz, in exchange for a hundred and twenty farms. (*Casting a bewildered glance at* LANDOLF *and adding at once:*) But this is no time for me to be speaking ill of bishops. (*Humbly, he turns back to* BELCREDI.) Believe me, I am grateful to you now, Peter Damian – truly grateful – that you prevented it. My life has been one long humiliation – my mother, Adalbert, Tribur, Goslar – and now this sackcloth you see me wearing. (*His tone suddenly changes, as if shrewdly studying how to play his part.*) It doesn't matter. Clearness of mind, perspicacity, firmness of attitude and patience in adversity. (*Then he addresses everyone on a note of sober penitence.*) I must put right the wrong I did. I humble myself before you, Peter Damian. (*He bows deeply and remains in that position, as if gripped by a sudden suspicion which forces him to add in a threatening tone, almost against his will:*) Provided, of course, it was not you who spread the obscene lie that my sainted mother Agnes committed adultery with Bishop Henry of Augsburg.

BELCREDI (*as* HENRY IV *still remains bowed, but with a finger pointing at him in accusation, he puts both hands on his breast in denial*): I never said such a thing. Never!

HENRY IV (*rising*): You never did, did you? Shameful! (HENRY IV *stares at him for a few moments, then says:*) I don't think you are capable of it. (*He goes to the* DOCTOR, *gives his sleeve a little tug and says with a sly wink:*) It's always "them", isn't it, Monsignore?

HAROLD (*in a whisper, as if prompting the* DOCTOR): Yes, of course, those rapacious bishops...

DOCTOR (*trying to carry off the part, but looking at* HAROLD): Them... oh yes, them.

HENRY IV: Nothing ever satisfied them! I was just a poor little boy, Monsignore... Even when you are king, without knowing it, you while away the time playing. I was six when they took me away from my mother. Little did I know that they used me against her, and even against the dynastic powers. They profaned everything. Thieves! Thieves, all of them – each one greedier than the other... Hanno worse than Stephen, Stephen greedier than Hanno!

LANDOLF (*softly, persuasively, calling his attention*): Your Majesty—

HENRY IV (*quickly turning to him*): Yes, of course! This is not the time to talk ill of bishops. But Monsignore, this shameful libel on my mother goes beyond everything! (*He*

looks at DONNA MATILDE *and his tone softens.*) And I
cannot even weep for her, my lady. You will understand,
for you have a mother's heart. About a month ago she
came all the way from her convent, just to visit me. Now
they tell me she is dead. (*A long pause, filled with emotion,
then he says, smiling sadly:*) And I cannot even weep for
her, because if you are here now and I wear *this* (*indicating his sackcloth*), it means I'm only twenty-six years old.

HAROLD (*gently, almost sotto voce, comforting him*): In that
case, she must still be alive, Your Majesty.

ORDULF (*as above*): Still in her convent.

HENRY IV (*turning to look at them*): True! Then I can postpone
my grief for another time... (*Almost foppishly he draws
DONNA MATILDE's attention to his dyed hair.*) Look! My
hair keeps its gold. (*Then quietly, as if in confidence:*) That
is just for you. I don't really need it, though I admit a little
external evidence is useful. It defines the boundaries of time,
if you follow me, Monsignore! (*He turns again to DONNA
MATILDE, examining her hair.*) Ah, but I see that you too,
Duchess... (*He winks and gestures expressively with his
hand.*) Ah... Italian women... (*As much as to say "fake",
but not in disdain – rather in mischievous admiration.*)
God forbid that I should show revulsion, or even surprise!
Wishful thinking! None of us can bear to admit that some
inscrutable and fatal power limits our will. We are all born,
and we all must die. Did you ask to be born, Monsignore? I
did not. And in between birth and death – neither of which
is something we wished for – so many things happen which
we all regret, but which resign ourselves to!

DOCTOR (*just to say something while he studies him attentively*): Too true, too true.

HENRY IV: And if we refuse to be resigned, out comes the
wishful thinking. A woman wants to be a man – an old man
wants to be young again. None of us lies or pretends. It can't
be denied: we are all genuinely convinced of our own worth.

But, Monsignore, while you stand firm, grasping your holy habit with both hands, something is slipping away down your sleeve, slithering away like a snake, without you even noticing it. Life, Monsignore, life! And you're astonished to see it slipping away from you before your very eyes. You're annoyed, angry with yourself. And remorseful... even remorseful! Ah, if you only knew how many regrets I have been faced with! Staring at me with a face like my own – yet so horrible that I was forced to look away... (*He turns to* DONNA MATILDE.) Has it never happened to you, my lady? Have you always been the same in your own eyes? Oh, God... that day, how could you... how could you do such a thing?... (*He stares so intently at her that she turns pale*.) Yes, you know what I'm referring to... Don't worry, though, I won't tell anyone. And you, Peter Damian... how could you befriend such a man?...

LANDOLF (*as above*): Your Majesty—

HENRY IV (*quickly*): No, no, I won't say his name! I know how it upsets him. (*He turns to glance at* BELCREDI.) You thought very highly of him, eh? Very highly... Nonetheless, we all hold firmly to our own conceptions – just as some people, when growing old, dye their hair. What matters if this dye does not fool you, and you are aware it's not my real colour? You, my lady, certainly don't dye your hair in order to deceive others – or even yourself – but in order to cheat your image in the mirror just a little... a tiny bit. I do it for fun – you do it in earnest. But I assure you, however serious you may be, you too are wearing a mask, madam! And I don't mean the venerable crown on your head, before which I bow, or your ducal robe. I simply mean this memory you wish to retain artificially of the golden hair which was once your pride and delight – or of the dark hair, if your hair was dark – the fading image of your youth. As for you, Peter Damian, the memory of what you were, of what you did, now appears only as the realization of past events, which remains with you – isn't that so? Like a dream. Well, that's how it is for me too – a dream – and when I think of it, there are so many inexplicable… What of it? It's not so astonishing, Peter Damian: what we are today will seem like that tomorrow. (*Suddenly, in anger, he grasps the sackcloth he is wearing.*) This sackcloth!… (HAROLD *and* ORDULF, *alarmed by the fierce relish with which he appears to be tearing it off, rush over to restrain him.*) By God!… (*He backs away from them and takes off the sackcloth, shouting:*) Tomorrow at Brixen, twenty-seven German and Lombard bishops will sign with me the deposition of Gregory the Seventh… He's no Pope – he's an evil monk!

ORDULF (*with the other two, begging him to stop*): For Heaven's sake, Your Majesty!

HAROLD (*encouraging him to put the sackcloth on again*): Sire, you shouldn't say such things!

LANDOLF: The Monsignore and the Duchess came to intercede for you. (*Surreptitiously he makes urgent gestures to the* DOCTOR *to say something.*)

DOCTOR (*confused*): Ah, yes, of course… to intercede for you.

HENRY IV (*suddenly contrite, almost terrified, he allows the* THREE YOUNG MEN *to help him back into the sackcloth, pulling it to him spasmodically*): Pardon, oh pardon, Monsignore, pardon! Pardon, my lady… Already I feel the weight of the excommunication upon me. (*He bends down, shielding his head with his hands, as if expecting something to crush him. He remains like that for a while, then, without moving, whispers confidentially to* LANDOLF, HAROLD *and* ORDULF, *in a different voice:*) Somehow, I don't know why, I can't humble myself before him (*with a furtive gesture towards* BELCREDI) today.

LANDOLF (*sotto voce*): But why do you persist in thinking that he is Peter Damian, sire, when we have told you he is not?

HENRY IV (*with a frightened look*): He is not Pietro Damian?

HAROLD: No, he's just a poor monk, Your Majesty.

HENRY IV (*sadly, with a sigh of frustration*): Ah, we can't
weigh what we do when we act instinctively. You, madam,
as a woman, perhaps can understand me better than the
others. [This is a solemn and decisive moment. Now look:
this very moment I could – as I talk to you – accept the help
of the Lombard bishops, seize the Pope and lock him up here
in the castle. I could rush to Rome and elect an antipope.
I could make an alliance with Robert Guiscard – Gregory
the Seventh would be lost! But I resist the temptation, and,
believe me, I am wise to do so. I recognize the spirit of
our times, and the majesty of one who bears himself as a
true Pope. Do you wish to laugh at me, seeing me in such
a state? You'd be stupid to do so: it would show you don't
understand the political wisdom of wearing this penitent's
sackcloth. I tell you, tomorrow our roles could be reversed.
Then what would you do? Would you laugh at the Pope
because he is a prisoner? No. We'd be equals then: I masquerading as a penitent today; he as a prisoner tomorrow.
But woe to him who does not know how to wear his mask,
be he king or Pope. Perhaps he seems to be acting a little
too cruelly at this moment. Yes, that may be so.] Perhaps
you think, my lady, that your daughter Bertha – I repeat, my
feelings have changed towards her… (*He suddenly turns to*
BELCREDI, *as if the man had contradicted him, and shouts
in his face:*) Changed, changed! Because of the love and
devotion she has shown towards me at this terrible juncture!
(*Shaking convulsively, he tries to curb his anger and groans
with remorse, then turns to* DONNA MATILDE, *once again
in a tone of gentle and sad humility.*) She has come with
me, my lady; she's down there, in the courtyard. She chose
to follow me like a beggar woman. And she is cold, frozen,
after two nights spent outdoors… in the snow! You are her
mother. That alone should move you to mercy and prompt
you to join him (*indicating the* DOCTOR) in pleading to
the Pope for my pardon. If he'd only grant us an audience!

DONNA MATILDE (*trembling, almost inaudibly*): Of course. At once.

DOCTOR: We will… we will!

HENRY IV: And another thing, another thing! (*He beckons them to come close, then whispers secretively:*) It is not enough that he should receive me. You know there's nothing he cannot do. Nothing, I'm telling you! He can even call up the dead! (*He beats his breast.*) I'm a proof of that! Look at me! There are no magic arts that are unknown to him! Well, Monsignore, my lady, my real punishment is in myself (*he taps his breast, then points to his portrait, as if fearfully*), or rather in *that*! For I can't free myself from this magic. I am repentant now, and I swear to you both that I shall remain penitent until he has received me. But I beg you, after he has lifted my excommunication, you must implore the Pope to grant me one other thing in his power: to separate me from *that* (*he points to the portrait again*), so that I may live my own life in its entirety, which I can't do now! I can't go on being twenty-six years old for ever, my lady! I beg this for your daughter's sake as well, so that I may love her as she deserves, and as I yearn to do now that she has proved her devotion to me. I have finished. That is all. I am in your hands. (*He bows.*) My lady! Monsignore! (*He is about to leave by the door through which he entered, but, noticing* BELCREDI *has crept forward to listen, and imagining he is going to steal the imperial crown from the throne, he runs to pick it up, stuffs it under his sackcloth and, with a sly smile on his lips and in his eyes, makes a series of bows, then goes.* DONNA MATILDE, *profoundly shaken, collapses into a chair, on the point of fainting.*)

CURTAIN

Act Two

Another room in the house, next to the throne room, austerely furnished in antique style. To the right, about eight inches above floor level, there is a raised platform with a wooden rail and supporting pillars. There are steps leading up to it from the front and side. On the platform are a table and five small period chairs, one at the head of the table and two on each side. The main entrance is at the rear. To the left are two windows looking out onto the garden, to the right a door to the throne room. It is late afternoon on the same day as Act One.

DONNA MATILDE, the DOCTOR and TITO BELCREDI are in the room. The two men are in the middle of a conversation, but DONNA MATILDE stands apart, looking glum and clearly annoyed by what the other two are saying, though she cannot help eavesdropping, because in her present state of uneasiness everything is of interest to her, in spite of herself, preventing her from working out a plan of action she can hardly resist – which she only sees vaguely and by which she is tempted. The two men's words attract her attention, because she instinctively feels a need, at that moment, to be held back.

BELCREDI: You may say what you like, Doctor, but this is my impression.

DOCTOR: I'm not saying you're wrong, but I assure you, it's only an impression.

BELCREDI: And yet, he said so himself, quite clearly. (*Turning to* DONNA MATILDE:) Didn't he, Marchesa?

DONNA MATILDE (*turning to him absent-mindedly*): Said what? (*Then, contradicting him:*) Oh, yes, he did... but not for the reason you think.

DOCTOR: He saw through our disguise... her cloak (*indicating the* MARCHESA), our Benedictine habits. It's all very childish.

DONNA MATILDE (*suddenly turning again, indignantly*): Childish! What do you mean, Doctor?

DOCTOR: In a sense – please allow me, madam – it was. On the other hand, it is more complex than you can possibly imagine.

DONNA MATILDE: Well, it's perfectly clear to me.

DOCTOR (*with the indulgent smile of someone who knows better*): Oh well, one needs to understand the peculiar psychology of mad people. You can be quite certain a madman is aware, fully aware, of any disguise worn in his presence, and that he sees through it, and yet he believes in it – just like children do, for whom it's both game and reality. That's why I say all this is childish. But at the same time, it is extremely complex... for he must, you see, be perfectly conscious of being an image, confronting himself... that framed image in the other room! (*He indicates the portrait in the throne room, on his left.*)

BELCREDI: He said so himself.

DOCTOR: Precisely. An image before which other images appear: ours – do you follow me? Now, in his mania – which is sharply perceptive and in its way logical – he has quickly detected the difference between our images and his. That is to say, that our images are a pretence. That made him distrustful. Every madman protects himself by means of constant and watchful suspiciousness. And that's all! It's too much to expect him to appreciate that we are playing this game based on his own game, for his own sake. And his game seems to us all the more tragic because – suspicious as he is – he felt the urge to expose it, as if to defy us... do you follow me? And he exposed his own game too – appearing before us with make-up and dyed hair and then saying he had done it on purpose, for fun!

DONNA MATILDE (*lashing out again*): No, Doctor, no! That's not it! That's not it at all!

DOCTOR: What do you mean?

DONNA MATILDE (*with passion and conviction*): I am absolutely certain that he recognized me!

DOCTOR and BELCREDI (*together*): Impossible, impossible! Oh, come!

DONNA MATILDE (*with still more conviction and intensity*): I tell you he recognized me! When he came close to me and stared into my eyes – straight into my eyes – he recognized me!

BELCREDI: But he was talking about your daughter...

DONNA MATILDE: No! He was talking about me!

BELCREDI: Well perhaps, when he said...

DONNA MATILDE (*quickly, ignoring* BELCREDI): About my own dyed hair. Didn't you notice how quickly he added "or of the dark hair, if your hair was dark"? He remembered perfectly well that in those days my hair was dark.

BELCREDI: Oh, nonsense!

DONNA MATILDE (*paying no attention to him, turning to the* DOCTOR): My hair really is dark, Doctor, like my daughter's. That's why he began talking about her.

BELCREDI: But he doesn't known your daughter... he's never seen her!

DONNA MATILDE: That's just it! Oh, you never understand a thing! By my daughter he meant me – me as I was then.

BELCREDI: God... this madness is contagious! Contagious!

DONNA MATILDE (*with quiet scorn*): What are you talking about, you fool?

BELCREDI: But, forgive me: have you ever been his wife? In his lunatic world, it's your daughter who is married to him: Bertha of Susa.

DONNA MATILDE: Exactly. Because I'm no longer dark, as he remembers me, but blonde, like this, and I presented myself to him as Adelaide, the mother of Bertha. My daughter doesn't exist for him – he has never seen her – you said so yourself. How should he know whether her hair is blond or dark?

BELCREDI: For goodness' sake, he was only talking in general when he said "dark" – wishing to evoke a youthful memory through the colour of the hair, be it dark or blond. But as usual, you start to fantasize. She says I shouldn't have come, Doctor, but she's the one who should have stayed away!

DONNA MATILDE (*at first visibly shaken by* BELCREDI's *words, she is momentarily absorbed in her thoughts, then recovers herself and says eagerly, because of her doubts*): No... no, he meant me. All the time he was talking to me, with me, about me—

BELCREDI: Oh please! You say he was talking about you all the time? He didn't leave me alone for a moment! Unless you thought he was also referring to you when he talked to Peter Damian?

DONNA MATILDE (*challengingly, almost without any restraint*): Who knows? Can you tell me why he took a dislike to you immediately, from the very first moment – to you and you only?

(*The tone of her question makes it clear that the implied answer is "Because he realized that you are my lover".* BELCREDI *understands immediately and, bewildered, hides behind a fatuous smile.*)

DOCTOR: If I may suggest... The reason could also be that only the Duchess Adelaide and the Abbot of Cluny were announced as visitors. So when he saw a third person with them, who had not been announced, he became suspicious at once—

BELCREDI: Exactly, and that's why he took me for an enemy – Peter Damian. But she stubbornly believes that he recognized her—

DONNA MATILDE: There is no doubt about it. I read it in his eyes, Doctor... you know, that look that ends every doubt... It may have been a moment – what can I say...

DOCTOR: We can't rule it out: a lucid moment...

DONNA MATILDE: Perhaps. But then... everything he said seemed full of regret for my youth and his – for the horrible thing that happened to him, which left him stuck with that mask... that mask from which he so longs to escape, but simply can't.

BELCREDI: Right. So that he can love your daughter... or rather you, as you like to believe... because he seems to have been touched by your pity for him.

DONNA MATILDE: Which is immense, believe me.

BELCREDI: So we see, Marchesa. So immense, a thaumaturge would believe that a miracle is more than likely.

DOCTOR: May I be allowed my say? I don't deal in miracles, because I'm a doctor and not a thaumaturge. I listened very carefully to everything he said, and I repeat that the elasticity of perception which characterizes all forms of consistent mania is in his case very – how can I put it? – relaxed. In other words, the elements of his mania are no longer holding together firmly. I think that just now he is slowly readjusting himself beneath his outer personality through sudden surges of memory, which pull him (and this is very encouraging) not out of a state of incipient apathy, but rather from smooth complacency into moods of reflective melancholy, which show a... yes, really considerable cerebral activity. I repeat, this is very encouraging. Well now, this violent shock we have planned for him—

DONNA MATILDE (*turning to the window, in the whinging tone of a sick person*): Why isn't the car back yet? It's been three and a half hours!

DOCTOR (*startled*): What's that you say?

DONNA MATILDE: The car, Doctor! It's been more than three and a half hours.

DOCTOR (*taking out his watch and looking at it*): Well, actually more than four!

DONNA MATILDE: It should have been back half an hour ago. But, as usual…

BELCREDI: Perhaps they can't find the dress.

DONNA MATILDE: But I told them exactly where it was! (*Impatiently:*) But where is Frida?… Where is she?

BELCREDI (*leaning out of the window*): I expect she's in the garden with Carlo.

DOCTOR: He'll calm her fears.

BELCREDI: She's not afraid, Doctor. Don't believe her. She just thinks it's a bore.

DONNA MATILDE: Well, please don't beg her to do it. I know what she's like.

DOCTOR: We must be patient and wait. After all, it will all be over in a moment… and we must wait till it gets dark. As I was saying, if we succeed in giving him a shock, and break the already-loosened threads which still bind him to his fantasy, thus giving him back what he begs for ("I can't go on being twenty-six years old for ever, my lady!" he said) and releasing him from what he himself sees as a punishment – well, in short, if we manage to make him suddenly regain the awareness of time past—

BELCREDI (*quickly*): —he will be cured. (*Ironically, spelling out his words:*) We'll have set him free!

DOCTOR: He will be like a clock that has stopped at a particular time. Yes, we'll hold our own watches in our hands till that precise time comes round again, and then give it a shake, hoping it will start up again and keep the correct time – after stopping for so long.

(*At this moment DI NOLLI enters from the main door.*)

DONNA MATILDE: Oh, there you are, Carlo. Where's Frida? Where has she gone?

DI NOLLI: She's coming... she'll be here in a moment.

DOCTOR: Is the car back?

DI NOLLI: Yes.

DONNA MATILDE: Oh, good. With the dress?

DI NOLLI: It's been here some time.

DOCTOR: Excellent!

DONNA MATILDE (*impatiently*): Where is the dress? Where is it?

DI NOLLI (*with a shrug and a sad smile, like a man reluctantly taking part in a game which he considers to be in bad taste*): Well, you'll see soon enough. (*He points to the door by which he entered.*) There you go.

(BERTOLD *appears on the doorway and ceremoniously announces:*)

BERTOLD: Her Highness the Marchesa Matilde of Canossa!

(FRIDA *enters, looking magnificent and extremely beautiful in the eleventh-century costume her mother wore as the Marchesa Matilde of Tuscany. She is the living image of the portrait in the throne room.*)

FRIDA (*with disdainful condescension, as she passes the bowing* BERTOLD): Of Tuscany! Of Tuscany, please! Canossa is just one of my castles.

BELCREDI (*struck with admiration*): Just look at her! Look! She's transformed!

DONNA MATILDE: It's me! God, don't you see? Stop, Frida. You see?... My portrait, come to life.

DOCTOR: Yes, yes. Perfect... perfect. Just like the portrait.

BELCREDI: Yes, no doubt about it. Just the same. Look, look... what a character!

FRIDA: Please... I'm about to burst out laughing... What a tiny waist you had, Mother! I had to breathe in before I could squeeze into this thing.

DONNA MATILDE (*very agitated, fussing with the dress*): Wait... stand still! These creases... Is it really so tight?

FRIDA: I'm suffocating! Let's get this over with quickly, please!

DOCTOR: Well, we need to wait till nightfall...

FRIDA: Oh no, please! I can't hold out... I can't hold out till then!

DONNA MATILDE: But why did you put it on so soon?

FRIDA: When I saw it, I simply had to. The temptation was irresistible.

DONNA MATILDE: You could at least have let me know. Let me help you. It's all crumpled up. Oh, dear!

FRIDA: I know, Mother. But they're old creases. It'll be difficult to smooth them out.

DOCTOR: Don't worry, Marchesa. The illusion is perfect. (*He invites her to place herself a little in front of her daughter without entirely concealing her.*) If you please... stand about here – yes, here – at a little distance from her. Just a little bit forward...

BELCREDI: To prompt an awareness of time past?

DONNA MATILDE (*with a slight turn to look at* BELCREDI): Twenty years later! It's frightening.

BELCREDI: Let's not exaggerate.

DOCTOR (*very embarrassed, trying to set things right*): No, not at all. I meant... I mean, it's also because... because of the costume... I mean to show...

BELCREDI (*with a laugh*): Oh, the costume, Doctor? That's not twenty years... more like eight hundred. It's an abyss. Do you really want to push him over with one shove? (*He points first to* FRIDA, *then to the* MARCHESA.) From here to there? You'll have to pick up the pieces afterwards. Seriously, think about it: for us it's just twenty years, two costumes and a masquerade. But if for him, Doctor, as you said, time has stood still – if he is living in Frida's day with her (*pointing at Frida*) eight hundred years ago – I'm telling you, the sheer vertigo of the leap will be such that when he drops down here among us… (*The* DOCTOR *shakes his head*.) You disagree?

DOCTOR: I do. Because, my dear Baron, life goes on. This life here – *our* life – will immediately become real for him too. It will take hold of him at once, tear away illusion and reveal to him that the eight hundred years you talk about are merely twenty. It's a trick… in a way, like the Masonic initiation: the leap into space… which seems God knows what, but is really only the depth of a stair tread.

BELCREDI: That's obvious, Doctor, but I'm not convinced. Look at Frida and the Marchesa. Who is the more advanced? The older people, Doctor. The young people think they are, but they're wrong. We're ahead by the amount of time we have between us.

DOCTOR: If only our past didn't force us so far apart from each other.

BELCREDI: But it doesn't. How should it? If they (*pointing at Frida and Carlo*) have to go through that which we already have, Doctor – growing old, making more or less the same stupid mistakes that we have… This is the common fallacy: that we leave this world through a door ahead of us. It isn't true. If we begin to die as soon as we are born, then whoever is born first is ahead of everyone else – and the youngest of all is Adam! Look at the Marchesa Matilde of Tuscany there! (*Pointing at Frida*.) Eight hundred years younger than us all! (*He makes a deep bow to her*.)

DI NOLLI: Please, please, Tito, let's not fool around…

BELCREDI: You think I'm fooling?

DI NOLLI: For God's sake, yes. Ever since you arrived here.

BELCREDI: How can you say that? I've even dressed up as a monk!

DI NOLLI: Yes, for a very serious purpose.

BELCREDI: Well, serious for the others… I agree. Serious for Frida here, for instance… (*Turning to the* DOCTOR:) But

Doctor, honestly, I still haven't understood what it is you want to do.

DOCTOR (*ruffled*): Well, you'll see. Just leave things to me. Of course, when the Marchesa is still dressed like that—

BELCREDI: Why? Has she also got to—

DOCTOR: Of course, of course! We have another dress for her next door – though he'll be convinced that he's in the presence of the Marchesa Matilde of Canossa...

FRIDA (*although talking quietly to* DI NOLLI, *she notices the* DOCTOR'*s mistake*): Tuscany, Tuscany!

DOCTOR (*as above*): Oh, what's the difference?

BELCREDI: Oh, I see. Now I begin to follow... He will be confronted with two of them?...

DOCTOR: Exactly. Two of them. And then...

FRIDA: Doctor (*Taking him aside with* DI NOLLI), please come here, listen...

DOCTOR: Coming... (*He walks over to where Frida and Carlo are and pretends to give some explanations.*)

BELCREDI (*quietly to* DONNA MATILDE): I say, now, for goodness' sake!...

DONNA MATILDE (*facing him squarely*): What?

BELCREDI: Are you really set on all this? I mean, taking part in this showdown? It's an extraordinary thing for a woman to do.

DONNA MATILDE: For some women, perhaps.

BELCREDI: No, no, my dear – for any woman, in this case. It's quite a sacrifice...

DONNA MATILDE: I owe it to him.

BELCREDI: Oh, come off it! You know you are not debasing yourself...

DONNA MATILDE: Then where's the sacrifice?

BELCREDI: Try, at least, if you do want to debase yourself in front of others, not to discredit me.

DONNA MATILDE: And who cares about you now?

DI NOLLI (*coming forwards*): Yes, yes, now... sure, sure, we'll do that... (*Turning to* BERTOLD:) Ah, Bertold... go and call one of those three men.

BERTOLD: Yessir. (*Goes out through the main door.*)

DONNA MATILDE: First we have to pretend to take leave of him, don't we?

DI NOLLI: That's right. I'll send one of them to let him know you're going. (*To* BELCREDI:) You needn't bother. You stay here.

BELCREDI (*shaking his head ironically*): Of course, I needn't bother... I needn't bother!

DI NOLLI: Also to make sure he doesn't get suspicious again, you see?

BELCREDI: Oh yes, of course... *Quantité négligeable*!

DOCTOR: He must be certain, absolutely certain that we have gone away.

(LANDOLF, *followed by* BERTOLD, *enters from the door on the right.*)

LANDOLF: May we come in?

DI NOLLI: Yes, come in, come in. Now then, your name is Lolo, isn't it?

LANDOLF: Lolo, or Landolf – as you please.

DI NOLLI: Good. Now listen: the doctor and the Marchesa will now take their leave of him...

LANDOLF: Very good. All we need to say is that the Pope has granted them an audience. Right now he's in his room, groaning, remorseful for all he's said, despairing of ever being pardoned. Please follow me... I'm afraid I'll have to ask you to put on your costumes again...

DOCTOR: Yes, yes, let's go... let's go...

LANDOLF: One moment. May I make a suggestion? Could we add that the Marchesa Matilde of Tuscany begged you to persuade the Pope to give him an audience?

DONNA MATILDE: You see? That means he *did* recognize me!

LANDOLF: No, madam, it doesn't. It's just that he fears the hostility of this Marchesa, because she entertained the Pope in her castle. It's a bit strange – as far as I know – well, I'm sure you know more than I do – Henry the Fourth was not secretly in love with the Marchesa of Tuscany, according to history, was he?

DONNA MATILDE (*quickly*): No, not at all. On the contrary: he hated her.

LANDOLF: I thought so. Well, he says he was once in love with her – he keeps saying that... And now he's afraid that her contempt for his secret love may prompt her to influence the Pope against him.

BELCREDI: We must persuade him there's no longer any hostility on her part.

LANDOLF: Excellent. I'll do that.

DONNA MATILDE (*to* LANDOLF): Very good, I agree. (*Then to* BELCREDI:) In case you don't know, it's historical fact that the Pope gave way only because the Marchesa and the Abbot of Cluny pleaded for him. And another thing, my dear Belcredi: it may interest you to know that when we organized that pageant I meant to use this to show him that I was by no means as hostile to him as he thought.

BELCREDI: But that's even better, then, Marchesa! Be truthful – be truthful to history...

LANDOLF: Indeed. In that case, Madam could spare herself the trouble of a double disguise and go with Monsignore (*pointing at the* DOCTOR) as the Marchesa of Tuscany.

DOCTOR (*protesting at once*): No, no... This won't do, I beg you! The confrontation must come as a shock! It must be sudden. No, no. Come on, Marchesa, we must go. You'll be the Duchess Adelaide again – mother of the Empress. And we'll take our leave of him. Above all, it's essential he believes we've gone. Come on, come on, let's not waste any more time. There's still so much to do.

(*The* DOCTOR, DONNA MATILDE *and* LANDOLF *go out by the door on the right.*)

FRIDA: I'm beginning to feel very frightened again.

DI NOLLI: Not again, Frida?

FRIDA: It would've been better if I'd seen him first.

DI NOLLI: Believe me, there's no need at all...

FRIDA: He's not violent, is he?

DI NOLLI: Of course not. He's as gentle as a lamb.

BELCREDI (*ironically, with mock sentimentality*): And *so* melancholy... Didn't you hear he's in love with you?

FRIDA: Oh, thank you – and that's why he's sad, right?

BELCREDI: He won't do you any harm.

DI NOLLI: It will all be over in a moment.

FRIDA: I know, but I have to be in the dark... with him...

DI NOLLI: Only for a moment. And I'll be close by. And the others will be just behind the doors, ready to rush in. You see, as soon as he's face to face with your mother, you'll have nothing more to do...

BELCREDI: What I'm worried about is that it'll all be a waste of time.

DI NOLLI: Now don't you start! It sounds like an excellent cure to me.

FRIDA: I agree, I agree. I have a good feeling about it. I feel all excited.

BELCREDI: But madmen, my dears (even though they themselves are not aware of it!) often possess a kind of happiness we are not aware of...

DI NOLLI (*irritated, interrupting him*): Happiness? What are you talking about?

BELCREDI (*assertively*): The inability to reason.

DI NOLLI: Sorry, what's reason got to do with it?

BELCREDI: What do you mean? According to our plan, he'll have to use his reason when he sees her (*pointing at Frida*) and her mother, won't he? But the whole thing has been concocted by us!

DI NOLLI: But where does reason come into it? We are merely confronting him with a double image of someone he's invented himself, as the doctor says.

BELCREDI (*with a sudden outburst*): You know, I've never understood why those people take degrees in medicine.

DI NOLLI: Who?

BELCREDI: Psychiatrists.

DI NOLLI: Well, what on earth should they take degrees in?

FRIDA: If they're going to become psychiatrists!

BELCREDI: You're proving my point! They should take Law, my dear! It's all balderdash! And the more they drivel on, the better they're taken to be: "Elasticity of perception!"; "awareness of time past!" And the first thing they say is that they can't work miracles – just when a miracle is the very thing one needs. But they know that the more they tell you they aren't thaumaturges, the more you'll take them seriously. Since they don't work miracles... they always land on their feet! Quite convenient!

BERTOLD (*who has been looking through the keyhole of the door on the right*): They're here, they're here! They seem to be coming this way...

DI NOLLI: Really?

BERTOLD: And I think he's coming too. Yes, yes, he is, he is!

DI NOLLI: We'll get out, then. Come on, quick! (*Turning to BERTOLD before going out:*) You stay here!

BERTOLD: Must I?

(*He gets no answer. DI NOLLI, FRIDA and BELCREDI go out quickly through the main exit, leaving him anxious and bewildered. The door on the right opens. The first to enter is* LANDOLF, *who stops, turns and bows swiftly. Then come* DONNA MATILDE, *in ducal robe and crown, as in Act One, and the* DOCTOR, *as the Abbot of Cluny, with – between them –* HENRY IV *in imperial dress.* ORDULF *and* HAROLD *bring up the rear.*)

HENRY IV (*continuing a conversation begun in the throne room*): Now I ask you: how could I be so cunning when they say I'm obstinate?

DOCTOR: Oh, no! Not obstinate! Good Lord, no!

HENRY IV (*with a pleased smile*): Then in your opinion I really am cunning?

DOCTOR: No, no... neither obstinate nor cunning!

HENRY IV (*He pauses, then says in a tone of gentle irony, as if to point out that things are not like that*): Monsignore! Since obstinacy is a vice that is rarely accompanied by cunning, I was hoping that by denying me the one, you would at least concede me a little of the other. I assure you I really need it. But if you are resolved to keep it all for yourself...

DOCTOR: Me? Do you think I am cunning?

HENRY IV: Oh no, Monsignore. Don't say that. Not in the least! (*He stops abruptly and turns to* DONNA MATILDE.) If you will excuse me, I'd like a word in private with Her Grace the Duchessa here by the door. (*He leads* DONNA MATILDE *a little apart and asks anxiously and secretively:*) Do you really love your daughter?

DONNA MATILDE (*bewildered*): Of course...

HENRY IV: And do you wish me to atone with all my love and devotion for the grievous wrong I have done her? Though you mustn't believe that I have been dissolute, as my enemies say!

DONNA MATILDE: No, I don't believe that. I have never believed that.

HENRY IV: Then is that what you wish?

DONNA MATILDE: What?

HENRY IV: That I love your daughter again? (*He gazes at her and then suddenly adds in a mysterious tone that expresses both warning and fear:*) Don't be a friend of the Marchesa of Tuscany, don't be her friend!

DONNA MATILDE: But I told you she begged and implored the Holy Father for your pardon as urgently as we have done.

HENRY IV (*quickly, with a shudder, quietly*): Don't tell me! Don't tell me! In the name of God, madam, can't you see how it upsets me?

DONNA MATILDE (*she looks at him, then speaks very softly, confidentially*): You still love her?

HENRY IV (*dismayed*): Still? Why do you say "still"? Perhaps you know? No one knows. No one must.

DONNA MATILDE: Perhaps she does know, since she has begged so hard for you.

HENRY IV (*stares at her, before speaking*): So you do love your daughter? (*Brief pause, then he turns to the* DOCTOR *and says, laughingly:*) Yes, Monsignore, it's absolutely true, I scarcely knew I had a wife until later... much, much later. And even now, I swear to you – although I know I have a wife, I must have one – I hardly ever think of her... It may be a sin, but I don't feel... I don't feel she has a place in my heart. What is extraordinary is that her mother doesn't have a place for her in her heart either! Admit it, madam... you don't care much about her!... (*He turns to the* DOCTOR *in frustration.*) She's talking to me about the other woman! (*More and more excitedly.*) And with a persistence – with a persistence that I am utterly at a loss to understand.

LANDOLF (*respectfully*): Perhaps, Your Majesty, to correct the opinion you had formed of the Marchesa of Tuscany. (*Dismayed at having dared to make such an observation, he quickly adds:*) I mean, of course, the opinion you *have* formed.

HENRY IV: So you too feel she acted like a friend to me.

LANDOLF: She is doing so now, Your Majesty.

DONNA MATILDE: Exactly. That's why—

HENRY IV: I see. I see. That means you don't believe I love her. I see... I see. No one has ever believed it – not even suspected it. So much the better. Now enough of it. Enough! (*He turns to the* DOCTOR, *with an altogether different mood and expression.*) What did I tell you, Monsignore?... The conditions under which the Pope is prepared to revoke my excommunication have nothing – nothing – to do whatsoever with the reason for imposing it in the first place. Tell Pope Gregory that we will meet again at Brixen. As to you, my lady, should you chance to meet your daughter in the courtyard of the Marchesa's castle, what would you like me to say? Tell her to come here. Let's see if I can keep her here, closely by my side, as wife and Empress. Many women have come before me, claiming... claiming to be your daughter – the wife I knew I had... yes, and even sought sometimes (I'm not ashamed – she's my wife). But when they said they were Bertha, hailing from Susa, they all giggled – I don't know why. (*As if confidentially:*) You see... in bed... without my dress... and she too... Well, for Heaven's sake! A man and a woman... what is more natural? At such a time we lose awareness of who we are... Our clothes dangle on hangers like ghosts... (*His tone changes, though remaining confidential.*) And I think, Monsignore... that ghosts are no more than little discombobulations of the spirit: images that we are unable to keep within the bounds of sleep. They come to us sometimes when we are awake, too, and they frighten us. I am really scared of them when they take shape before me at night... muddled figures who laugh after jumping off their horses. Sometimes I'm even afraid of my own blood pulsing through my veins in the silence of the night – like thumping footsteps in a far-off room. But I have kept you standing here far too long. I remain your servant, my ladyship. My respects, Monsignore. (*He accompanies them to the main*

doorway, bidding them goodbye and receiving their bows.
MATILDE *and the* DOCTOR *go out. He closes the door,
then turns around abruptly, completely changed.*) Clowns!
Clowns! Clowns! It was like playing a piano of colours!
At one touch... she turned white, red, yellow, green! And
as for that other idiot... Peter Damian... Ha ha! He was
perfect – most appropriate! He was scared of showing
his face again... (*As all this pours from him in a gush of
cheerful frenzy, he walks up and down and looks around,
until his attention is caught by* BERTOLD, *who is terrified,
rather than dumbfounded, by this sudden transformation.*
HENRY IV *pulls up in front of him, derisively pointing
him out to the other three, who are also bewildered and
astonished.*) Look at this imbecile here, staring at me with
an open mouth! (*He shakes him by the shoulders.*) Don't
you understand? Don't you see how I make them dress and
spruce up – how I force them appear before me at will,
those terrified clowns? And they are only scared of this:
that I might tear off their ridiculous masks and reveal their
disguise for what it is! As if it wasn't me who made them
put it on – to satisfy my whim... of acting like a madman!
LANDOLF, HAROLD, ORDULF: What? What are you saying...
You mean... (*Looking at each other in shock and
amazement.*)
HENRY IV (*turns towards them as they speak, and says imperiously*): That's enough! Let's put an end to this! I'm bored
with it all! (*Then he continues quickly, as if, on consideration, this is something that torments him and he finds
impossible to believe.*) My God, the impudence of it! To
come before me, dragging her paramour with her! And
pretending to be moved by compassion, in case they should
upset a poor lunatic who's already detached from the
world, from time, from life! Otherwise, do you think that
someone like him would submit to this kind of abuse? They
always expect – every second, every day – that everyone

should be as they wish them to be... That's not abuse, is it?... Oh no, no... that's merely their way of thinking, of seeing things... of feeling! Everyone has his own way. Even you, right? Of course. But what *is* your way? That of the herd... Do you feel miserable, feeble, doubtful? Well, they take advantage of that... they subject you to their will, so that you feel and see the way they do! Well, that's what they think! For, after all, what can impose on you? Words!... Words which everyone understands and uses in their own way. That's how so-called current opinion is formed. And Heaven help anyone who some fine day finds he's been labelled with one of these words which everyone repeats! "Mad", for instance, or "cretin". But tell me – would you be happy if you discovered someone was busy trying to persuade others that you are as he sees you – to have you classified for all time in their minds as mad... "Mad!" "Mad!" I am not talking about now – now that I'm pretending to be mad – but before I fell from my horse and cracked my head... (*He stops suddenly, seeing the others more agitated and astonished then ever.*) Why do you look at each other like that? (*He mockingly mimics their expressions.*) Oh! Ah! Well, have you made up your minds? Am I or am I not? Very well... yes, I *am* mad! (*His expression becomes frightening.*) But then, by God, on your knees... on your knees! (*He forces them to kneel, each in turn.*) I order you to kneel in front of me – like this – and touch the floor with your forehead three times! Down! Everyone must prostrate himself before a madman! (*As he sees the four kneeling figures, his savage merriment evaporates, turning to scorn.*) Get up, you sheep, up! You obeyed me? You could have put me in a straitjacket. To crush a man like that, with a single word! It's nothing – like swatting a fly... Our entire life is crushed under the weight of words. The weight of the dead. Do you seriously believe that Henry the Fourth is still alive?... Yet, look, I speak to you, who are alive, and give you orders. That's how I want you to be. Do you think this is also a joke – that it's the dead who continue to shape life? Yes, it's a joke in here... but go outside, into the world of the living... It's daybreak. Time lies before you. A new dawn. "This day which is about to begin," you say, "we will shape it ourselves". Really? You? How about all the old traditions – all the customs? And when you open your mouths, you'll repeat the same old platitudes. Do you think that's living? You're just chewing the cud left by the dead! (*He stops in front of* BERTOLD, *who by now is completely stunned.*) You don't understand a thing, do you? What's your name?

BERTOLD: Me? Oh... er... Bertold.

HENRY IV: Bertold my foot, you fool! Just between you and me... what's your name?

BERTOLD: Well... er... to tell you the truth, it's Fino.

HENRY IV (*noticing that the others are making slight warning signs to* BERTOLD, *he turns to silence them*): Fino, eh?

BERTOLD: Yessir – Fino Pagliuca.

HENRY IV (*turning again to the others*): I've often heard what you call each other when you're by yourselves. (*To* LANDOLF:) Your name's Lolo, isn't it?

LANDOLF: Yes, sir. (*In delighted realization:*) Oh my God, then you're...

HENRY IV (*brusquely*): What?

LANDOLF (*suddenly turning pale*): Nothing, I mean...

HENRY IV: Not mad any more? Of course I'm not. Can't you see?... Now we can all laugh behind the backs of those who believe I am. (*To* HAROLD:) Your name's Franco, I know. (*To* ORDULF:) And yours is... wait a minute...

LANDOLF: Momo.

HENRY IV: Yes, Momo... That'll be great, won't it?

LANDOLF (*as above*): But then... oh my God!...

HENRY IV: Then nothing! We can have a good long laugh together! (*He laughs loudly.*) Ha, ha, ha, ha, ha, ha!

LANDOLF, HAROLD, ORDULF (*looking at each other in dismay and bewilderment, half cheerful, half frightened*): Is he cured? Can it be true? How could it be?

HENRY IV: Shh, shh! (*To* BERTOLD:) You are not laughing? Are you still offended with me? Don't be. I wasn't talking about you, you know? You see, it suits everyone... it suits everyone that certain people should be considered mad: it's an excuse for locking them up. And you know why? Because they can't bear to hear them talk. What shall I say of those people who just left? That one's a whore, one's a dirty libertine and the third's an impostor. Oh, it's not true... No one can believe it. But they'd all stand there listening to me in horror. Well, I'd like to know why, if it's not true. Can you believe a word of what a madman says? Yet that won't stop them listening to me with their eyes wide open in fear. Why? Tell me – you tell me – why? You see, I'm quite calm now.

BERTOLD: Perhaps because... because they think that—

HENRY IV: No, no, no, my dear boy... look me straight in the eye! I'm not saying it's true... don't be alarmed. Nothing is true. But look into my eyes.

BERTOLD: Well then?

HENRY IV: You see? You see? You too!... There's fear in your eyes too... because at this moment you think I'm mad. There's the proof... there's the proof! (*He laughs loudly.*)

LANDOLF (*taking courage, he speaks for the others in frustration*): What proof?

HENRY IV: This dismay of yours – because once again you think I'm mad. Yet you know this already. You believe – you've always believed, till now – that I am mad. Isn't it so? (*He holds their gaze and realizes they are frightened.*) You see? Don't you feel that this dismay can turn into fear, as if the earth might give way under your feet, taking away the very air you breathe? Of course, my friends!

How else can you feel before a madman – before a man who shakes from its very foundation everything you've built up within and around yourselves... the logic, the very logic of all your constructions? What else do you expect? Madmen construct without logic – lucky them! – or with a logic of their own that flutters like a feather... Changeable! Changeable! Today's one thing and tomorrow God knows what. You cling to your own beliefs – they don't. Changeable! Changeable! You say: "This cannot be!" – and for them everything is possible. "But that's not true," you say. Why? Because it's not true for you, or you, or you (*pointing at three of them*), and a hundred thousand like you. Ah, my friends! We should see what seems real to these hundred thousand who are not considered mad! Ah, what a wonderful show they make of the things they agree on – the pinnacle of logic! What I know is that when I was a child I believed that the moon in the well was real. So many things seemed real to me! And I believed in all the things they told me – and I was happy. God help you if you don't cling with all your might to what seems true to you today – or to what seems true to you tomorrow, even if it's the opposite of what was true for you yesterday! God help you if you were to fix your thoughts on this terrible thing, which can really drive you out of your mind: that if you find yourselves next to someone and look into their eyes – the way I used to look into the eyes of a certain person – you see yourself as a beggar at a gate you are forbidden to enter. Whoever is able to get in, it won't be you, with your inner world, that you alone can see and touch, but someone you don't know, who sees and touches you in their own impenetrable world, like the other. (*A long pause. It has grown darker, and in the gloom the four young men in a mask seem to have become even more perplexed and alarmed, increasingly detached from the great Masked Man, who is absorbed in the contemplation of the terrible plight which he – not he alone, but all mankind – finds himself in. Then he shakes off his mood, and peers around, as if trying to look for the others, who he realizes are no longer next to him.*) It's got dark in here.

ORDULF (*promptly, coming forward*): Would you like me to get the lamp?

HENRY IV (*ironically*): Oh yes, the lamp... Do you think I don't know that as soon as I've turned my back and gone off to bed with my oil lamp you switch on the electric light for yourselves – here and in the throne room too? I pretend not to notice.

ORDULF: Oh well, in that case, shall we...

HENRY IV: No, it would dazzle me. I want my lamp.

ORDULF: Right. It's just behind the door. (*He steps out through the main door and returns at once carrying an antique oil lamp, similar to a sea lantern.*)

HENRY IV (*taking the lamp and pointing to the table on the platform*): There we go... a little light. Sit there, round the table. No, not like that. More at ease, more relaxed. (*To* HAROLD:) There, like this... (*arranging him on the chair; then to* BERTOLD:) And you like this... (*as before*) that's better. (*Goes to his chair and sits down.*) And me here... (*Turning his head to face a window:*) We should be able to command a nice decorative moonbeam from the moon. She's very beneficial to us, the moon. As for me, I need her a lot: I often lose myself watching her from my window. To look at her up there, who would believe that she knows eight hundred years have passed and that I, seated at my window and gazing at her like any poor nobody, cannot really be Henry the Fourth? But look – look what a magnificent night picture we make! The Emperor among his trusty counsellors... don't you like it?

LANDOLF (*in an undertone to* HAROLD, *not wishing to break the spell*): Do you realize... if we had known it was all make-believe...

HENRY IV: What was make-believe?

LANDOLF (*hesitant and apologetic*): Oh, nothing. It's just that... well, this morning I was saying to him (*indicating* BERTOLD), while we were showing him the ropes... that it was a pity that, dressed as we are and with so many other fine costumes in the wardrobe... and... a hall like that... (*Gestures towards the throne room.*)

HENRY IV: Well? What was a pity?

LANDOLF: Oh... er... just that didn't know...

HENRY IV: That you playing out this comedy for fun?

LANDOLF: Well, we thought...

HAROLD (*coming to his assistance*): Well, yes, that it was all true.

HENRY IV: And isn't it? Don't you believe it is true?

LANDOLF: Well, if you say—

HENRY IV: I say that you are a pack of fools! You should have acted out this sham for yourselves, not for me and any occasional visitors – just like this, as you are now, your good old natural selves, every day, in front of no one else. (*To* BERTOLD, *taking him by the arm:*) Your part in this pretence allows you to eat, sleep and scratch yourself, if you feel an itch. (*Addressing the others too:*) You can feel that you are truly living in the year 1100, here in the Court of your Emperor Henry the Fourth. You can tell yourselves here, in this remote time, so colourful and sepulchral, you can tell yourself that at a distance of eight centuries from it, the people of the twentieth century will be squabbling and torturing themselves in relentless agony to find out what lies in store for them, how everything that worries them and makes them anxious will be settled. While you, meantime, are here – with me – in history! However sad my lot, however horrible the events, harsh the struggles or bitter the circumstances, it's all history. They won't change – they can't change – any more, do you understand? It is all fixed for ever.

And you may sit there in peace and quiet, observing how every effect obediently follows its cause with perfect logic – how every event takes place precisely, coherent in its smallest detail. So satisfying, so satisfying! Well, that's the great joy of history!

LANDOLF: Wonderful! Wonderful!

HENRY IV: Yes, it's wonderful, but now it's over. Now that you know, I can no longer go on. (*He picks up the lamp and is about to go to bed.*) Nor, for that matter, could you, if you have not understood the reason I've done it. I'm sick of it now. (*Almost to himself, suppressing his fury:*) By God, she'll be sorry she came here! Dressing up as my mother-in-law! And he as an abbot!... Dragging a doctor along to examine me. Perhaps they were hoping to cure me?... The clowns! But I must have the pleasure of slapping one of them in the face... That man! Famous swordsman, is he? He'll run me through? We shall see, we shall see. (*There is a knock at the main door.*) Who is it?

VOICE OF GIOVANNI: *Deo gratias.*

HAROLD (*cheerfully, at the thought of playing yet another joke*): Oh, it's Giovanni – it's Giovanni, coming to play the monk, as he does every evening...

ORDULF (*as above, rubbing his hands*): Oh, good! Let him do it! Let him do it!

HENRY IV (*quickly, sternly*): You fool! You see? Why? Just to have a laugh at the expense of a poor old man who does this out of love for me?

LANDOLF (*to* ORDULF): It must seem for real, don't you understand?

HENRY IV: Exactly. For real! That is the only way to stop truth becoming a mockery. (*He goes to the door and admits* GIOVANNI, *who is dressed as a humble friar and carries a scroll of parchment under his arm.*) Come in, Father, come in. (*He assumes a tone of tragic gravity and gloomy resentment*.) All the evidence of my life and reign that was favourable to me was deliberately destroyed by my enemies. The only thing that has survived is this account of my life, written down by a humble monk who is devoted to me... and you'd make fun of him? (*He turns affectionately to* GIOVANNI *and invites him to sit at the table*.) Sit down, Father. Here. Take the lamp. (*He places on the table, next to* GIOVANNI, *the lamp he was holding*.) Now write, Father, write.

GIOVANNI (*Unrolls the parchment and prepares to be dictated*): I am ready, Your Majesty.

HENRY IV (*dictating*): The peace edict proclaimed at Mainz benefited the poor and the good-hearted as much as it harmed the wicked and powerful. (*The curtain begins to fall*.) It brought wealth to the former, hunger and poverty to the latter...

CURTAIN

Act Three

The throne room is dark. The back wall is just visible. The two portraits have been removed from their frames, and in their place stand FRIDA, *in the Marchesa of Tuscany costume she wore in Act Two, and* CARLO DI NOLLI, *dressed as* HENRY IV. *Both have assumed the exact postures of the portraits.*

When the curtain rises, the stage is momentarily empty. Then the door on the left opens and HENRY IV *enters, holding the lamp by its handle and turning to speak to the* FOUR YOUNG MEN, *who presumably are in the adjoining room with* GIOVANNI, *as at the close of Act Two.*

HENRY IV: No. Stay – stay there. I can manage by myself. Goodnight.

(*He closes the door and, wearily and dejectedly, begins to cross the hall, making for the second door on the right, which leads to his apartments.*)

FRIDA (*When she sees he has gone a little way past the throne, she whispers from her niche, as if about to swoon in terror*): Henry...

(*He stops abruptly, as if he feels a knife in his back, and, turning in alarm to peer at the wall behind him, instinctively raises his arms, as if to defend himself.*)

HENRY IV: Who called my name?

(*It is not really a question, but a flickering exclamation of fright: it expects no reply from the darkness or from the terrible silence of the hall. He is struck with the sudden fear that perhaps, after all, he really is mad.*)

FRIDA (*although his terrified reaction does nothing to calm her own fears, she repeats a little louder*): Henry...

(*While doing her best to play the part she has been assigned, she cannot help craning forwards a little from her niche and looking towards the other.* HENRY IV *shouts out in horror and drops the lamp. Covering his head with his hands, he runs, as if to flee.*)

FRIDA (*jumping from the frame onto the ledge, screaming like a madwoman*): Henry... Henry... I'm scared! I'm scared!

(*Meanwhile,* DI NOLLI *also leaps onto the ledge and then onto the floor. He runs to* FRIDA, *who continues to scream uncontrollably and is on the point of fainting. From the door on the left all the others rush in – the* DOCTOR, DONNA MATILDE, *also dressed as the Marchesa of Tuscany,* TITO BELCREDI, LANDOLF, HAROLD, ORDULF, BERTOLD *and* GIOVANNI. *One of them promptly switches on the light, which has a strange effect, coming from bulbs hidden in the ceiling, and is strong only above the scene.* HENRY IV *stands watching. Although jolted out of his momentary terror by this unexpected invasion, his whole body is still shaking. The others pay no attention to him, but crowd solicitously round* FRIDA *to comfort her.* DI NOLLI *holds her in his arms as she still trembles and sobs. Everyone talks confusedly.*)

DI NOLLI: It's all right, Frida, I'm here. I'm here with you.
DOCTOR (*arriving with the others*): That's it, that's it. We don't have to do anything else now.

DONNA MATILDE: He's cured, Frida! Look, don't you see? He's cured.

DI NOLLI (*incredulous*): Cured?

BELCREDI: It was all a joke! Don't be worried!

FRIDA (*as above*): No, I'm scared. I'm scared!

DONNA MATILDE: Of what? Look at him. It wasn't for real. It wasn't.

DI NOLLI (*as above*): Not real? What are you saying? Cured?

DOCTOR: So it appears... although in my opinion...

BELCREDI: But he is! (*Indicating the* FOUR YOUNG MEN:) They told us all about it.

DONNA MATILDE: Yes, he's long been cured. He confessed it to them.

DI NOLLI (*more angry than astonished*): But only a moment ago...

BELCREDI: Well, it was all an act – to have a laugh at your expense. And we, acting in good faith, were his victims too...

DI NOLLI: I can't believe it! His own sister too, right up to her death?

HENRY IV (*During this exchange, he has approached the various groups, looking at each person in turn as they rain accusations and abuse on him for what they believe has been a cruel joke, now unmasked. His glowering look shows that he is contemplating revenge, although it is unclear to him what shape this will take, because of the tumultuous anger still raging inside him. Deeply stung, he decides to behave as though the pretence they have mischievously planned for him were true. He shouts at his nephew*): Go on! Go on – say it!

DI NOLLI (*startled at his shouting*): Say what?

HENRY IV: That it was only *your* sister who died.

DI NOLLI (*as above*): *My* sister! I said *your* sister... whom you compelled to come here as Agnes, your mother, right to the end.

HENRY IV: And was she not *your* mother?

DI NOLLI: Of course, of course, my mother!

HENRY IV: Your mother died when I was "old and far away". You've jumped down right now from *there (pointing at the niche)*. How would you know if I have mourned her for years, in secret, even though I'm dressed like this?

DONNA MATILDE *(in consternation, looking at the others)*: What's he talking about?

DOCTOR *(studying him closely, with concern)*: Gently, gently, for God's sake!

HENRY IV: What am I talking about? I am asking you all if Agnes was not the mother of Henry the Fourth. *(He turns to FRIDA as if she really were the Marchesa of Tuscany.)* You, of all people, ought to know, Marchesa.

FRIDA *(still in a frenzy, clinging to DI NOLLI)*: No! I don't, I don't!

DOCTOR: He's getting delusional again. Please... be gentle with him...

BELCREDI *(contemptuously)*: Delusional my foot! He's play-acting again!

HENRY IV *(quickly)*: Am I? It was *you* who have emptied those niches... and he's standing before me as Henry the Fourth...

BELCREDI: This stupid game has gone on long enough!

HENRY IV: Who said it's a game?

DOCTOR *(loudly, to BELCREDI)*: Don't provoke him, for God's sake!

BELCREDI *(ignoring the DOCTOR's plea, even more loudly)*: That's what they told me!... *(He points again at the FOUR YOUNG MEN.)* Them! Them!

HENRY IV *(turning to look at the FOUR YOUNG MEN)*: You? Did you say it was a game?

LANDOLF *(timid, embarrassed)*: No... in fact, we only said you were cured.

BELCREDI: Then let's put an end to this farce! *(To DONNA MATILDE:)* Don't you think the sight of him *(indicating DI*

NOLLI) and you, Marchesa, in that dress, is now intolerably childish?

DONNA MATILDE: Oh, shut up! Who cares about the dress if he's really cured?

HENRY IV: Yes, I am cured. I'm cured. (*To* BELCREDI:) But that doesn't mean the story ends here so easily as you think. (*Aggressively:*) Do you realize that over the last twenty years no one has ever dared to appear before me dressed like you and this gentleman here? (*Indicating the* DOCTOR.)

BELCREDI: Of course I know. In fact, this morning I too dressed up before you as—

HENRY IV: As a monk, yes.

BELCREDI: And you took me for Peter Damian. And I didn't laugh, because I really thought that—

HENRY IV: That I was mad. And does it make you laugh to see her in that dress, now that you know I'm sane? Yet you could think that she now, in my eyes, looks... (*He breaks off with a sudden gesture of contempt.*) Ah. (*He turns swiftly to the* DOCTOR.) You're a doctor?

DOCTOR: Yes, er... I am.

HENRY IV: And was it your idea to have her dressed up as the Marchesa of Tuscany too? Do you realize, Doctor, that you ran the risk of plunging my mind back into darkness?... For God's sake, making those paintings speak and jump out of their frames! (*His gaze falls on* FRIDA *and* DI NOLLI, *then moves to the* MARCHESA *and finally to the clothes he is wearing.*) Well, wonderful combination. Two couples. Bravo, bravo, Doctor! For a madman like him... (*He makes a slight gesture towards* BELCREDI.) But to him now it just seems an out-of-season carnival masquerade, doesn't it? (*He turns to face* BELCREDI.) Well, I'll get rid of my own fancy dress now. Then I can come away with you, can't I?

BELCREDI: With me? You mean with all of us!

HENRY IV: Where? To the club? Tails and white tie? Or together at home with the Marchesa?

BELCREDI: Wherever you like. I'm sure you don't want to continue to stay here now, on your own, living in this world of make-believe you've created since that unfortunate carnival? I'm still wondering how – how on earth – you managed to keep it up all these years after you recovered from the accident.

HENRY IV: Well, you see, the thing is, after I fell from my horse and cracked my head, I really was mad... I don't know how long for.

DOCTOR: Oh, I see, I see. For a long time?

HENRY IV (*very quickly, to the* DOCTOR): Yes, Doctor, a long time – about twelve years. (*He promptly resumes his conversation with* BELCREDI.) Which means, my dear friend, that after that carnival I didn't know a thing about what was happening in your world (not mine), how circumstances were changing, how I was being betrayed by friends – for example, who had occupied my place... well, say, in the heart of the woman I loved – about the people who had died, who had moved away... all this was not, for me, the joke you think it was, you know?

BELCREDI: No, no... I didn't mean that. I was talking about *later*.

HENRY IV: Oh yes, later. One day... (*He stops, turning to the* DOCTOR.) A most interesting case, Doctor: examine me – examine me closely. (*He begins to shudder as he speaks*.) One day, without warning... whatever fault I had in here... (*touching his forehead*) who knows how, it was corrected. Little by little, I began to see straight again – at first I wasn't sure if I was dreaming or not. Then I realized I was awake: I touched this and that object... I could see things clearly again... Well, as he said (*indicating* BELCREDI), off, off with this masquerade... with this nightmare! Let's open the windows: let's breathe in fresh air! Come, come – let's run outside! (*He pulls himself up suddenly.*) But where to? And to do what? To have everyone point at me secretly and say "Look, there's Henry the Fourth" – not as I am now, but arm in arm with you, among my dearest friends?

BELCREDI: They wouldn't. What makes you think that?

DONNA MATILDE: They wouldn't dare... it's inconceivable... they know it was due to that accident.

HENRY IV: But they already said I was mad even before it happened. (*To* BELCREDI:) You know that. You, more than anyone else, raged against those who tried to defend me.

BELCREDI: Oh come now. That was only in jest.

HENRY IV: And look at my hair now. (*He shows the hair at the back of his neck.*)

BELCREDI: Well, I'm going grey too!

HENRY IV: But there's a difference! I went grey here, as Henry the Fourth – do you understand?... And I didn't notice it. I noticed it suddenly one morning, opening my eyes again. It was a terrible shock... because I realized at once that it wasn't just my hair that had gone grey, but everything else... all had crumbled, all was over. I was like someone who arrives, hungry like a wolf, at a banquet which is already finished.

BELCREDI: Yes, but all the others...

HENRY IV (*quickly*): I know – they couldn't be expected to wait for me to be cured. Not even those who crept up behind me and viciously pricked my horse until it bled.

DI NOLLI (*stunned*): What? What?

HENRY IV: Yes, it was foul play – to make it rear up, and to make me fall off.

DONNA MATILDE (*quickly, horrified*): It's the first I've heard of this!

HENRY IV: Perhaps that too was "only in jest"...

DONNA MATILDE: But who did it? Who was behind us?

HENRY IV: Does it matter to know who it was? All those who
went to the banquet, leaving me with a few flabby morsels
of pity, Marchesa, or perhaps a scrap of remorse sticking to
their dirty plates. (*Abruptly turning to the* DOCTOR:) Now,
Doctor, don't you think my case is really new in the annals
of lunacy? I preferred to remain mad… I found everything
was here to hand for this novel pleasure: to live my madness
out – completely aware of what I was doing – and in this
way revenge myself on the stone which played havoc with
my head. Squalid and empty though it seemed when my
reopened my eyes, I decided to dress up this solitude again in
the colours and splendour of that distant carnival day when
you – (*looking at* DONNA MATILDE *and indicating* FRIDA
to her) yes, there you are, Marchesa – shone in all your glory,
and oblige all those who came before me to continue to play
out that masquerade of long ago which, for you, but not for
me, had been the whim of a day – make it no longer a pretence, but a permanent, madman's reality: everyone dressed
in costume… the throne room, my four Privy Counsellors
– all traitors, of course! (*Turning on them suddenly:*) I
wonder what you gained by letting them know I am cured!
If I am cured, I no longer need your services – so you'll end
up without a job! It was certainly mad of me to confide in
someone. Ah yes, but it's now my turn to accuse you! Do you
know that they planned to go on acting this charade with
me behind your backs? (*He laughs loudly. The others laugh
feebly, with the exception of* DONNA MATILDE.)

BELCREDI (*to* DI NOLLI): Did you hear that? I can't believe it.

DI NOLLI (*to the* FOUR YOUNG MEN): You?

HENRY IV: You must forgive them! This dress (*grasping his
clothes*) – which is obviously and intentionally a caricature
of that other masquerade which goes on all the time, every
minute, and in which we involuntarily act as clowns…
(*indicating* BELCREDI) dressing up as the people we think
we are – this dress, their dress, forgive them, they still don't

see it as their own identity. (*Turning again to* BELCREDI:)
You soon get used to it, you know? It's easy enough to walk
about like this... pretending to be a character in a drama...
(*acting it out*) especially in a room like this! Look, Doctor!
I remember once seeing a priest – I'm sure he was Irish...
quite a handsome man too – asleep on a bench in a park in
the November sun, with his arm behind his head. He was
lost in the golden delight of that warmth, which must have
seemed to him like a breath of summer. I'm sure that at
that moment he forgot he was a priest – or where he was!
He was dreaming – of Heaven knows what! And a cheeky
little boy came by, carrying a flower he'd torn up by the
roots – and as he passed the priest, he tickled his neck with
the flower. The priest opened his shining eyes, and I saw he
was smiling, unaware, with the blissful joy of his dreams...
But then he suddenly sat up and was the priest again, uptight
in his cassock, his eyes burning again with an expression as
serious as the one you've seen in mine – because Irish priests
defend the seriousness of their Catholic faith with as much
zeal as I defend the sacred rights of hereditary monarchy. I
am cured, my friends... because I'm perfectly aware I play
at being mad – and I do it quite calmly. The trouble with
you is that you live out your madness in a state of constant
agitation – without being aware of it, without seeing it.

BELCREDI: Oh, look... so in conclusion, we are the madmen
now!

HENRY IV (*in a sudden burst which he tries to suppress*): But
if she (*indicating the* MARCHESA) and you were not both
mad, would you have come to see me?

BELCREDI: To tell the truth, I came because I believed *you*
were mad.

HENRY IV (*quickly and loudly, indicating the* MARCHESA):
And she?

BELCREDI: Well, I can't speak for her... She seems struck dumb
by what you say – spellbound by this "conscious" madness

of yours. (*Turning to her:*) You know, Marchesa, dressed as you are for the role, you could stay here and live it out…

MATILDE: You're so insolent!

HENRY IV (*quickly, trying to calm her*): Ignore him… ignore him… He's always provoking. Even though the doctor warned him not to be provoking. (*To* BELCREDI:) Don't think I'm still upset by what happened between us – by the part you played with her in my misery. (*To* DONNA MATILDE, *indicating* BELCREDI:) Or by the part he now plays in your life. My life is this. It's not yours. Your life, in which you have grown old, does not belong to me. (*To* DONNA MATILDE:) Was that what you wanted to tell me – to show me – with this sacrifice of yours, dressing up like this on the doctor's advice? Oh, well done, Doctor, like I said to you! "What we were then and what we are now, eh?" But I'm not a madman in the way you think, Doctor! I know only too well that he (*indicating* DI NOLLI) can't possibly be me, because *I* am Henry the Fourth – I, here, for the last twenty years, do you understand? Fixed in this perpetual mask! You (*Indicating the* MARCHESA) have lived and enjoyed these twenty years, and have become… look at her… a woman I no longer recognize. This is the woman I know. (*He indicates* FRIDA *and goes over to her.*) For me she will always be like this. You all seem to me like children I can easily scare. (*To* FRIDA:) And you're scared too, child, aren't you, by the trick they persuaded you to play on me – without realizing that for me it couldn't be the trick they meant it to be, but this terrible miracle: my dream coming to life in you, more vividly than ever! Up there, in that picture frame, you were just an image – they have turned you into flesh and blood. And you are mine – mine, mine! You're mine by right! (*He grasps her in his arms, laughing madly, while the others cry out in fright. They rush to free* FRIDA *from him, but he becomes furious and calls to the* FOUR YOUNG MEN:) Hold them! Hold them! I order you to hold them!

(*The* FOUR YOUNG MEN *are so mesmerized by him that they automatically try to restrain* DI NOLLI, *the* DOCTOR *and* BELCREDI.)

BELCREDI (*freeing himself easily and hurling himself at* HENRY IV): Let her go! Let her go! You're not mad!
HENRY IV (*in a flash, draws the sword from* LANDOLF's *scabbard*): Not mad, eh? Then take that! (*He wounds* BELCREDI *in the stomach. There is a shriek of horror, and the others rush to help* BELCREDI, *shouting confusedly*:)
DI NOLLI: Are you hurt?
BERTOLD: He's hurt! He's hurt!
DOCTOR: I told you!
FRIDA: Oh God!
DI NOLLI: Frida... come here!
DONNA MATILDE: He's mad! He's mad!
DI NOLLI: Hold him!
BELCREDI (*protesting furiously as they carry him out through the door on the left*): No... you're not mad! He's not mad! He's not mad!

(*They exit by the door on the left. Their shouts continue until we hear a sudden piercing scream from* DONNA MATILDE, *then silence.*)

HENRY IV (*Still on stage, surrounded by* LANDOLF, HAROLD *and* ORDULF. *His eyes are wild. He is astounded his own pretence was so lifelike that he was suddenly compelled to commit a crime*): Now yes... I've no choice... (*He draws them around him, as if to protect him.*) Here, together... here, together... for ever!

CURTAIN

CAPS AND BELLS

Il berretto a sonagli (1917)

Translated by Carlo Ardito

Characters

CIAMPA, *a clerk*
BEATRICE FIORÌCA
ASSUNTA LA BELLA, *her mother*
FIFÌ LA BELLA, *her brother*
SPANÒ, *a police officer*
LA SARACENA, *old clothes dealer*
FANA, *Beatrice's old retainer*
NINA CIAMPA, *Ciampa's young wife*

A small inland town in Sicily

Note on the Text

Caps and Bells was first performed in 1917 in Sicilian dialect. An Italian version was published in 1918, but was not staged in that language until 1928.

Ciampa the clerk is a wronged husband, who will only tolerate his wife's infidelity as long as he is not forced to admit that others believe he is aware of it. Once that line is crossed, he is honour-bound to kill his wife – and her lover – if caught in the act.

The role of Ciampa requires an exceptionally able actor. Many distinguished leading men essayed the part over the years, but it is generally agreed that the finest performances were given by actor and playwright Eduardo de Filippo in his own translation into Neapolitan from 1936 onwards. Pirandello himself, after watching Eduardo in the role, is quoted as having said to him: "Ciampa has waited twenty years to point at you as his true interpreter."

– Carlo Ardito

Act One

Living room in the Fiorìca household, lavishly furnished in a provincial style. Main door upstage centre; two doors stage right and left, draped with curtains.

When the curtain rises, BEATRICE *is sitting on the sofa, sobbing.* LA SARACENA *is sitting opposite her, looking cross.* FANA *is standing by.*

FANA (*pointing at her weeping mistress*): Happy now? Aren't you ashamed of the damage you've done? Is this the way to upset the family?

LA SARACENA (*a thick-set, formidable woman, about forty; showy, with a large yellow silk scarf, and a pale-blue silk shawl with long fringes, tight at the waist. She rises and rounds on* FANA): What the devil do you think you're saying? Me? Ashamed? Don't talk rubbish!

BEATRICE (*about thirty, pale, hysterical, blowing hot and cold and continuing to sob*): Pay no attention to her... let her say what she likes.

LA SARACENA: Excuse me: tell her rather that all I did was to carry out a specific order you gave me, no more and no less.

BEATRICE: I don't need to justify myself to her.

FANA: You certainly don't! I'm only a servant here. I know that. But you are required to justify yourself to God – we all have to!

BEATRICE (*angrily*): Out! Back to the kitchen! And mind your own business!

LA SARACENA (*seizing* FANA *by the arm*): Oh no. Not so fast. Wait, please, madam. And you too. We all have souls in the eyes of God, masters and servants. I'll allow no reflections on my character. What about *your* conscience?

How can you bear to see your mistress shed tears of blood, suffer the tortures of the damned and say: "It's nothing. It is the will of God. Offer it up to him!" You call that right?

FANA: It is. For those who fear God.

BEATRICE: I see! So when a man hurts you, treats you like dirt, that's God's will too, is it?

FANA: No. I say we should offer it up to God, ma'am. You can't grab a man by the scruff of the neck and face him head on! You can't use force with someone stronger than we are! Gently, gently does it. Tact and good manners will bring a man back to his hearth again!

LA SARACENA: Nonsense! If women carried on like that, men would turn us all into doormats!

FANA: That could never apply to my mistress. That master is ever so gentle... and respects her. Gives her everything she asks for. He treats her like a queen.

BEATRICE: Do keep quiet! Gentle, you say. Respectful. And generous. But what does he get up to when he's not at home? What about *my* heart, *my* peace of mind? You're judging his behaviour when he's at home, and are blind to the way he carries on when he's out!

LA SARACENA: Is that what you call conscience? Where I come from it's called hypocrisy. In a nutshell: did you or did you not fetch me from home and bring me here?

FANA: I did as I was told.

LA SARACENA: So did I. "Saracena..." – your mistress's words – "...help me! My husband... and so-and-so... I suspect them... Find out if it's true. It's hell at home. I've got to leave at all costs!" (*To* BEATRICE:) Isn't that what you said?

BEATRICE: Yes, yes, and I'm leaving. Immediately. Once and for all!

FANA: Holy Mother of God!

LA SARACENA: Leave the Mother of God alone! A house where jealousy prevails is finished, done for! It's a constant earthquake, you listen to me! And if there were children around...

FANA: That's the real trouble: there are no children.

LA SARACENA: So? Do you want her to die, the poor woman? She wants to get out!

FANA: That's what she says, but look at her crying!

BEATRICE: Because I'm furious, that's why I'm crying! If he were here I'd murder him! Tell me, Saracena, is there a chance of catching them together... tomorrow?

LA SARACENA: Like two birds in their nest. What time is he expected back?

BEATRICE: At ten.

LA SARACENA: Then rest assured that by ten thirty you'll catch them both together, alive and cooing. Lodge a complaint with the Police Inspector. I'll do the rest. Tell me something: is it true that your husband is passing through Palermo on his way to Catania?

BEATRICE: Yes. Why?

LA SARACENA: Well... because... I heard – no. It's nothing...

BEATRICE: Tell me, tell me... What have you heard?

LA SARACENA: A little matter of a present he promised to bring her from Palermo.

BEATRICE: A present? For her?

LA SARACENA: A beautiful necklace, yes. With pendants.

FANA: You're not a woman! You're a witch!

LA SARACENA (*to* BEATRICE): Write out the complaint.

BEATRICE (*consumed with uncertainty*): No... no. It's better if I... oh God, I'm going mad! It's better if we get Inspector Spanò over here. He's a family friend. Owes everything to my father, may he rest in peace. He'll tell me what to do. In fact, you go and fetch him, Saracena, tell him to come and see me.

FANA: Think it over, madam, please! Think of the scandal!

BEATRICE: I don't care.

FANA: I warn you you're courting disaster!

BEATRICE: I'll be rid of him! Rid of him! I'm leaving him! Please go, Saracena, don't let's waste any more time.

FANA (*holding* LA SARACENA *back*): Just a moment. Just a moment. (*To* BEATRICE:) Think carefully, please. Have you given any thought to the woman's husband... to Ciampa?

BEATRICE: I've thought of everything, don't you worry, him included. Don't interfere. I know where to send him.

LA SARACENA: Send him... where? There's no need. They'll take care of that, don't you worry. The moment your husband gets back to the office, Ciampa'll turn round and leave of his own accord.

FANA: Who? Ciampa? Are you mad? Are you trying to tell my mistress that Ciampa knows everything and is keeping quiet?

LA SARACENA: You be quiet! You know nothing!

FANA: You're wrong. You're making a big mistake!

LA SARACENA: Oh yes? You think it's all like a fireworks display. Bang! Bang! Then it's over? Don't be taken in! He's seen his wife with the finest earrings, four rings on her fingers... tomorrow she'll show off the necklace with pendants. What'll he think? That she paid for them out of her savings? A likely story! When your master's at his desk in the office, where is Ciampa? Out in the street with his head in the air, walking around with nothing to do.

FANA: He follows orders, the poor man. He's sent out on errands, and does as he's told. But everyone knows that whenever he leaves the office, he bolts and bars the door leading to his living quarters.

LA SARACENA: Yes. And the master unlocks it.

FANA: Ciampa's got a great big padlock!

LA SARACENA: The master's got a key to it, too.

BEATRICE (*to* FANA): Stop it! I told you to get out and stop interfering! (*To* LA SARACENA:) I know how to get rid of

Ciampa. I'll send him off this very evening. As a matter of fact... Fana... come here... But for goodness' sake don't let on to him... Can I trust you?

FANA: Can you trust me? I held you in my arms when you were a baby! (*Bursts into tears.*)

BEATRICE: Come, come, stop crying.

FANA: Look: there's your brother... your mother. Let them advise you, they're your own flesh and blood. They won't let you down.

BEATRICE: Stop it, I said. I don't need anybody's advice. Go and fetch Ciampa, this minute! And you, Saracena, get me Inspector Spanò. Tell him I want to see him. Immediately.

LA SARACENA: No. Let's do it the other way round.

BEATRICE: What do you mean?

LA SARACENA: Send her (*points at* FANA) to get the Inspector. I'll get Ciampa.

BEATRICE (*to* FANA): Do you know the way to the police station?

FANA: If that's really what you want me to do, I'll find it.

LA SARACENA: Come, come, both of you. There's not going to be a tragedy, believe me. Not a bit of it! (*To* BEATRICE:) All you're going to do is teach him a lesson, that's all. It'll be quite enough. My husband... now my husband... four years ago I kicked him out of the house. Result? He follows me round like a poodle, and daren't leave my side unless I give him my special look – like this! – guaranteed to terrify him out of his wits. Shakes like an aspen leaf, he does! So there – a little lesson, that's all. You'll see. Men! It's a pleasure to watch them with their tail between their legs. I'm off. We're all agreed, then. You've made up your mind.

BEATRICE: Yes, I have. Absolutely.

LA SARACENA: Tomorrow's the day?

BEATRICE: Tomorrow.

LA SARACENA: Then I kiss your hands and I'll go and call Ciampa. (*Begins to make for the upstage door when the doorbell rings loudly.*) Someone at the door!

BEATRICE (*to* FANA, *who goes to answer the door*): Wait. It's probably my brother. If it's him, not a word! (*Makes a sign enjoining silence.*)

FANA: I won't say a thing, don't worry. (*Goes out of the room by the upstage door to answer the front door.*)

BEATRICE: I've asked him to come specially, so we can arrange Ciampa's departure.

LA SARACENA (*visibly annoyed*): There was no need! When it comes to these things, the fewer people involved the better. Even Fana we could have done without.

BEATRICE: Fana can be trusted, have no fear. As for my brother, let me deal with him. I've got an idea.

(FIFÌ LA BELLA *enters upstage centre. He is about twenty-four, elegant, good-looking.*)

LA SARACENA (*bowing*): Your servant, sir.

FIFÌ (*regarding her with contempt*): You... here?

LA SARACENA: I was about to leave...

BEATRICE: Yes, you'd better. We're agreed, then. I'll be expecting Ciampa.

LA SARACENA: He'll be here directly. Your servant... (*Goes.*)

FIFÌ: Are you having dealings with that hag?

BEATRICE: Me? Well, she's doing something for me.

FIFÌ: Don't you know a lady can't possibly receive that creature without damaging her reputation?

BEATRICE: Oh? Because she knows all about the shameful tricks you men get up to, and you're afraid she'll let on to your wives and mothers?

FIFÌ: Bull's-eye! Go on thinking that and I know where you'll end!

BEATRICE: I know exactly where I'll end. Don't you worry. As far as you are all concerned I'm supposed to sit here quietly, I'm to be kept in the dark about everything that goes on.

FIFÌ: We are on edge today!

BEATRICE: Did you bring the money?

FIFÌ: I have.

BEATRICE: No wonder you're so scathing with me. Remember what you said when you needed the money? "Please, little sister... help me! You're always so good and kind – please save me. I've been gambling. I've lost. Think of the dishonour!" You know perfectly well I was forced to resort to this "hag" no lady can receive without damaging her reputation. I did it for you, since I sent her to Palermo to pawn earrings and a bracelet behind my husband's back.

FIFÌ: I see. You got her here over that business.

BEATRICE: Give me that money. Is that all of it?

FIFÌ (*reaching for his pocketbook*): Not quite.

BEATRICE: I knew it. How much?

FIFÌ: If only you could have waited... not that long... say a fortnight... I can't make out why you're in so much of a hurry.

BEATRICE: It's vital that both earrings and bracelet should be back here tomorrow. I've sent for Ciampa for this very reason: I'm sending him to redeem them right now.

FIFÌ: Did your husband suspect anything? He isn't due till tomorrow.

BEATRICE: That's right. That's the reason.

FIFÌ: I don't get it. Is it absolutely necessary that you display all your finery on your husband's return tomorrow?

BEATRICE: Yes it is. You can't imagine the welcome I've in mind for him. You'll see. It'll be quite a party! (*The door-bell rings.*) That'll be Ciampa. Give me the money. Is there much missing?

FIFÌ (*taking the money out of his pocketbook*): Here you are. You count it. I'm not sure. I think there's three one-hundred lire notes.

BEATRICE (*counting*): ...And one fifty note. One hundred and fifty is missing.

FIFÌ: As I said, if only you'd waited.

BEATRICE: Never mind. I'll make up the difference. You may go now.

FANA (*enters upstage centre*): Ciampa's here. Can he come in?

BEATRICE: Show him in. But wait... come here first. (*Takes her to one side and whispers.*) You go straight where I told you.

FANA (*equally soft*): To the Inspector's?

BEATRICE: Tell him I'd like him to come here. If he comes straight away, make him wait in the study. Take the key and go. Be quick.

FANA: Yes, madam. I'll get my wrap and go. (*Goes.*)

FIFÌ: Will you tell me what you're up to? What's all this mystery?

BEATRICE: Be quiet. Here's Ciampa.

(CIAMPA *enters upstage centre. He is about forty-five, with long, thick hair brushed backwards, somewhat untidily. He has no moustache, but sports broad brush-like sideboards which overrun his cheeks up to his eyes, which sparkle harshly and cruelly, with a hint of insanity. A pen is stuck behind his ear. He wears an old frock coat.*)

CIAMPA: I kiss your hands, madam. Sir. Madam, I'm yours to command.

BEATRICE: Always mine to command, dear Ciampa! Always on parade.

CIAMPA: As you say, always on parade... often like Christ on the cross. But in this case "yours to command" means, unless I'm mistaken, that I'm your humble servant.

BEATRICE: You? A servant? We're all masters here, my dear
    Ciampa. No distinctions between us: you, FIFÌ here, my
    husband, *me, your wife*... we're all equal. In fact I'm not
    even sure whether I'm not a little beneath you all.

CIAMPA: What? That's heresy, madam! What are you saying?

FIFÌ: Let her have her say. All women, according to her—

BEATRICE: Not all women, only *certain* women. There are
    others who know how to sweet-talk you men, how to flatter
    you... like this. (*Strokes her brother's cheek.*) ...Now they
    stand above all others, even if they come from the streets.

CIAMPA: Excuse me, madam. You happened to mention my
    wife.

BEATRICE: I was generalizing, that's all: Fana, my mother,
    me, your wife...

FIFÌ: All women... all equal.

CIAMPA (*to* BEATRICE): Forgive me. (*Turns to* FIFÌ.) And
    you too, sir. But I feel that my wife... even if you're
    having a general discussion, shouldn't really be brought
    into it. She's as out of context as Pilate is in the Creed.
    I am at your service, that's understood, but my wife
    is perfectly looked after and in her own home. It's
    my duty to see that she's not talked about, either for
    or against.

BEATRICE: Are you so jealous you can't even bear to have her
    mentioned? That's rather overdoing it!

CIAMPA: It's a matter of principle with me, where wives, sar-
    dines and anchovies are concerned. Sardines and anchovies
    under glass; wives under lock and key. And here's the key.
    (*Takes a key out of his pocket and displays it.*)

FIFÌ: A splendid principle for my sister.

CIAMPA (*places his hands on* FIFÌ's *chest*): Each to his own, sir.

BEATRICE (*to* FIFÌ): There's always the risk you bolt the door
    and leave the window open.

CIAMPA: Still, it's the husband's duty to shut the door.

BEATRICE: I never suspected you'd be such a tyrant.

CIAMPA: Me? A tyrant? Never. I like things to be arranged neatly. There is the window. The door I've already shut, of course. Lean out of the window, by all means. But mind no one comes up to me and says: "Ciampa, your wife is about to break her neck trying to jump out of it!" Does this make me a tyrant? Man realizes that a woman needs to take a little air at the window. And a woman recognizes that a man has the duty to lock the door. That's all. You wanted me for some service, madam?

BEATRICE: FIFÌ, I'm sorry... I've something to discuss with Ciampa.

FIFÌ: You want me to leave just to tell him to...

BEATRICE: I'd sooner not go into it in front of you.

FIFÌ: Why not? You may speak freely. I've paid off my loan.

BEATRICE: I suppose so. Well... listen, Ciampa: I need you. I know I can trust you. You're more than a member of the family. I am grateful.

CIAMPA: I am very devoted to you all.

BEATRICE: I know you are. And I am very grateful for that... and *everything else*.

CIAMPA: I must warn you that I'm not that slow.

BEATRICE: I beg your pardon?

CIAMPA: I've a feeling... the way you're talking this morning... you sound as if you've been eating lemons.

BEATRICE: Lemons? Why, never. Honey. I've had honey for breakfast. Anyway, you were saying?

CIAMPA: Dear God, it's not words I'm talking about. We're not children! You're trying to tell me something the words aren't saying.

BEATRICE: What? What do you mean? If you've got a guilty conscience...

CIAMPA (*turns to* FIFÌ): I appeal to you, sir. What does she mean by saying that I'm more than a member of the family? I tell her I'm devoted to the family, and she adds: "...and I'm grateful for *everything else*". What am I to make of

that *everything else*? What does she mean by saying that
we're all masters here, without any distinction, my wife
included? I haven't got a guilty conscience. But she's trying
to get at me. Why?

FIFÌ: She's not trying to get at you. She's against everyone.
It's a serious business.

BEATRICE: Will someone tell me what I'm supposed to have
said that's so terrible? Can't one open one's mouth any
more?

CIAMPA: That's not it. Would you like me to explain what the
matter is? The instrument's out of tune.

BEATRICE: Instrument? What instrument?

CIAMPA: What I call the social spring. I must point out that
we all possess three watch springs, as it were, in our heads.
(*His right hand clenched, with his thumb and forefinger
close together as if they were holding a watch key or
winder, he mimes a watch-winding gesture first on his
right temple, then in the middle of his forehead, and
finally on his left temple.*) They have separate functions:
one serious, one social, one insane. We need the social
spring above all, as we are social animals – that's why
it's placed right in the centre of our forehead. Without
it, dear lady, we'd all devour one another like so many
savage dogs. That wouldn't do. (*Turns to* FIFÌ.) I'd eat
you up, for example. And that's not allowed. So what do
I do? I give the winder a little turn, walk up to you all
smiles and put out my outstretched hand: "I am delighted
to see you, my dear fellow!" (*To* BEATRICE:) You see
what I mean? But at some point the waters might look
troubled, in need of the proverbial oil. Therefore I first
wind up the serious spring, then set about clearing matters
up, give my reasons, state things plainly, without frills,
as is my duty. If that produces no results, then I give the
insane spring a good turn... but then I lose my head...
and God help us all!

FIFÌ: Excellent! Splendid! Bravo, Ciampa!

CIAMPA (*to* BEATRICE): I think that you, madam, begging your pardon, must have given several turns, for reasons best known to yourself – which are none of my business – to either the serious or the insane springs, which are causing your head to buzz like a swarm of hornets! Meanwhile, you'd like to talk to me by means of the social spring. Result? The words you utter flow from the social spring, but they're out of tune. Am I making myself clear? Be advised by me, stop using it. Ask your brother to leave… (*Approaches* FIFÌ.) I beg you, sir, you'd better leave…

BEATRICE: Why? Let him stay.

FIFÌ (*to* CIAMPA): You want to deny me the pleasure of listening to you?

CIAMPA (*pointedly, to* BEATRICE): Because you should now, right there – will you allow me? – on your right temple… wind up the serious spring and have a private talk with me, a serious talk, for your own good and mine.

BEATRICE: I'm being serious, too. I'd like a serious talk.

CIAMPA: Very well, then. Here I am. But let me say this though, I must warn you that unless you wind up the serious spring in time, you might well wind up the insane one, or cause others to do so.

FIFÌ: I've a feeling it's you, Ciampa, who is off key at the moment.

BEATRICE: I think so too. I've felt it for some time. I don't understand…

CIAMPA: Please forgive me. (*With a sudden outburst, to* FIFÌ:) My father's forehead was often split open.

FIFÌ: How does your father come into this?

CIAMPA: When he was a youngster, my father, rather foolishly, instead of protecting his head, when he stumbled and fell… preferred to save his hands. So when he tripped and as he fell, do you know what he did? He instinctively put his hands behind his back and fell flat on his face. No wonder he split his forehead. But I, sir, fall down with my hands well forwards. Why? Because I'd sooner my forehead were unharmed, free of all marks or encumbrances.

FIFÌ: That's all very well, but if you don't know the reason why my sister sent for you, why put your hands forwards, so to speak?

CIAMPA: I take your point. Very well: I'll disable the serious spring and call into service the social. (*To* BEATRICE, *bowing:*) I'm yours to command.

BEATRICE: I'd like you to leave tonight for Palermo.

CIAMPA (*starting*): For Palermo? How?... The master returns tomorrow.

BEATRICE: Do you think he'll need your services the moment he's back?

CIAMPA: Naturally. Otherwise why should he employ me in the office?

BEATRICE: I know he pays you to guard the safe, and consequently gives you living accommodation in the rooms next to the office.

CIAMPA: That's not the only reason. You mustn't belittle my services. I am his clerk. I write.

FIFÌ (*to his sister*): Note, my dear, the pen behind his ear.

CIAMPA: Just so. It's my badge of office. Just as the innkeeper displays a vine leaf and a jug – that's his sign. I'm a clerk: I carry a pen.

FIFÌ: A clerk and a journalist, no less!

CIAMPA: Don't mention journalism! That's just a hobby of mine, something I dabble in at night, in my spare time. I write on behalf of my employer: I keep his ledgers, I look after the business. You don't imagine we just pass the time of day at the office, telling each other stories? I'm not just an onlooker. Has your husband ever complained about me?

BEATRICE: What? My husband? Complained about you? Never! He won't hear a word against you.

CIAMPA: So. You'd like me to go to Palermo. Tonight.

FIFÌ: Why not? I see no harm in it.

BEATRICE: I'll tell my husband I've sent you. Am I not allowed to send you on a special errand?

CIAMPA: On an errand? But of course you are. You are the mistress here. (*To* FIFÌ:) Can you imagine how I feel at the prospect of taking a breath of fresh air in a big city like Palermo? Why, that'll be heaven on earth! I am choking out here. I can hardly breathe! But the moment I step out into the avenues of a big city... why, I'm in paradise! Ideas flow freely within me! The blood courses blissfully through my veins! Ah, if only I'd been born in a city, somewhere on the mainland... God knows what I might have become!

FIFÌ: An academic... a member of parliament... a minister... a...

CIAMPA: King! Let's not fantasize, though. (*To* FIFÌ:) After all, we're puppets, aren't we? The divine spark enters into us and pulls the strings. I'm a puppet, you're a puppet... we're all puppets. It should be enough for us all to be puppets as instruments of God's will. No, sir! Each one of us turns himself into a puppet of his own accord, into the puppet he could be or believes himself to be. That's when the rows begin. (*Turns to* BEATRICE.) Because you see, dear lady, every puppet demands respect, not so much for what he really believes himself to be, but for the part he plays in public. Let's be honest with ourselves: no one is happy with the role he plays. If each of us were faced with the image of the puppet he really is, he'd spit in its face. But from others... ah, from others he asks for, nay demands respect. For example (*addressing* BEATRICE), within these walls, madam, you are a wife, true?

BEATRICE: A wife... well, yes... at least...

CIAMPA: One can tell immediately you're not happy with your lot. Nevertheless, as the wife you evidently are, you wish to be respected.

BEATRICE: Naturally. And how! I demand it – God help those who refuse it!

CIAMPA: You see? Just as I said. And everyone's the same. As far as you are concerned, if you knew my respected employer the Cavaliere Fiorìca only as a friend, you might get on with him in perfect amity. The actual war is waged between the two puppets: the husband-puppet and the wife-puppet. Within they tear out each other's hair. But outside, in the public glare they walk hand in hand: both of them having activated the social spring, also employed by us bystanders: we raise our hats, smile, make way for the happy pair. And the two puppets glow with pride and satisfaction.

FIFÌ (*laughing*): You're a character, my dear Ciampa, you really are!

CIAMPA: This is life, my dear sir! Madam: it's vital to keep the respect of others. We should hold our puppet high – whatever its nature – so that everyone reverently raises his hat. Have I made myself clear? But let's get down to business. What do you want me to do in Palermo?

BEATRICE (*shaken, with an abstracted look*): In Palermo, did you say?...

FIFÌ (*drawing her attention to the matter being discussed*): Wake up, Beatrice.

BEATRICE: What? Oh... I thought I heard Fana come in...

CIAMPA: Have you changed your mind?

BEATRICE: Certainly not. (*To* FIFÌ:) Where is the money?

FIFÌ: Over there, on that table.

BEATRICE: Here it is. Now, Ciampa, here's three hundred and fifty lire. (*Hands the money to Ciampa.*)

CIAMPA: What do you want me to do with it?

BEATRICE: Wait. I'll get another hundred and fifty from the other room... and two tickets.

CIAMPA (*looking at* FIFÌ *with some severity*): Pawn tickets?

FIFÌ: That's right. And don't look at me like that!

CIAMPA: Me? I was not, sir! I'm waiting for instructions.

BEATRICE: It's a question of redeeming the items. A pair of earrings and a bracelet, in two cases. I'll get the tickets. (*Goes right out.*)

FIFÌ: My sister pawned the stuff to do me a favour. Her husband doesn't know.

CIAMPA: Bear in mind, sir, that he's my employer.

FIFÌ: I can be quite open about it. I've repaid the loan to my sister. And she wants the jewels back by tomorrow.

CIAMPA: Tomorrow? By tomorrow? And what excuse will she give her husband for sending me out of town on the eve of his return?

FIFÌ: Have no fear. Women are never short of excuses.

CIAMPA: Surely he's been away a number of days... she could have sent me earlier, so he wouldn't hear of it at all.

FIFÌ: As a matter of fact I've only just returned the money.

CIAMPA: I smell a rat. I suspect your sister is up to something.

FIFÌ: I tend to agree with you. She's acting a little strangely. What can it be? Maybe it's the old old story – jealousy.

CIAMPA: Is that why she's sending me to Palermo?

(BEATRICE *enters, looking flustered, as if emerging from a disquieting argument.*)

BEATRICE: Right. Here I am. Here I am.

FIFÌ: What's the matter now?

BEATRICE (*attempting to compose herself*): Why... nothing's the matter.

FIFÌ: You look to me... a bit...

BEATRICE (*now at ease*): It's nothing, don't worry. I couldn't
   find the tickets at first and I was worried. (*Hands* CIAMPA
   the tickets.) Here are the tickets. And the rest of the money.

CIAMPA: Very well. But how are you going to justify my
   absence to your husband? Have you thought of that?

BEATRICE: I've thought of everything! (*Shows a roll of banknotes she has been holding in her other hand.*) You see?
   This is for your fare, and another hundred and fifty lire.

FIFÌ: Well, well, look at those banknotes!

CIAMPA: As long as we have banknotes...

BEATRICE: So? What do you mean? Out with it! (*To her
   brother:*) It's my own money. Part of my savings. (*Turning
   to* CIAMPA:) You were saying... as long as we have
   banknotes?...

CIAMPA: All I meant was that the money enables you to pull
   strings and send another puppet all the way to Palermo.

BEATRICE: I take no pleasure in doing that, I assure you.
   You know perfectly well why I'm sending you. Now then,
   with the extra one hundred and fifty lire I want you to buy
   me a necklace, Ciampa – and that will give me pleasure!
   Shall I tell you what kind of necklace it is I want? One
   with pendants.

CIAMPA: I see.

BEATRICE: With pendants. I'll tell my husband that I've seen
   a friend of mine wear the same necklace and I liked it so
   much that... well, it's just a whim of mine. My husband
   will understand.

CIAMPA: Frankly I don't know whether I'm competent enough
   to select...

BEATRICE: Don't worry. If you can't manage it, just say you
   couldn't find one when you get back.

CIAMPA: But then why give me the money at all?

BEATRICE: Because I'd really be very glad if you'd get me the
   necklace. I'd like one that's *exactly the same* and *bought
   by you.*

CIAMPA: I don't get it. Bought by me? What do you want from me? Exactly the same as what? I've no idea what it looks like.

BEATRICE: I'll tell you. Go to our jewellers, Mercurio. I know my friend's necklace was definitely bought at their shop. Go there and you'll find it. I'd like you to leave as soon as possible.

CIAMPA: I'm stunned. Stunned? I'm petrified, I tell you.

FIFÌ: Admit though, it's a marvellous excuse she's thought of.

BEATRICE: It is, even if I say so myself. Can you think of a nicer surprise for my husband? When he sees me tomorrow, wearing the necklace, why... There's a train leaving at six. You haven't much time.

FIFÌ (*consulting his watch*): He's got an hour.

CIAMPA: A couple of minutes is all I need. I'll lock up the office, secure the door to my rooms with lock and bolt, and go to the station. (*Addressing* BEATRICE:) However, I'd like you to make use of the hour that's left before the train is due to leave.

BEATRICE: How?

CIAMPA: You might like to pause and think things over.

BEATRICE: What is there to think about?

FIFÌ: Let's make a move, Ciampa. I'll come with you. Au revoir, Beatrice.

BEATRICE: Goodbye.

CIAMPA (*to* BEATRICE): Let me remind you once again of the case of my father, who failed to use his hands for protection.

BEATRICE: Not again!

CIAMPA: I'm on my way. Good day. (*Having reached the door, he retraces his steps.*) Madam, would you like me to bring you my wife?

BEATRICE: Your wife? Here? (*Laughs scornfully.*) That's all we need! That really is a good one! Why?

CIAMPA: For my own peace of mind.

BEATRICE: Really! Are you mad? What would I do here, with your wife?

CIAMPA: Naturally, a lady like you would have little in common with... still, just as I said, for my own peace of mind.

BEATRICE: But you'll have her under lock and key, in accordance with your principles! Isn't there a steel bar as well?

CIAMPA: And a padlock, madam. I'll bring you the keys.

BEATRICE: There's no need for that. Keep your keys.

CIAMPA: Sorry, but no. If you refuse to have me bring my wife here, allow me at least to leave the keys with you. I'm not going to budge.

BEATRICE: Oh, very well. But don't waste any more time.

CIAMPA (*to* FIFÌ): Let's go, then. (*Begins to leave. At the door, turns again.*) You were saying... with pendants?

BEATRICE (*impatiently*): Not again! Yes! With pendants.

CIAMPA: I kiss your hands. (*Goes with* FIFÌ.)

(BEATRICE *rushes to the door on the right.*)

BEATRICE: Inspector... come in... come in... at last!

(*Inspector* SPANÒ *enters. He is about forty, the typical comic country policeman, bearded and generally hirsute. He gives himself heroic airs, and now and then, as he talks, shows the depth of his bigotry.*)

SPANÒ: I am astonished. As if struck by lightning. You know the kind of lightning I'm referring to... followed by a deafening clap of thunder right at my feet!

BEATRICE: We've little time for small talk, Inspector. We must agree on a plan. Imagine: he wanted to bring his wife here and leave her with me!

SPANÒ: His wife? He... Here?

BEATRICE: What better proof do we need? What have we come to?

SPANÒ: Calm yourself. Yes. Absolute calm is of the essence.

BEATRICE: How can I? I want to give him a lesson he'll never forget. In front of witnesses.

SPANÒ: Of course. Of course. But the consequences... have you thought of the consequences?

BEATRICE: You mean... I'll have to seek a separation. I am ready for that. But not on an amicable basis, as they say. No. First I'll revile him in front of everyone, then we'll split up. It must never be said that I was in the wrong. I want a scandal – a big scandal. The whole community must be made aware of the kind of man the Cavaliere Fiorìca is... this man they all cherish and respect! I'll lodge the complaint with you officially. You're an officer of the law and can't object.

SPANÒ: Yes, madam... of course... if you lodge a complaint...

BEATRICE: I'll draw it up now. Tell me how to do it and I'll get down to it.

SPANÒ: No, no. That's not possible. You want me to tell you how to write it out?

BEATRICE (*coquettishly and with a hint of irritability*): Won't you help me? Inspector... won't you help me?

SPANÒ: Naturally I want to help you. But bear in mind I'm a friend of the family as well.

BEATRICE: Aren't you on the side of justice?

SPANÒ: Yes... well... I'm on the side of the law. It is my sworn duty to be impartial. And I go forwards with my head held high, even in the presence of God Almighty. But as you know I honour the memory of your late sainted father, who was a father to me too. You know he loved me, madam. The things he taught me! On the other hand here's this... the question of these little sins of the flesh... hardly mortal sins...

BEATRICE: Little sins? Is that what you call them?

SPANÒ: Let's call them... diversions, if you like. I speak as a friend.

BEATRICE: As *his* friend?

SPANÒ: Yes. I mean: no! I'm your friend as well...

BEATRICE: I like that: diversions. Sweet, charming, harmless diversions! You call yourself a man of justice? Is that the way you give a helping hand to a weak, wronged woman who cannot defend herself? I want to lodge a complaint. Now. This instant. How do I set about it?

SPANÒ: The complaint itself is pretty standard. It's the investigation that follows that's the problem. Not at all simple. It's all most delicate and fraught with difficulties. I shall have to carry out inquiries unnoticed... study the lie of the land. You've no idea... Clues... proof...

BEATRICE: There'll be no need for any of that, Inspector. You know Saracena?

SPANÒ: She's one of our informants.

BEATRICE: Better still. Send for her. She'll give you chapter and verse.

SPANÒ: Madam, I've already talked to her. We are always one step ahead, believe me. Two doors are involved: one into the office, the other, on the opposite side, leading to the two rooms next to the office, that is to say Ciampa's living quarters. Now then, is there a door in between, yes or no? Between the office and Ciampa's two rooms? Of course there is. And Ciampa usually locks it up from the office, with bar and bolts and padlock, right? What next? I raid the place with a couple of officers, both sides at the same time. Result? They won't open the door till they have secured the middle door, and by the time we gain access, one'll be in the office, the other in the private section.

BEATRICE: Can nothing be done?

SPANÒ: Ah, there comes into play the art of successful policing, madam. Something can and will be done! Supposing, madam, you had the key to the office—

BEATRICE (*cutting in*): I have! That is, Ciampa is going to let me have it right now, before he leaves. I'm waiting for him.

SPANÒ (*stunned*): What? Ciampa's going to let you have the key?

BEATRICE: Yes. I didn't even have to ask him for it. He insisted... he forced me to accept. As a matter of fact I didn't want it at first.

SPANÒ: I don't understand. No. It must mean that... you can be sure that Ciampa hasn't the least suspicion. None!

BEATRICE: What are you saying? Why then did he want to bring his wife here?

SPANÒ: Because... dear me... because the whole village knows... if you'll allow me...

BEATRICE: That I'm jealous? Is that it? And using the fact I'm jealous, my husband's always done as he pleased... I'm going to show them all whether or not my jealousy is justified! You say that once we have the key we're home and dry? You get into the office before he's had time to secure the middle door and...

SPANÒ (*smiles commiseratingly*): Me? Open the office door? Yes, then what happens? Do you think your husband is so careless as to pay the lady a visit having taken the naive precaution of locking the office door? He'll have barred it as well. So where am I now? How do I open a door barred from the inside? First I utter my warning: "Open up, in the name of the law!"... followed by various prescribed cautions... Then I proceed to break the door down... While all this is going on, the Cavaliere will have had ample time to lock and bolt the central door. Madam, if that's all there was to policing, I'd be the happiest inspector in the force.

BEATRICE: Oh my God! What are we going to do?

SPANÒ: What indeed... Now... Your husband gets in at ten tomorrow. Very well. I'll tell you what we do. One of my men will be in hiding in the office... in the cubbyhole where the Cavaliere stores the duplicator... let's say half an hour before his arrival... that is to say... (*with the air of a conjurer producing a rabbit out of a hat*)... at half-past nine! That's it. Caught on the wing!

BEATRICE (*triumphantly*): Well done, Inspector! Bravo! And now, please help me with the written complaint. (*The doorbell rings.*)

SPANÒ (*with a knowing air*): There's someone at the door, unless I'm mistaken.

BEATRICE: Right again! It'll be Ciampa, with the key. You'd better disappear, in there. (*Points to the door on the right.*)

SPANÒ: We'll catch them in full flight! (*Goes out right.*)

CIAMPA (*behind the curtain of the upstage door, carrying an overnight case*): May I come in?

BEATRICE: Come in, come in, Ciampa. (*Registers surprise and indignation as* CIAMPA *enters together with his wife.*) What's this?

CIAMPA: I've brought my wife.

BEATRICE (*enraged*): Take her back, take her back this minute!

CIAMPA: Let me explain...

BEATRICE: I'm not going to listen! Off with her, now! I won't have her here!

CIAMPA: But madam... my wife is clean... modest...

BEATRICE: I'm sure she's perfectly clean... and modest, naturally! But I won't have her here. (*Turns to* CIAMPA's *wife.*) I am surprised at you, daring to come here with your husband... you don't belong here!

NINA (*she is about thirty, more fastidious than modest. She dresses neatly, aiming at a ladylike effect: elegant shoes, silk shawl, earrings, rings. She answers softly but clearly, her eyes downturned*): It was my husband who ordered me to come.

CIAMPA (*jubilant*): Just so!

BEATRICE: You could have saved yourself the journey. I specifically told your husband he was not to bring you.

NINA (*her eyes still lowered, answers in a clear voice*): I was not to know that, madam.

CIAMPA: Indeed she did not.

BEATRICE: You've trained her well, haven't you?

CIAMPA: No, madam. She's telling you the truth, quietly and in all modesty – as she should. I alone am responsible for bringing her here. You won't have her?

BEATRICE: I thought I'd made it abundantly clear!

CIAMPA: You could keep her in the kitchen. Or in the coal cellar. She could sleep under the kitchen range, with the cat.

BEATRICE: Are you set on provoking me? Don't make me say what should be left unsaid.

CIAMPA: Say it, say it! Out with it. I wish you would!

BEATRICE: Go. Just go. That's all!

CIAMPA: Very well. You won't have her. That's established. I've brought her here and you refuse to keep her. That's also established. Therefore, here are the keys. I'm on my way. Remember that now I am in your hands. (*Hands over the keys. Then he approaches his wife and pretends to wind up an imaginary spring on her forehead.*) Wait, Nina: social spring activated. A little curtsy, eyes suitably averted and straight home!

NINA (*bowing slightly*): Your servant.

CIAMPA: Excellent! (*Follows his wife up to the door. By the door he turns her round and addresses* BEATRICE, *pretending to wind up the serious spring on his right temple.*) If you'd care to open…

BEATRICE: I'm opening nothing!

CIAMPA: Then keep everything shut tight!

CURTAIN

Act Two

The next day.

BEATRICE (*angrily, her hair dishevelled, is standing by the door on the left, yelling at* FANA *somewhere off left*): It doesn't matter! Bring it here, now! I've got to be out of the house by this evening! Away from this wretched place!

(*The doorbell rings.*)

FANA (*enters left, laden with clothes*): Holy Mother of God, who could that be?

BEATRICE: Go and answer it. If it's the Inspector, show him in and tell him to wait and be patient. I can't receive him like this.

(BEATRICE *goes out right.* FANA, *still carrying the heap of clothes and puffing, goes out through the upstage centre door to answer the door. Shortly after we hear voices off.* ASSUNTA LA BELLA *enters, followed by* FIFÌ LA BELLA, *who has seized* FANA's *arm and is shaking her vigorously. Mother and son are clearly agitated.*)

ASSUNTA (*rushes out towards the right door, then crosses the stage to the left, shouting*): Beatrice! Beatrice! Where is she? Where is she? Beatrice! (*Goes out left, still shouting.*)

FANA (*attempting to disengage herself from* FIFÌ): Why are you cross with me?

FIFÌ (*still shaking her angrily*): Because it was your duty to come to me and warn me!

ASSUNTA (*enters left*): Where is my daughter? Tell me where she is! Beatrice! Beatrice!

193

BEATRICE (*enters right at the summons and falls into her mother's arms*): Mother! Mother! (*She bursts into tears.*)

ASSUNTA: Beatrice, what have you done? You're ruined!

FANA (*still trying to shake off* FIFì): It was entirely her own idea. She won't listen to anyone. I said it to her many times – haven't I, madam? I said: "Talk to your brother. He's a man. But first seek your mother's advice!"

ASSUNTA: How could you keep it all from me, your own mother! How could you go to such lengths without telling a soul!

FIFì (*seizing his sister by the arm away from her mother*): What's the use of tears now? Are you aware the whole town is seething with rumours?

ASSUNTA: They've arrested him, did you know? They've arrested him!

FANA: The master? Mother of God!

ASSUNTA: And they've arrested *her*.

FANA: Ciampa's wife as well?

BEATRICE: Both of them? Hurrah! I'm delighted! Good! Exactly as I planned.

ASSUNTA: What are you saying, Beatrice…

FIFì: The shame of it all. The scandal.

BEATRICE: Yes, yes! The scandal. The shame: his shame!

FIFì: Your shame, too! What do you think you're going to get out of this fine mess?

BEATRICE: I will tell you, since you ask. This: (*takes a deep breath of relief and exhales*) I can breathe again now. I've taught him the lesson he deserved. And I'm free now! Free!

FIFì: Free? You're mad, that's what you are! You're free to hide in my house, and never show your face in public again. You call that free? You'll have no status…

BEATRICE: I don't care. As long as I don't have to set eyes on him again. I was getting ready to leave. I've been packing since last night.

FIFì: Don't forget I was here yesterday. Was it that witch I found you plotting with yesterday?

FANA: Yes, yes – she was the one. The very person.

ASSUNTA: Who are you talking about?

FANA: Saracena.

ASSUNTA: My God! How could you, Beatrice? How could you have dealings with a… creature like that? (*To* FIFÌ:) Didn't you suspect anything?

FIFÌ: I certainly never suspected she'd go that far.

FANA: They sent me to fetch Inspector Spanò…

FIFÌ: Spanò?

ASSUNTA: Inspector Spanò? How could you?

FIFÌ (*to* FANA): Did I hear you say Inspector Spanò?…

ASSUNTA (*to* BEATRICE): You mean to tell me that Inspector Spanò – who owes everything to your father – allowed you to go through with it, without advising you against it?

FIFÌ: You're such an innocent, Mother. He can't have believed his luck when he saw the chance to put one over his betters! Don't you understand?

ASSUNTA: To think I've lived to see such shame heaped upon the women of our family!

FANA (*to* ASSUNTA): You've always been known as a paragon of prudence by one and all… Never a word out of place.

ASSUNTA: And yet I could tell you things, Fana, you know that.

FANA: The world is not what it was, madam.

ASSUNTA (*to* BEATRICE): Why didn't you think of me, daughter? I am an old woman. I can't take these blows. I'll probably be dead by tomorrow… Only God knows how I'm feeling just now…

FIFÌ: Calm down, Mother. Calm down, or I don't know what I'll do! She wanted to get herself into a mess – let her get out of it!

ASSUNTA: Oh yes? Have you forgotten she's my daughter? Your sister? What a thing to say!

FIFÌ: Now she thinks she's my sister. I was here, with her, yesterday. What can we do? All we can do is take her home with us, because she clearly can't stay here with her husband!

BEATRICE: Who wants to stay here?

(*The doorbell rings. They all start in anticipation.*)

ASSUNTA (*dismayed*): Who could that be?

BEATRICE: I'm not afraid of anyone!

FIFÌ (*to* FANA): Go and answer it. Don't worry: I'm here.

FANA (*to* FIFÌ): Come with me, sir, please. I'm scared.

FIFÌ (*to his mother and sister*): Go into the other room, both of you. (*To* FANA:) Don't make a fuss. Answer the door.

ASSUNTA: Come, come with me, Beatrice... (*Goes out right with* BEATRICE.)

FIFÌ (*now alone, faces the door upstage centre.* FANA *opens it, followed by* INSPECTOR SPANÒ): Ah, it's you, Inspector.

SPANÒ: Always at your service, sir.

FIFÌ: And a fine service you've done us, Inspector. The whole family has reason to be grateful to you.

SPANÒ: You're being unfair, sir.

FIFÌ: Am I? Was that the way to treat a family who – let's not mince words – did so much for you?

SPANÒ: That's exactly why I'm telling you you're being unfair. I am deeply hurt! Surely you realize I am a public servant!

FIFÌ: Thank you very much. Don't I know it! Is it a friend I am talking to? You came here—

SPANÒ (*cutting in*): ...At your wife's request!

FIFÌ: ...Be that as it may... and accepted a written complaint?

SPANÒ: Accepted? Wait... I'm cut to the quick, sir. In the first place I did all I could to dissuade her. But she – where is she? She could tell you... I did all I could to stop her.

FIFÌ: You might have checked with me first.

SPANÒ: She'd put her signature to the complaint already. What could I do?

FIFÌ: You could have made her withdraw it.

SPANÒ: All I can say then is that you don't know your own sister. Dear God, she threatened that unless I cooperated she'd take it straight to the Commissioner and tell him that I refused to... ah, here she is... (ASSUNTA *and* BEATRICE *enter right.* SPANÒ *rushes to kiss* ASSUNTA's *hand, who refuses the advance.*) Please, please let me kiss your hand... (*Turns to* BEATRICE.) And you, madam, please tell your brother—

ASSUNTA (*interrupting*): It's no use, my dear Inspector... (*Turns to* FIFÌ.) It's no use at all to go on pretending...

BEATRICE: Frankly, I think the Inspector is right.

SPANÒ (*to* FIFÌ): You see?

BEATRICE: I alone was responsible. No one else.

SPANÒ (*to* FIFÌ): What did I tell you? That was gospel truth you've just heard. How can you hold me responsible, sir, or (*addressing* ASSUNTA) you, dear lady. I worship you as if you were my own mother. You see? You see what you've reduced me to? I'm crying, sir, yes, crying because if I'm at fault at all it's due to... an excess of friendship! You can't imagine how difficult it is for me to carry out my filthy duties – excuse the expression, madam – in this town of ours. Forgive me, but how could I possibly dare apprehend the Cavaliere myself? Do you know what I did? I made matters even worse. Blame me for that, sir, if you like. You'd be quite justified.

FIFÌ: I've no idea what it is you did. What else have you done? Tell me.

SPANÒ: The fact is... as I couldn't possibly... bring myself to make the arrest myself... I entrusted the task to someone else... my fellow officer Logatto. He's a stranger... (*with a hint of contempt*) from Calabria. And what did he do, the blockhead?

FIFÌ: Don't tell me: he arrested them both, my brother-in-law and the lady.

BEATRICE: He did his duty, you mean. He acted as he was meant to.

ASSUNTA: Do be quiet, Beatrice. You don't know what you're saying!

FIFÌ: Were they caught together? Go on, out with it!

SPANÒ: Well... yes and no... together and yet not together...
That is... not quite in the act... Now, you'll admit that's
some consolation. In fact I'd go so far as to say that with
the evidence so far available, nothing conclusive can be
proved. Nothing at all!

FIFÌ: In that case... why were they arrested?

SPANÒ: Why? Because I wasn't there, that's why! Because that
jackass from... Calabria... was in charge! I admit that that
was entirely my fault, and I shall live to regret it. But have
no fear, sir, the Cavaliere will be released immediately,
tonight! I promise and swear it to you! Or my name is not
Alfio Spanò!

FIFÌ: You'd better tell me the whole story, from beginning to
end.

SPANÒ: Very well. This is what happened. My wretched colleague, using the key obtained from Mrs Beatrice, let himself into the office and hid in the cubbyhole next to the
office. Now, when the other officers knocked at the front
door of Ciampa's rooms, and asked to be let in in the name
of the law etc... the Cavaliere – as soon as the lady opened
up – the Cavaliere made as if to open the connecting door
with the office—

BEATRICE (*triumphantly*): There you are! You see? So he was
in Ciampa's rooms. He's opened the connecting door!

SPANÒ (*baffled*): Yes... but...

BEATRICE: How could he have opened it, if Ciampa had locked
it and brought me the key? That's your proof.

SPANÒ (*recovering*): No. I'm afraid that's no proof at all.

BEATRICE: Why not?

SPANÒ: Let me explain. It's an English lock. Two keys are
always provided.

BEATRICE: Two keys, fine! One with Ciampa, the other in my
husband's pocket.

SPANÒ: May I proceed? According to the verbal disposition,
Cavaliere Fiorìca stated that having just detrained from

Catania, and unable to make out why Ciampa was not at his
desk, and furthermore needing to freshen up after the journey – I sympathize with the poor gentleman – and in addi-
tion wishing to take sight of the correspondence received
in his absence – let me remind you: these are the very words
of the deposition – he says he knocked at the door to ask
Ciampa's wife whether he could possibly wash his hands.

BEATRICE (*laughing stridently*): His hands... Wash his hands
indeed! Just fancy that!

SPANÒ: Yes, his hands. The poor gentleman wanted to open
his correspondence.

FIFÌ: Pay no attention to my sister, Inspector. Go on.

SPANÒ: That's when she... Ciampa's wife that is... when she
slipped him the other key under the door.

BEATRICE: Fancy that! Under the door, really? How convenient.

SPANÒ (*continuing*): It was in fact proved conclusively, madam,
that there is sufficient clearance between the door and the
floor for the key to be slipped under the door from one side
to the other. Moreover the Cavaliere was found to be in his
shirtsleeves, in other words decently clad.

BEATRICE: Oh yes? What about her? How was she... dressed?

SPANÒ: Well now... well... she was...

BEATRICE: Say it! Say it! After all it's all in the deposition,
isn't it?

SPANÒ: I can definitely tell you that she was not wearing a
blouse.

BEATRICE: She must have been naked. Was she naked?

SPANÒ: Of course not! What are you implying? What I meant
was that she was wearing more than just a blouse... A
skirt *and* a blouse: you know the kind of clothes women
wear about the house... women of the people, I mean...
at this time of year. What with the heat... I swear to you
I'm slightly perspiring myself... She was properly dressed,
I assure you! A slightly plunging neckline, granted... short
sleeves... a summer blouse that is...

BEATRICE: So as long as you didn't find them completely naked—

ASSUNTA (*interrupting*): I forbid you to talk like this! Is that my daughter speaking?

FIFÌ: Shame on you! And in front of a man! (*Points to* SPANÒ.)

BEATRICE: You call that a man?

ASSUNTA: Beatrice!!

BEATRICE: Let's all pretend then! Let's pretend it never happened. Let's sweep it all under the carpet. The shame is in talking about it, not in the actual act.

FIFÌ: I'm not quite clear about one thing, Inspector. Why were they both arrested if the accusations proved groundless?

SPANÒ: I was coming to that. The woman was arrested owing to her... *excessively* plunging neckline, you understand... that amounts to disturbing the peace. As for the Cavaliere... Well, picture the scene: the moment they set about arresting him he lost his control. He was furious. Had I been present I'd have understood and overlooked his outburst. He could have slapped me about and I'd have put up with it, out of friendship. But my colleague from that benighted province of Calabria... put his foot down and apprehended him for resisting arrest. Have no fear, sir: he'll be released. Tonight! And God help my colleague if he doesn't shut up. I'll fix him, I promise you! I'll fix him!

FIFÌ: In other words, you're telling me no offence was committed.

SPANÒ: None. A thorough search was made, including the suitcase and the jacket the Cavaliere had taken off.

BEATRICE: His jacket, too? What about his briefcase? Tell me, didn't they find by any chance a necklace – with pendants – which he had promised her as a gift from Palermo?

FIFÌ: Would that be why you wanted Ciampa to get you an identical necklace?

BEATRICE: Yes. (*To* SPANÒ:) Was such a necklace found during your search?

SPANÒ: Forgive me, madam, but who mentioned such a neck-lace to you? Saracena?

FANA: That's it! She's the culprit.

SPANÒ: I know all about it, of course. She mentioned it to me. It's all nonsense, and this is how it started: Ciampa's wife is forever bickering with her neighbours, who make fun of her because of all the rings she wears. Well, she bragged that one of these days she'd surprise them all by appearing on her balcony looking like Our Lady and wearing a huge necklace – with pendants! That's all there is to the story. Would you really like to know what was found in the Cavaliere's suitcase? A prayer book. A small, beautiful prayer book, bound in ivory-tinted leather, with gilt pages.

ASSUNTA: You see, Beatrice? It was meant for you.

SPANÒ: Wait. That is not all. We also found a box of candied almonds.

ASSUNTA (to BEATRICE): Your favourites!

FANA: Haven't I always said he treats you like a queen?

FIFÌ: Ungrateful wretch!

(BEATRICE *falls tearfully into her mother's arms, repentant and highly emotional*.)

SPANÒ (*evidently pleased with the effect he has produced, nods and winks at* FIFÌ): I think it would be prudent, sir, if your sister were not at home when her husband returns. I am hoping to release him before the evening is out.

ASSUNTA: An excellent idea.

FIFÌ: We'll take her home with us.

SPANÒ: For a few days, at least. We must sympathize with him. The poor man is furious and is threatening all kinds of mischief.

FIFÌ: He's right. Absolutely right. I don't know what I'd do in his place!

SPANÒ: It'll all blow over. You'll see. Give him a few days, he'll be back to normal. He'll be himself again. Isn't domestic peace a wonderful thing?

(*A long pause, as if the status quo had been restored. Suddenly, a persistent ring at the door breaks the hush.*)

FANA (*starting with fear*): Help us, dear Lord! It's him! Ciampa!

FIFÌ: I'd forgotten all about Ciampa.

SPANÒ: Of course! Ciampa! And his wife in prison!

ASSUNTA: What do we do now? What can we do for the poor man?

SPANÒ: It might be better not to let him in.

FIFÌ: No. I think we should receive him. And give him chapter and verse, sensibly.

SPANÒ: I'm not sure about that. The man might react… irrationally.

FIFÌ: Let him! As long as in the end…

FANA (*cutting in*): I'm shaking with fear!

BEATRICE (*meekly*): Mama and I should leave the room perhaps…

FIFÌ (*glaring at her and shouting*): I should think so too!

ASSUNTA: Come, come, Beatrice. Let's leave the men to their own devices… (*Goes out right with* BEATRICE.)

FIFÌ (*to* FANA, *who is following the women out of the room*): Where do you think you're going? Answer the door! (FANA *exits upstage centre.*)

FANA (*enters immediately, backwards*): Mother of God! He's dead! He tripped and fell!

FIFÌ and SPANÒ: What? What's happened?

(*They rush towards the upstage door to help.* CIAMPA *enters, cadaverous, his clothes soiled with mud, his forehead bruised, his collar and tie undone. He is holding his spectacles.* FIFÌ *and* SPANÒ *go to his help and brush his clothes with their hands.*)

FIFÌ: What on earth... My dear Ciampa, what's happened?

SPANÒ: Did you have an accident?

CIAMPA: That's it: an accident. It was nothing. But my glasses are broken.

FIFÌ (*runs to get him a chair, while* SPANÒ *gets another;* FANA *does the same*): Here, sit down... sit down here.

SPANÒ: Here's a chair.

CIAMPA: Thank you. I prefer to stand.

FIFÌ: But why?

CIAMPA: I'd sooner not.

SPANÒ: But you can hardly stand up!

CIAPMA: Have no fear. I have nine lives, like a cat. I'll be better presently. Never mind. I'll be leaving soon. (*To* FIFÌ:) Where is your sister?

SPANÒ: She's in the room next door.

FIFÌ: You'll understand, Ciampa, that right now she can't talk to you.

CIAMPA: Talk? There's no need to talk any more. The deed is done.

FIFÌ: The deed, as you call it my dear Ciampa, is not perhaps what you think it—

SPANÒ (*cutting in, officiously*): The verbal deposition is totally negative!

FIFÌ: There! Straight from the horse's mouth. And if the Inspector tells you, you can believe him. No reason for you to be upset.

CIAMPA: I have your assurance?

SPANÒ: My assurance? It's the legal document itself that provides the assurance, do you understand, Ciampa?

CIAMPA: Ah well, if the document—

FIFÌ: That's it! There was no foundation to any of the accusations...

SPANÒ: ...And the document carries legal authority!

FIFÌ: Will you accept the Inspector's word?

CIAMPA: Very well. I have something here to deliver to your sister.

FIFÌ: The items you collected in Palermo? You may hand them over to me.

CIAMPA: Very well. Might it not be better, since the Inspector is here, if I leave the items with him?

FIFÌ: Leave them with him or with me, as you please. (*To* SPANÒ:) A few articles Ciampa redeemed from...

SPANÒ: Fine, fine.

FIFÌ (*to* CIAMPA): You could even leave them on that table. (*Points with patrician disdain at the small table next to the sofa.*)

CIAMPA: Why do you attach so much weight to a verbal declaration?

FIFÌ: A verbal deposition is a statement of fact, as the Inspector explained.

SPANÒ: Precisely. It's legally binding.

CIAMPA: Very well. I'd like the following declaration to carry legal weight as well: that I hereby deliver to the Inspector, having been sent by the mistress—

SPANÒ (*interrupting*): I know all that!

CIAMPA: You do, do you? I was sent away on this particular errand, and I require you to take note of the fact that I, a humble servant, went and returned, having discharged the errand and turned over to you these two items. (*Takes two jewel cases out of his pocket.*) One... two. That's all. (*Begins to leave.*)

FIFÌ: What are you doing now?

CIAMPA: Nothing. I'm going.

FIFÌ: Just like that?

CIAMPA: There's nothing further for me to do here. I wanted to speak to your sister. It seems I can't. Therefore I'm going.

FIFÌ: What have you got to say to my sister?

(FANA, *behind* CIAMPA, *shakes her head at* FIFÌ *hoping he'll drop the subject, a hand under her chin.*)

CIAMPA (*suddenly turns round and surprises* FANA *in mid-gesture. He replicates her gesture*): Have you a sore throat? Breathing problems maybe? For your information I've got eyes at the back of my head, and they don't require glasses! (*To* FIFÌ:) Are you afraid that if I talk to your sister—

FIFÌ (*interrupting*): Why should I be afraid? The fact is that my sister, at this particular moment, is not in a position to talk to anyone. The Inspector here, my mother, who's in the other room with her, and I myself have made her see the folly of her ways. And now she's sorry she acted as she did... she's most contrite. Isn't that so?

SPANÒ: Too true. Floods of tears...

CIAMPA: Floods of tears, you say...

FIFÌ: Yes. Frankly she's also been crying because I've given her a piece of my mind. I've been blunt in the extreme.

SPANÒ: Too true. A veritable avenging angel...

FIFÌ: Let me assure you, Ciampa, that you couldn't possibly add to the string of home truths I subjected her to.

CIAMPA: Come now, what do you think I'd say to the lady? All your sister did was to take my name – my puppet that is... you remember yesterday I talked about puppets – my own puppet. She threw it to the ground and stamped on it... like this. (*Throws his hat on the floor and stamps on it.*) Why? Because she – the poor puppet! – felt herself trodden under as well. Our positions, mine and hers, are on the whole identical. What could I say to her? I wanted to put only one question to her. Not to the lady herself, but to her conscience.

FIFÌ: And what would that question be?

CIAMPA: My question would be addressed to her conscience. (*Turns to* SPANÒ *and opens his frock coat wide.*) Inspector – search me!

FIFÌ (*pushing him away*): Don't be absurd!

SPANÒ: We know you're a gentleman, Ciampa.

CIAMPA: Inspector. I'm glad, very glad you're here, looking at me as my heart bleeds, and I weep tears of blood: yes, blood, because I've been assassinated! (*He bursts into sudden and uncontrollable sobs.*)

FIFÌ and SPANÒ: Come... come. There's no need for that. Please, please, Ciampa! Control yourself!

CIAMPA: I'll control myself. But... may I put this one question to the lady?

FIFÌ: Of course! I'll call her right now. (*Calls out in the direction of the door on the right.*) Beatrice! Mama! Come, Beatrice! (BEATRICE *enters with* ASSUNTA.) I want you to listen to Ciampa. He wants to ask you a question.

ASSUNTA: The poor man! Are you hurt?

CIAMPA: It's nothing. The trouble is... it's just my glasses... they're broken. My vision is a trifle blurred. In any case there's nothing left for me to see. (*To* BEATRICE:) One question only. Do you believe... and let's leave aside everything that happened this morning... everything... do you believe in all conscience you were right in acting as you did, despite the fact that yesterday I, in your brother's presence—

ASSUNTA (*attempting to interrupt him*): Yes yes, we know everything, my good man!

FIFÌ: You even brought your wife here!

CIAMPA: Please allow her – allow her to answer the question. It's just possible that your sister intended to injure me as well, in the belief she had every reason to do so. Answer me... truthfully.

BEATRICE (*hesitantly*): No... I... with you...

SPANÒ: She meant no harm towards you, Ciampa. In fact she took care to keep you out of it by sending you to Palermo.

BEATRICE: Quite so. As the Inspector says... I...

CIAMPA: No, madam! It isn't possible you didn't include me. Yesterday, in this very room for over two hours I put my hands well forwards...

BEATRICE: Yes. That's exactly why I sent you to Palermo. In order to have a free hand here, to deal with your wife and my husband.

CIAMPA: Without considering me?

BEATRICE: Without considering you.

CIAMPA: I see. Then what was I? A nonentity? Some dirt? Something you picked up between thumb and forefinger and flung away again, into any old corner, as if I didn't count at all? But I want to let it all out now, madam, and look into the very depths of your conscience, and declare that you did intend to injure me! And why? Because according to you I knew *everything* and kept quiet! Am I right? Answer me. Am I right?

BEATRICE: Since you say it yourself... yes. That's the way it was.

CIAMPA: I see. So if someone, let's assume, is blind, you stick a notice on his back saying: "Look everyone – he's blind!"

BEATRICE: No. That's beside the point.

CIAMPA: Let's ignore the blind man, then, after all everyone knows his condition without any need for a notice on his back. You must prove to me that one solitary person – one only – in the whole town could suspect me of knowing what you suspected I knew, and come up to me and say to my face: "Ciampa, you're a cuckold and are well aware of the fact!"

FIFÌ (*cutting in*): Impossible. Never. Not a soul!

SPANÒ (*chiming in*): Who could ever even think such a thing?

ASSUNTA (*chiming in*): No one, no one!

FANA (*chiming in*): What a thing to say!

CIAMPA (*out-shouting the others*): But she could always say that even if the others didn't know... *I knew*, and that'd be enough! Is it true? Don't deny it! Never mind the verbal declaration – I need to know what you think deep down! Is it true? The truth!

BEATRICE: Yes. It is true.

(*A sudden stir of surprise and consternation among the others. Silence.*)

CIAMPA (*wounded, shaking his head*): Ah, at last. It's my turn to speak now... Not about myself. In general terms. (*Addressing* BEATRICE:) How could you know why someone steals, or kills... Because, you see, that someone – who might be ugly, old, poor – might love a woman who holds his heart in a tight grip, as in a vice – yet he won't yell with pain. No. She can quickly put an end to his suffering with a kiss, and the old man is suddenly intoxicated with joy! How could you know how much suffering the poor man experiences, how cruel his torture really is, to the point that he'll even agree to share the woman's love with another man, someone rich, young, handsome, especially if the woman gives him to understand that he is still the master, and that no one will be aware of the arrangement? I'm generalizing, madam, naturally. I'm not speaking of myself. This is a festering wound I'm talking about, full of shame and cleverly concealed. And what do you do: stretch out your hand and uncover it for all to see? Let's change tack and come to ourselves. Madam, I know you suspected my wife and your husband. Ah, jealousy. Who hasn't experienced it who truly loves someone? I can feel sympathy for crimes. How could I not feel for you if you're jealous? I came here to see you yesterday so you could talk about it, unburden yourself! If you had your suspicions, I was not the one to relieve you of them. I know only too well that with suspicions of this kind, the more you try to root them out, the sturdier they grow. If you'd only opened your heart to me, I'd have gone straight home and said to my wife: "Pack up – we're leaving." Today I'd have said to your husband: "Cavaliere, I kiss your hands and here's my resignation." "But why, my dear Ciampa?" "Because I can't stay with you any longer. I've other things to attend to." That's the way it's done, madam. Why else do you think I brought my wife here with me yesterday? So you'd explode, so you'd let out all the anger that's been building up inside you! I begged you: "Speak out! Speak out!" But you said nothing. You pushed me aside and... murdered me as it were... What do you want me to do now? Tell me what to do. Shall I wear my disfigurement with pride? Shall I buy myself a cap with two antlers and display myself to the entire neighbourhood? So that the children can follow me mocking and yelling, "Boo! Boo!"? And there I am, all smiles, bowing and thanking them right and left?

FIFì: Why? Disfigurement? Where? A cap... children? Nothing's happened, I tell you!

SPANò: Absolutely nothing!

CIAMPA: Of course, that's what the deposition states. And who's going to believe any of that after all the scandal? Policemen, dawn raids, arrests...

SPANò: Even so: everything's been explained. Therefore—

CIAMPA (*interrupting*): Inspector, this is a great deal of mud we're talking about! A lot of it will stick. They'll say: "He's an important man. They've fixed it all up among themselves." Where does that leave me? I agree that you, madam, could have indulged in the luxury of teaching your husband a lesson if you thought he was having an affair with a girl... a girl without brothers or a father to breathe down her neck and cry vengeance. Everything could have been arranged neatly and without any bother. But someone else was involved. I was involved, and you ignored that completely. I repeat: am I a nonentity? Well, you've had your little joke, your little diversion. The whole community has had a good laugh and tomorrow you'll kiss and make up with your husband. What about me? As far as you are concerned everything's back to normal. But... what about me? I'm left with a verbal deposition that states nothing out of the ordinary has taken place. From tomorrow onwards I'll have to put up with everyone coming up to me looking suitably concerned: "Nothing's happened at all, Ciampa. Mrs Fiorìca was joking!" (*Turns to SPANò with a sudden movement.*) Inspector... feel my pulse! (*Stretches out his wrist.*)

SPANÒ: Why?

CIAMPA: Feel my pulse. You'll find it's normal. I am calm and relaxed, you're all witnesses to this, and I'm telling you that either tonight or tomorrow, as soon as my wife is home again, I'll split her head open with an axe. (*A very short pause.*) But she'll not be the only one to be done away with. If that was all, the dear lady here would be only too pleased. I'll mete out the same treatment to the Cavaliere. It's only fair.

FIFÌ and SPANÒ (*seizing CIAMPA, while the women weep and cry*): What's that? What are you saying? You're mad! You're not going to kill anybody!

CIAMPA (*pale, convulsed, with a hint of a smile*): Both of them! I've no choice. I didn't start all this.

FIFÌ: You're not going to kill anyone. You've no reason and no right to do so, and you know it. And if you try we'll be there to stop you!

SPANÒ: I for one!

CIAMPA: Inspector, you may be able to stop me today—

SPANÒ: ...And tomorrow!

CIAMPA: ...But the day after tomorrow I'll kill them! You know what we say here in Sicily: "Woe betide the man who is dead in another's heart!" I am not in any way excited, Inspector. As you are my witness, I never wanted any of this to happen. But I've been forced into a corner! I can't walk about disfigured as I am for all to see! Bear in mind that I won't rest until—

BEATRICE (*cutting in*): What if I tell you now, Ciampa, that you have no reason, no reason at all to—

CIAMPA: Now you tell me? Now you recognize you shouldn't have put a man through this ordeal? It's too late.

FIFÌ: Forgive me, but if she herself admits that nothing has happened, surely...

CIAMPA: You call that nothing, sir? You ought not to say that to me.

FIFÌ: What you call a scandal was due to a moment of madness, I tell you.

ASSUNTA (*chiming in*): Sheer madness!

SPANÒ: While the balance of her mind was disturbed – the lady admits it!

FIFÌ: She has admitted it. We confirm it, all of us. A moment of madness.

THE ASSEMBLED COMPANY: Madness! Madness! That's all!

CIAMPA (*while everyone is busy shouting "Madness! Madness!" his gloom gives way to joy, as if struck by a welcome idea*): Thank you, dear God! This is wonderful. Wonderful! Yes, ladies and gentlemen! All can be solved peacefully! What a relief! I could dance… leap about with joy! What a weight off my chest! I needn't soil my hands with crime… they can stay clean… and I kiss them! Look at me: I'm kissing my own hands! (*To* BEATRICE:) You go and get ready. Right now!

BEATRICE (*dumbfounded*): Me? Why?

CIAMPA: Do as I tell you, please, go and get ready. Let's not waste any time. (*Consults his watch.*) You'll make it. You'll make it in time.

BEATRICE: What? Where am I going?

FIFÌ: What is it now?

SPANÒ: Where is she supposed to go?

CIAMPA: She'll make it, I tell you. Fana! And you (*to* ASSUNTA), madam… go help her pack. Put a few things in a suitcase. But hurry up, please. We've no time to lose!

BEATRICE: Where am I going? Why must I hurry? Are you quite mad?

CIAMPA: I most decidedly am not. But you are. Everybody here is agreed. Your brother, your mother, the Inspector – we all agree that you are mad. If we all say so it must be true. You're mad and you're off to the madhouse. It's all perfectly simple.

FIFÌ: What? Who?…

ASSUNTA: My daughter? To the... What are you saying?

BEATRICE: The madhouse? Me?

CIAMPA: Let's not call it that. Let's call it a nursing home. Three months. An extended holiday.

BEATRICE (*indignantly*): If anyone's for the madhouse, that's you! Get out of my house! This instant!

CIAMPA: Why send me away? I've your best interests at heart.

SPANÒ: Is that the way to talk to the lady?

FIFÌ: This is intolerable!

CIAMPA (*to* FIFÌ): Intolerable? Intolerable? Don't you see this is the only remedy at hand? It's for her sake! For her husband's sake! For everybody's sake! Can't you see your sister has made her husband ridiculous, and owes him an apology before the whole community? On the other hand if we say: "She's insane!" – that settles everything. "She's insane, let's lock her up and that's that." In this case I shall be fully vindicated. Disarmed. I say to myself: "The woman's mad, nothing I can do about it!" That's all. And my employer will no longer feel any embarrassment among friends. And you, madam, enjoy a splendid three-month vacation! Come, admit it: there's no better solution. But she's to leave right now.

FIFÌ: What a brilliant idea! That's it! (*To* BEATRICE:) Don't you see? It's all a game of make-believe!

BEATRICE: What? Me? To the madhouse? Did you hear that, Mother – I'm to go to a madhouse...

ASSUNTA: A nursing home, dear. It's all for the best, you know...

SPANÒ (*ponderously, to* BEATRICE): It's the perfect solution. Bound to satisfy the judicious *and* the judicial. Think of the Cavaliere, too...

BEATRICE: Are you all out of your minds? You want them all to think I'm mad?

CIAMPA: One moment. It was you who branded three people with the mark of infamy before the whole town. The first

as an adulterer, the second as a whore, the third as a cuckold. Perhaps you merely want to *say* it was a moment of
madness. That's not enough, dear lady. You must *show*
them you're really mad – mad enough to be committed to
an institution.

BEATRICE: You're the one who should be locked up!

CIAMPA: No. Definitely not me. You're the one. For your own
good. All of us here know you're mad. Now the whole town
must be made aware of it. Don't be alarmed, it'll be quite
painless. It's no hardship to appear insane. I'll tell you how
you set about it: tell everyone the truth. Nobody'll believe
you. They'll all think you're insane.

BEATRICE (*convulsed with rage*): So you do know I am right,
that I had to act as I did!

CIAMPA: No. Certainly not. Turn over the page, madam. If
you turn the page you'll see that there's no clearer sign
of insanity than the belief that one is right. Go on – give
yourself the treat of being really insane for three whole
months. Do you think that's nothing? If only I could allow
myself that luxury! (*Points to his left temple.*) Oh, how
wonderful it would be to wind up the spring of insanity
to its limit, pull down over my ears the cap and bells of
madness and parade myself in the town square, spitting
out the truth at them all! Man's maximum lifespan might
turn out to be not one hundred, but two hundred years!
It's injustice, cruelty, brutality, all the bitter pills we're
made to swallow that shorten our lives and poison our
systems… the fact that we can't let off steam… that we
can't open the valve of insanity! But you can. Yes! Give
thanks to God you can open it, madam! You'll live for
another hundred years. Make a start: yell to your heart's
content!

BEATRICE: Me? Yell?

CIAMPA: Yes. Right here. In front of your brother! (*Pushes* FIFÌ
forwards.) Go on! In front of the Inspector! (*Pushes* SPANÒ

forwards.) Go on! In front of me, too! And bear in mind that only the insane are allowed to shout: "Boo!" to my face.

BEATRICE: Very well. Boo! You see, I'm doing it. Boo! Boo!

FIFÌ (*attempting to restrain her*): Beatrice, really!

SPANÒ: Madam, please!

ASSUNTA: Stop it!

BEATRICE (*with fury*): No! Am I not insane? Very well, I'll have to make it clear to him: Boo! Boo! Boooo!

CIAMPA (*the others endeavour to take* BEATRICE *away, as she continues to yell as if really unhinged*): She's mad. Do you hear that? She's stark raving mad! Isn't it wonderful? She'll have to be locked up! Locked up! (*Dances with delight, clapping his hands. There is a great deal of confusion, and uninvited neighbours suddenly appear, attracted by the noise, enquiring more through gestures than words as to the cause of the mayhem.* CIAMPA *continues to clap his hands, exhilarated, answering questions.*) She's mad! Mad! They're about to take her to the loony bin! She's mad, I tell you!

(FIFÌ *and the* INSPECTOR *gently clear the assembled neighbours from the room, who exit murmuring sadly among themselves.* CIAMPA *collapses on a chair, centre stage, and bursts into a heart-rending laugh, full of rancour, savage relish and despair, as…*)

THE CURTAIN FALLS

HONEST AS CAN BE

Il piacere dell'onestà (1917)

Translated by Donald Watson

Characters

ANGELO BALDOVINO

AGATA RENNI

SIGNORA MADDALENA, *her mother*

THE MARCHESE FABIO COLLI

MAURIZIO SETTI, *his cousin*

THE PARISH PRIEST OF SANTA MARIA

MARCHETTO FONGI, *stockbroker*

FOUR DIRECTORS

A MAID

A SERVANT

A NURSE (*non-speaking*)

The action takes place in a city in central Italy, about 1920.

ANGELO BALDOVINO: *About forty, serious, tawny unkempt hair, short reddish rather bristly beard, penetrating eyes, a deep voice with a somewhat slow delivery. He is wearing a heavy brown suit. Fingers almost always holding pince-nez. His general slovenly appearance and his way of speaking and smiling denote a broken man whose life has taught him to keep well hidden the bitterest and most tempestuous memories, from which he has derived a strange philosophy combining irony and self-indulgence. All this specially in the first act and partly in the third. In the second he appears, superficially at least, transformed: soberly elegant, self-possessed but dignified, a gentleman, with well-kept hair and beard and no longer clutching his pince-nez.*

AGATA RENNI: *Twenty-seven. Proud, almost severe with the effort it takes to overcome the risk to her reputation. Desperate and rebellious in the first act, she then presses proudly and compliantly on to fulfil her destiny.*

LA SIGNORA MADDALENA: *Fifty-two. Elegant, still beautiful, but accepting her age. Passionate for her daughter, she can only see though the latter's eyes.*

THE MARCHESE FABIO COLLI: *About forty, upright and well-mannered, with that touch of awkwardness which predisposes some men to be unlucky in love.*

MAURIZIO SETTI: *Thirty-eight. Smart and free-and-easy, a good talker, a man of the world.*

MARCHETTO FONGI: *Fifty, an old fox, a shady little character, misshapen and listing to one side. Shrewd all the same, not lacking in wit and with a certain gentlemanly air.*

Act One

An elegant drawing room in the Renni household. Main entrance to the rear. A door to the right, a window to the left. The stage is empty when the curtain rises – the main door opens, the maid comes in and ushers in MAURIZIO SETTI.

MAID: Please take a seat. I'll go and say you're here, signore. (*She goes out on the right. After a while* SIGNORA MADDALENA *enters through the same door, anxious and upset.*)

MADDALENA: Good morning, Setti. Well?

MAURIZIO: He's here. Arrived with me this morning.

MADDALENA: And it's... all arranged?

MAURIZIO: Everything.

MADDALENA: You made it all clear to him?

MAURIZIO: I explained everything. Don't upset yourself.

MADDALENA (*hesitantly*): But quite clear? How did you put it to him?

MAURIZIO: Oh Lord! Well... I told him... exactly how things stand.

MADDALENA (*shaking her head, bitterly*): And what things!... Oh yes!

MAURIZIO: Signora, I had to tell him straight out.

MADDALENA: Why yes, of course... but...

MAURIZIO: Circumstances change the way it looks. Rest assured it all depends on the sort of people involved, the whole situation.

MADDALENA: Why yes of course, you're right.

MAURIZIO: And don't doubt I put him completely in the picture.

MADDALENA: What kind of people we are? Who my daughter is. And he agreed? No problem at all?

MAURIZIO: None. Stop worrying.

MADDALENA: Worrying?... Oh, my dear friend, how can I help it? But what's he like? At least tell me what he's like.

MAURIZIO: Well... nice-looking. Lord, I don't mean an Adonis, but pleasant, you'll see. He presents well. A sort of dignity about him, but without affectation. Aristocratic family in fact. He's a Baldovino.

MADDALENA: But his opinions? His attitude?

MAURIZIO: Of the very best, believe me.

MADDALENA: And he knows how to talk... express himself, I mean?

MAURIZIO: Oh, signora, he's from Macerata! They're good talkers, you know, in those parts.

MADDALENA: No, you see... I wonder how discreet he will be. You understand, that's what really matters. One word out of place... without a certain... (*she hardly whispers her words, as if it hurts her even to utter them*) a bare minimum of... Oh dear, I just don't seem to know how to put it. (*She takes out a handkerchief and starts crying.*)

MAURIZIO: Look on the bright side, signora.

MADDALENA: It could be so distressing for my poor Agata.

MAURIZIO: No risk of that, signora. Not an unseemly word, I promise you. He's extremely reserved. Restrained. A perfect gentleman, I tell you. Quick on the uptake, too. Nothing to fear on that score. Promise you.

MADDALENA: My dear Setti, believe me, I don't know where I am in the world today... I feel helpless... Suddenly have to face such a crisis. It's like one of those nightmares... you know?... When the door gets left open for any Tom, Dick or Harry to walk in and spy on you.

MAURIZIO: Well in life, you know...

MADDALENA: And that poor daughter of mine! Such a sensitive soul. If you knew what she's going through! It's too dreadful.

MAURIZIO: I can imagine. You know, dear lady, that I've done my very best to—

MADDALENA (*interrupting and grasping his hand*): Oh, I know! Of course I do! You see the way I trust you? You're one of the family. More than a cousin, more like a brother to our dear Fabio.

MAURIZIO: Is he here?

MADDALENA: Yes, he's in there now. He probably can't leave her on her own yet. He has to keep a close eye on her. As soon as she heard you'd arrived, she dashed to the window.

MAURIZIO: Good God! Because of me?

MADDALENA: No, not for *you*! Because she knows why you went to Macerata and who'd be coming back with you.

MAURIZIO: But all this... I'm sorry, but I thought she...

MADDALENA: No! Just imagine! She's in turmoil, in a desperate state. She frightens me.

MAURIZIO: Forgive me, but... wasn't it all settled? Didn't she agree to it herself?

MADDALENA: Of course she did. But that's just the point.

MAURIZIO (*in consternation*): She's changed her mind?

MADDALENA: No! But could she really *want* this to happen? There was no choice. She *had* to agree.

MAURIZIO: Of course. And make the best of it.

MADDALENA: Oh, Setti! She'll never survive it!

MAURIZIO: She will, signora, you'll see that...

MADDALENA: It will kill her! If she doesn't do something dreadful first. I know I've been too indulgent. But I trusted Fabio... I was sure he'd be more responsible. You shrug your shoulders? You're right. What else can we do? But close our eyes and let shame take over?

MAURIZIO: Now don't talk like that, signora. When we're doing our best to...

MADDALENA (*hiding her face in her hands*): No, please! Don't remind me, it makes it worse – at first I was only conscious of my own weakness. Now, I promise you, all I feel is remorse.

MAURIZIO: I'm aware of that, dear lady.

MADDALENA: But you'll never understand! You, you're a man. And not even a father. How can you ever understand the torment it is for a mother to watch her daughter getting older and losing the first bloom of youth. You no longer have the strength to be as strict as prudence would advise or honour would dictate. Oh! Respectability, my dear Setti, makes a laughing stock of us all. When your daughter gazes at you with eyes begging for pity, what can her mother say, a mother who for good or ill knows the ways of the world and has been in love herself? So as not to give the game away, we pretend not to notice. And this pretence, together with our silence, make us accomplices... until we come... to this! But I really did hope, as I said, that Fabio would be more sensible.

MAURIZIO: Yes, dear lady... but good sense is not always...

MADDALENA: I know! I know!

MAURIZIO: If he could have...

MADDALENA: I know... I can see, it's as if he's quite distraught too, the poor thing. Had he not been an upright man of integrity, how else would we have reached this point?

MAURIZIO: Fabio is a gentleman.

MADDALENA: And we knew he was unhappy. Separated from that worthless wife of his. And this very fact, which should have altered us, is precisely what led us into this mess. You are sure aren't you, in all honesty, that if Fabio had been free he would have married my little girl?

MAURIZIO: No doubt about it.

MADDALENA: Please be perfectly frank with me.

MAURIZIO: Can't you see for yourself, signora, from the state he's in now, that he's hopelessly in love?

MADDALENA: It is true, isn't it? You'll never know what a consolation it is, to have even the slightest reassurance at a moment like this.

MAURIZIO: But what can be in your mind, signora? You know how much I respect you both, how sincerely devoted I am to you and Signorina Agata!

MADDALENA: Oh thank you! Thank you!

MAURIZIO: Please, you must believe me. Or I'd never have become so involved.

MADDALENA: Thank you, Setti. A woman, you see, a poor young girl, who has honourably waited so many years for a partner with whom she could spend her life, at last meets a man worthy of her love. And she finds him hurt and embittered by the unfair treatment he has suffered at the hands of another woman. Believe me, she is sorely, irresistibly tempted to prove to him that all women are not the same. That there exists at least one who can match love for love and appreciate the good fortune his wife has stamped on.

MAURIZIO: Oh yes! You're right, dear lady. Stamped on, poor Fabio never deserved that.

MADDALENA: Sound sense tells us all in our hearts: "No, you can't, you shouldn't do it." She knows it and, if he's an upright man, he knows it as well. So does her mother, who watches anxiously from the wings. For a time you keep silent, you try to do the right thing and you stifle your doubts...

MAURIZIO: ...And in the end, the moment comes...

MADDALENA: It comes all right! It creeps up on you... One perfect evening in May. Her mother was leaning out of the window. Outside, the flowers and stars. Inside, heartbreak and torment. And she murmured to herself: "Doesn't my daughter, for once in her life have a right to them too? Those flowers and those stars?"... And so I stayed there in the shadows, mounting guard over a misdemeanour that the whole of Nature connived at, while still knowing that the next day society and our own conscience will condemn it. But at the time one is glad to let it happen, strangely content emotionally, and proud to face the abuse whatever the cost tomorrow... That's how it was, my dear Setti... I ask for no excuse, only compassion. One ought to die afterwards. But one doesn't. Life goes on and needs the support of all the conventions we cast aside in one single moment of madness.

MAURIZIO: Yes, I know. And that's why we need to keep our heads. You acknowledge that up to now the three of you, you in one way, Fabio and Agata in another, have all let your feelings run away with you.

MADDALENA: Of course we have!

MAURIZIO: Well then, now is the time to control and restrain them. And then listen to the voice of common sense?

MADDALENA: Indeed it is.

MAURIZIO: We have to move forward. There's no time to lose... Ah! Here's Fabio.

(FABIO *comes in from the door on the right, desperately anxious and upset. He makes straight for* MADDALENA.)

FABIO: Please go to her at once. Don't leave her alone!

MADDALENA: Yes, of course... But I thought...

FABIO: Go, please go!

MADDALENA: Yes, of course... (*To* MAURIZIO:) Forgive me! (*She goes off to the right.*)

MAURIZIO: What's this? You in a bad way too?

FABIO: For God's sake, Maurizio, not another word! You think you've found the answer, do you? You know what you've done? I'll tell you! Offered a sick man a placebo.

MAURIZIO: I have?

FABIO: Yes, you. A palliative. The illusion of a cure.

MAURIZIO: But it's what you asked for! Let's get this straight. I never wanted to be your guardian angel.

FABIO: I'm in pain, Maurizio. Going through hell for that poor young girl. And all because of that solution you proposed. I'm sure it's the right one, but that only makes it worse.

Do you see? It's cosmetic, a cover-up, that can do no more than save appearances.

MAURIZIO: And they don't matter any more? Four days ago that's what you were desperate to do, save appearances. And now it's possible you can...

FABIO: I only know how wretched I feel. Isn't that natural?

MAURIZIO: Maybe. But that way you lose everything. Appearances do matter. So you have to create them for yourselves. *You* can't be objective about it. I can. And I must bully you, give you a good shake... make you take the placebo, as you put it – he's here with me now. We came together. As we have to move fast...

FABIO: Yes, you're right...Tell me about it... But it's no good! Did you make it clear I won't let him handle any finance? Not one penny.

MAURIZIO: I did.

FABIO: And he agrees?

MAURIZIO: He's here, isn't he?... However, he does ask – and it seems fair enough to me – in order to fulfil all the terms of your mutual agreement and in view of the conditions, that you wipe out his past life and pay off a few debts.

FABIO: How many? A lot? I bet there are!

MAURIZIO: No. Only a few. My God, Fabio, a man with no debts, did you expect that too? He doesn't have many. But he insisted I told you that if he hasn't acquired more it's not because he wasn't ready to. His creditors no longer trusted him.

FABIO: Oh, that's rich!

MAURIZIO: At least it's honest! You do realize that if he'd still had any credit left, he wouldn't have had to...

FABIO (*his head in his hands*): For pity's sake, that's enough! Tell me how you put it to him... What's he like? Shabbily dressed? In bad shape?

MAURIZIO: He's a bit run down since I saw him last. But we can put that right. I've done something already. Morale is important, you know, for a man like that. The bad things he's felt compelled to do...

FABIO: Gambling? Stealing? Cheating at cards?...

MAURIZIO: He used to gamble. For a while now he's been banned. He was so bitter I felt sorry for him. We spent a whole night walking round, outside the walls of the town. Ever been to Macerata?

FABIO: No.

MAURIZIO: For me, I tell you, it was a fantastic night. Walking round that avenue in the flashing of thousands of fireflies with that man beside me. He was alarmingly frank: startling thoughts from the depths of his being darting into your mind like fireflies before our eyes. I don't know how but I seemed to be out of this world, in a strangely mournful mysterious dreamland. He was master of it. Where the weirdest and most improbable things could happen and yet appear familiar and everyday. He knew what I was feeling. He doesn't miss much. And he smiled. Then started talking about Descartes.

FABIO: Who?

MAURIZIO: Descartes, the philosopher... Oh yes, as you'll see, he's a highly cultured man too. Above all, philosophical. He said that Descartes...

FABIO: But in God's name, now of all times, what do I care about Descartes?

MAURIZIO: Listen and you'll find out. When Descartes, he told me, was investigating our notion of reality, he had one of the most terrible thoughts any human has had to face. If our dreams came to us with any regularity, we'd be hard pressed to distinguish our waking life from our sleep. Have you ever noticed how strange it is when the same dream crops up time and time again? It hardly seems possible that it's not real, because our whole grasp of the reality of our world hangs on a most tenuous thread: the re-gu-lar-ity of our experiences. We whose lives are governed by repetition can't divine what may seem real or believable to a man like Baldovino, who has no rules to live by... So you can see how eventually it was easy for me to put our proposal to him. He mentioned some of his own projects. Highly plausible to him. To me so bizarre and unattainable that my scheme suddenly looked so blatantly simple and obvious, you couldn't think of anything more straightforward. Anyone would have accepted it... And surprise, surprise! I wasn't the first to mention money. It was he who at once indignantly protested there'd be no question of payment. He wouldn't dream of it... And do you know why?

FABIO: Why?

MAURIZIO: Because, according to him, it's easier to be a hero than a gentleman. You can be a hero for once in your life, but a gentleman must remain one all the time. Which is far from easy.

FABIO: I see. (*Anxious, gloomy and disturbed, he starts pacing the room.*) So... it seems he's quite a character?

MAURIZIO: A man of many talents!

FABIO: Who's made little use of them... apparently!

MAURIZIO: Far too little. Even as a boy. We were at school together as I told you. Gifted as he was, if he'd wanted he could have gone far. But always he studied only what suited him, things of no use to him at all. Education, he says, is the enemy of wisdom. Because you need to learn so many things which, if you were wise, you'd be wiser to ignore. He was brought up a member of the upper class: tastes, habits, ambitions – and then vices too... But chance stepped in. His father went bankrupt and... After that, it's no wonder!

FABIO (*resuming his pacing*): And... and you say he's a fine-looking man.

MAURIZIO: Yes, very presentable... What's wrong? (*He laughs.*) Come on now, confess you're beginning to feel a trifle nervous I might have chosen too well!

FABIO: Oh please! It's just... he's too much of a good thing. A highly cultured intellectual...

MAURIZIO: A philosopher too! Not inappropriate, I think, given the circumstances.

FABIO: Don't take it so lightly, Maurizio! Can't you see I'm on edge? I'd rather have someone less... unusual, that's all, more modest, ordinary...

MAURIZIO: Who'd give the game away at once? Who wouldn't have looked the part? Think about it. We had to consider the kind of house he was coming to... A middle-aged nonentity would have seemed very odd. We needed a man of distinction to inspire respect and consideration. It had to be possible for people to believe that our signorina would agree to marry him... And I'm sure that...

FABIO: Then what?

MAURIZIO: That she will... And what's more that she at least will be more grateful to me than you are!

FABIO: Oh yes! She'll be grateful all right! If you could hear her now!... Did you tell him it all has to be settled as soon as possible?

MAURIZIO: Of course! You'll see how quickly he fits into the family.

FABIO: Meaning what exactly?

MAURIZIO: Oh, good Lord, only so much as you want him to!

(*Enter the* MAID, *and then* MADDALENA.)

MAID (*from the door on the right*): Signor Marchese, madam would like to see you for a moment.

FABIO: I can't just now. I have to go out with my cousin. (*To* MAURIZIO:) I must see him. And talk to him. (*To the* MAID:) Ask madam to wait a little. I can't come now.

MAID: Very well, signore. (*She goes.*)

MAURIZIO: It's only a few doors from here. The nearest hotel. But in the state you're in...

FABIO: I'm out of my mind... This is driving me crazy. What with her in there in floods of tears and you out here bullying me...

MAURIZIO: Remember we're not committed yet. And if you really don't want…

FABIO: I want to see him, I tell you, and talk to him first.

MAURIZIO: Well, let's go then. He's only round the corner.

MADDALENA (*bursting in, alarmed*): Fabio! Fabio, please come at once! Don't leave me alone with her!

FABIO: Oh God!

MADDALENA: She's hysterical! Please, I beg you!

FABIO: But I've simply got to…

MAURIZIO: No, Fabio… Go to her now!

MADDALENA: Yes, Fabio, *please*!

MAURIZIO: Shall I bring him here? With no commitment. It might be better for you to talk to him here. For Agata as well.

FABIO: Yes, go and fetch him. Without obligation, mind! Not before he's had his talk with me. (*He goes out through the door on the right.*)

MAURIZIO (*shouting after him*): A few minutes! I'll come straight back. (*He exits through the main door.*)

MADDALENA (*after him*): You're bringing him here? (*She is making for the door on the right when Agata and Fabio rush in.*)

AGATA (*dishevelled, and struggling wildly to break away from* FABIO): Let me go! No! Let me go! I must get away, away from here!

MADDALENA: But darling, where do you want to go?

AGATA: I don't know. Just away.

FABIO: Agata, for God's sake!

MADDALENA: This is madness.

AGATA: Leave me alone! I will go mad or I'll die! There's no other way out. I can't bear it! (*She collapses into a chair.*)

MADDALENA: Wait at least until Fabio's seen him and talked to him. Till you've seen him too.

AGATA: Me? No, not me! Can't you both see how awful it is, what you want me to do? It's monstrous.

MADDALENA: But, my darling, it was you yourself...

AGATA: No! I won't do it! I won't!

FABIO (*desperately, resolutely*): Well then, you shan't! If you don't want to, neither do I. Yes, it *is* monstrous. It's horrible for me too. But in that case are you ready for us to face it together?

MADDALENA: What are you thinking, Fabio? You're a man! Can't you see that *you* can shrug the scandal off? We're just two poor women on our own. All the shame will be ours to bear. It's a choice between two evils. Either public disgrace for us all...

AGATA (*quickly*): ...Or a private one! That's it, isn't it? I'm the only one who will be utterly shamed. To have to live with this man and see him every day. A man who must be absolutely vile and loathsome to agree to such an arrangement. (*Springing to her feet and trying to reach the main door before being pulled back.*) No! No! I won't! I won't see him! Let me go away!

MADDALENA: But where? What will you do?... Face the scandal alone? If that's what you want, I don't know what I...

AGATA (*throwing her arms round her and sobbing helplessly*): No it's for your sake, Mamma... no, for your sake...

MADDALENA: For my sake? Oh no, darling. Why for my sake? Don't worry about *me*. We can spare each other the pain. Or run away from it. We have to stay and endure it, all three of us, try and help each other, because we all have our share of the blame.

AGATA: No, not you, Mamma... Not you!

MADDALENA: I'm more to blame, my darling. And I swear I'm suffering even more than you!

AGATA: No, Mamma. I suffer for you too.

MADDALENA: And I above all for you. It's even worse for me. I can't share my pain because, darling, you are everything to me. Hold tight... wait... we must wait and see...

AGATA: It's dreadful, so awful!

MADDALENA: I know... but let's meet him first.

AGATA: I can't, Mamma! I can't!

MADDALENA: But if we're here with you!... None of us will be taken in, we're not hiding anything. We'll stay here with you, Fabio and I, right beside you.

AGATA: But he'll come and live here! Imagine! Always here with us, Fabio... Someone who knows our secret.

FABIO: But it will be in his interest to hide it too, to keep our secret for all our sakes. And he'll stick to our arrangement. If not, all the better for us! As soon as he shows signs of breaking it, I'll have an excuse to send him packing. After a time we won't need him.

MADDALENA: You see? Why think it's for ever? Only for a while.

FABIO: Just a short while. It'll be up to us to see it's not for long.

AGATA: No, no! He'll always be with us.

MADDALENA: Let's meet him first... Setti has made quite sure...

FABIO: We'll find a way to make it work.

MADDALENA: He's a very intelligent man and he... (*A knock at the front door to the rear. A pause for alarm and then:*) Oh, that's it! It must be him now...

AGATA (*jumping up and clutching her mother*): We can't stay! Let's go, Mamma! Oh God! (*She drags her mother to the door on the right.*)

MADDALENA: Yes, all right. Fabio can talk to him... We can both go in here. (*They both leave on the right.*)

FABIO: Don't worry!... Come in!

(*The* MAID *appears through the front door.*)

MAID: Signor Setti and another gentleman.

(*Exit* MAID. *Enter* MAURIZIO *and* BALDOVINO.)

MAURIZIO: Ah, here we are... Fabio, this is my friend Angelo Baldovino. (*Fabio bows to* BALDOVINO.) The Marchese Fabio Colli, my cousin. (BALDOVINO *bows.*)

FABIO: Please sit down.

MAURIZIO: You have things to discuss, so I'll leave you. (*To* BALDOVINO, *shaking his hand:*) See you later back at the hotel. All right? Bye, Fabio. (*Exit* MAURIZIO *through the main door.*)

BALDOVINO (*sitting, his pince-nez on the tip of his nose, his head tilted back*): First, I'd like to ask you a favour.

FABIO: Please go ahead.

BALDOVINO: Signor Marchese, I'd like you to be quite open with me.

FABIO: Why, naturally... There's nothing I want more.

BALDOVINO: Thank you. But maybe what *you* understand by "open" is not exactly what I mean.

FABIO: But... I don't know... "open"... frank and sincere... (*and as* BALDOVINO *waves his finger at him*) so what do *you* mean by it?

BALDOVINO: Something more than that. You see, Marchese, inevitably we reinvent ourselves. Let me explain. I arrive here, and immediately in your presence I become what I'm meant to be, what I'm able to become... I construct myself... that is, I adopt a new self to suit the relationship I'm meant to establish with you. And of course you do the same thing with me. But basically, behind the façade we present to each other, behind our shutters and our blinds, our true selves lie hidden inside, with our most secret thoughts, our most intimate feelings – what we know ourselves to be, quite separate from the two of us who both wish to reach agreement... Do I make myself clear?

FABIO: Yes, admirably... very clear. My cousin told me how intelligent you are.

BALDOVINO: I see. So you probably think I just wanted to show off.

FABIO: No, no... all I meant was... you expressed yourself very
clearly and I agree with you.

BALDOVINO: So, if you allow me, I'll start with some plain
speaking. For some time, Marchese, I've been deeply,
unspeakably disgusted by the deplorable picture of myself
I've had to invent in my relations with... if I can say it
without offence... my peers.

FABIO: No... please go on...

BALDOVINO: I see myself doing it, continually watching myself,
Marchese. And I think: "Look at what you're doing now!
It's shabby, revolting!"

FABIO (*disconcerted, embarrassed*): No, but for God's sake
why?

BALDOVINO: I'm sorry, but it is. So, you may ask me why I go
on doing it? Why indeed? Partly the fault is mine, partly
of others, and this time through force of circumstances.
I cannot help myself. It's easy to want to live this way or
that. It's hard to be what you really want to be. We are
not quite alone, you see. There's us... and then the beast
we rise on. You can strike him, but you'll never teach him
to think... try to train a donkey to keep off the edge of a
cliff. You can try, beat or whip him, but go there he must.
And when you've finished kicking or thumping him, just
look at his sorrowful eyes. Can you help feeling sorry for
him? Pity doesn't excuse him... Excuse brutishness and it
brutalizes the mind. But compassion's not the same thing
at all. Is it?

FABIO: No, of course not... But can we now talk about us?

BALDOVINO: Marchese, we are. I've told you all this so you
realize that, feeling as I do about our arrangement, I need
to keep my self-respect too. Which means being honest and
open... Pretence would be odious, not to say demeaning,
even vulgar. The truth!

FABIO: Definitely, quite right... Now let's try and reach an
understanding...

BALDOVINO: So I have a few things to ask you, if you don't mind.

FABIO: What now?

BALDOVINO: A few questions please.

FABIO: All right then. Ask away!

BALDOVINO: Here goes. (*He takes his pocketbook out.*) The situation in a nutshell. I've made some notes. It's best for us both to treat it seriously. (*He opens it, leafs through it and begins his questioning, rather like a judge but without severity.*) You, Marchese, are the young lady's lover...

FABIO (*jumping in to cut him short and avoid further use of the pocket-book*): No, no! I'm sorry but is this...

BALDOVINO (*smiling calmly*): You see? You jib at the very first fence!

FABIO: Of course I do! Because...

BALDOVINO (*suddenly severe*): ...It's not true? Is that what you're saying?... Well then (*rising*) I'm sorry, Signor Marchese, I told you, I'm a proud man. I could never lend myself to a dreary humiliating farce.

FABIO: What do you mean? It's your attitude that seems to me...

BALDOVINO: Mistaken? I can only maintain my self-respect – for what it's worth – so long as you deal with me as you address your own conscience... Either that, signore, or we'll get nowhere. I will not involve myself in unseemly fictions... Nothing but the truth ... Will you answer me?

FABIO: Well... it's yes. But no more notebook, for God's sake! You mean Agata Renni?

BALDOVINO (*goes on searching regardless, finds the entry and repeats*): Agata Renni, that's right... aged twenty-seven?

FABIO: Twenty-six.

BALDOVINO (*consulting the notebook*): On the ninth of last month. So she's in her twenty-seventh year. And... (*another look in his notebook*) there's a mother?

FABIO: Oh really!

BALDOVINO: Just being conscientious, you know. That's all. It makes it easier for you to trust me. Always meticulous, as you'll find.

FABIO: Well, yes. Her mother is here.

BALDOVINO: And… forgive me, how old is she?

FABIO: Oh… I'm not sure… about fifty-one or two…

BALDOVINO: Is that all?… It's just that… Frankly, it would be easier without one. A mother's an inconvenient complication… But I knew about her… So shall we stretch a point and say fifty-three? You, sir, will be roughly my age… I'm a bit worse for wear. I look older, but I'm forty-one.

FABIO: So I'm a bit more. I'm forty-three.

BALDOVINO: Bravo! You don't look it. Perhaps if I took more care… Forty-three then… Now I'm afraid I have to bring up another very sensitive matter.

FABIO: My wife?

BALDOVINO: You're separated. I know you're not at fault. You're a perfect gentleman. Incapable of wrongdoing. So it's tempting to wrong *you*. The fault must be your wife's. And here you found consolation. But life is a hard taskmaster. For every joy it brings, we pay a hundredfold in trouble and strife.

FABIO: Too true!

BALDOVINO: I should know! Now, Marchese, it's your turn to pay up. The threatening shadow of the creditor looms over you. Settlement without delay. And I come to stand surety and offer a guarantee that your debt will be honoured. You won't believe, sir, the joy it gives me to wage a vendetta against society when it distrusts my signature. I long to validate it and say: here stands a man who has taken from life what he has no right to, and now I am paying his debt for him because if I didn't, decency would be jeopardized and a family's honour made bankrupt. For me it's a source of great satisfaction, signore, I'm getting my own back! Believe me, that's my only motive. You doubt my word?

You've every right to. Because I'm like... do you mind if I make an analogy?

FABIO: Why no, of course, go on.

BALDOVINO (*continuing*): ...I'm like a man come to spend gold coin in a land where the currency is banknotes. At first no one trusts gold, it's only natural. I'm sure you're inclined to refuse it, aren't you? But rest assured. It's real gold, Marchese. I never could squander it, because it weighs heavy in my soul, not in my pocket. Otherwise...

FABIO: Fine! Well done! Excellent! I couldn't ask for more, Signor Baldovino. Honesty and kindness of heart.

BALDOVINO: I have memories of my own family too. Dishonesty can cost me so much: endless bitterness, disgust, abhorrence and the sacrifice of my self-respect. How could honesty cost me as much? You're inviting me... yes, I mean it... to a double wedding. Apparently I'm taking a wife. But my true bride will be honesty.

FABIO: Yes, exactly, that's fine by me. Enough said!

BALDOVINO: Enough? You think that's enough? I'm sorry, Marchese, but what does all this entail?

FABIO: Entail? I don't follow.

BALDOVINO: Consequences, sir... I can see you feel awkward in my presence, when you're struggling so hard to come to terms with this painful situation and find a way out... but you seem to take it all very lightly.

FABIO: No, on the contrary! Why do you say lightly?

BALDOVINO: Let me put it to you, sir. Do you wish me to be honest or not?

FABIO: Of course I do! It's the one condition I insist on.

BALDOVINO: Excellent. Because I am honest. I feel it in my bones. I wish it, I intend to act accordingly, and I shall prove it to you. So what do you say?

FABIO: Exactly what I said before. That's fine by me.

BALDOVINO: But, I'm sorry, sir, what are the consequences? Listen. What is it, the sort of honesty you want from me?

236

Think about it – it's nothing. An abstraction. Pure form…
may we call it an absolute? Now if I'm to be scrupulously
honest, I shall simply have, in a way, to breathe life into an
abstraction, to embody a concept, to experience this pure,
absolute honesty within myself. And what will that lead to?
First of all, now listen, that I must act as a tyrant.

FABIO: A tyrant?

BALDOVINO: Inevitably! But not because I want to! Only as
pure form dictates, of course – nothing else concerns me –
but for form's sake, to be honest in the way you wish and
I desire, I warn you I must become tyrannical. I shall want
appearances meticulously observed. And that is bound to
occasion great sacrifice on your part, you, the signora and
her mother: a most distressing curtailment of freedom and
respect for all the abstract conventions of good form in
society. And if only to prove how seriously I take all this,
may I point out bluntly, signore, the way people will react
at once? How what happens between us will look in other
people's eyes? Have no illusions that in your dealings with
me – honest as I'll be – any wrongdoing will be laid at your
door, not mine. Only one thing matters to me in this whole
unhappy affair: the chance you all give me – and which I
accept – to be an honest man.

FABIO: Yes, but you can understand, my dear signore – you've
already said it yourself – that I'm not in the mood just now
to grasp all this. You're extremely eloquent, but do let's
come down to earth!

BALDOVINIO: Down to earth! Me? Impossible.

FABIO: I'm sorry, but why not? What do you mean?

BALDOVINO: I can't, just because of the position you put me
in – I'm compelled to dwell in the abstract. If I become
earthborne, I'm done for. Reality is not my element, that's
your preserve. You can keep your feet on the ground. You
talk and I'll listen. I'll be the intelligence that finds no excuse
but feels compassion for…

FABIO (*suddenly, pointing to himself*): ...The donkey?...

BALDOVINO: I'm sorry. It has to be.

FABIO: Why yes, you're right. Of course you are. So let me talk now. It's the beast talking. You know, down to earth, straight out? And you can listen and be compassionate. That way we'll reach an understanding...

BALDOVINO: With me, you mean?

FABIO: Of course, who else?

BALDOVINO: No, signore. An understanding with yourself! I know all about it already. I've done so much talking – I don't usually talk so much, you know – because I want to be sure you're quite able to carry it through.

FABIO: Me?

BALDOVINO: Yes, you. I am already, it's easy for me. What do I have to do? Nothing but incarnate form. The active part – and not an agreeable one – is your prerogative. It's something you've started already and it's up to me to repair the damage. You keep on with it. It'll be the cover-up. But to make this work, in your interest and above all the signorina's, you must respect me. And the role you've chosen to play yourself won't be easy for you. The respect is not for me, but for the form I embody: the honest husband of a respectable woman. That is what you expect, isn't it?

FABIO: Naturally.

BALDOVINO: And you do realize, don't you, that the more honest you want me to be, the more strict and tyrannical this form must be? That's why I warned you of the out-come. Not for my sake but yours! My philosophy, you see, improves my vision. And to justify my conduct in this case, all I need is to look on the wife who will be mine in name only... as a mother-to-be.

FABIO: That's exactly right.

BALDOVINO: And to see that my relations with her are always governed by the thought of that little baby to come. The

function I'm called on to fulfil – a decent noble function
– is dictated by the innocence of a child. Is that all right?

FABIO: Oh yes! That's excellent.

BALDOVINO: Careful now! All right for me. But for you,
Marchese, the more you agree, the harder you make it for
yourself.

FABIO: I'm sorry, I don't... but why... I don't see what problems there are.

BALDOVINO: It's my duty, I believe, to point them out. You are
a gentleman. Force of circumstances has led you to behave
dishonestly. But for you, honesty is essential. So unable to
be honest yourself, you ask me to stand in for you: which
means playing the honest husband of a lady who can never
be your wife, the honest father of a child you can never
acknowledge as yours. That's true, isn't it?

FABIO: Yes, yes, that's true.

BALDOVINO: But if the lady is yours and not mine... If the
child is yours and not mine, don't you see that it's not
enough that I alone should be honest? You, signore, must
be honest with me too... If I'm to be honest, so must we
all. There's no alternative.

FABIO: How's that? I don't see why. Wait a minute...

BALDOVINO: Now you can feel the ground shake under your
feet.

FABIO: No, but I mean... if our ways have to change...

BALDOVINO: Of course they must! It's you who are changing
them. The appearances you wish to save don't only concern other people. There'll be one that concerns you too...
One that you yourselves have demanded and wanted me to
represent. Your own honesty. Have you thought about that?
It won't be easy, you know.

FABIO: But if you know how things stand.

BALDOVINO: Precisely. It's because I *do* know!... It won't make
things easier for me, but what else can I do? I advise you,
Marchese, to give it careful thought.

(*A pause.* FABIO *stands up and starts pacing about excitedly, in consternation.* BALDOVINO *stands up and waits.*)

FABIO (*still pacing*): It's true that if… you realize… that if I…

BALDOVINO: Yes, believe me, you'd better think a bit more about what I've said. And discuss it, if you think it wise, with the signorina too. (*With a brief glance at the door on the right:*) That may not be necessary, because…

FABIO (*suddenly turning to him, angrily*): What? Do you imagine…

BALDOVINO (*sadly, with great calm*): Oh, after all, why shouldn't she know? I'll leave you – you'll inform me or send word to the hotel, what you've decided. (*He makes to leave, then turns round.*) Meanwhile, Marchese, you can count on my complete discretion.

FABIO: I do.

BALDOVINO (*slowly, seriously*): I too have many things weighing on my conscience. I don't think anyone's to blame for what's happened here. It's just unfortunate. Whatever you decide, please know how grateful I shall always be – in private – to my old school friend for trusting enough in my honesty to let me involve myself in this troublesome affair. (*He bows.*) Signor Marchese…

CURTAIN

Act Two

Grand parlour in what has become the BALDOVINO *household. Several pieces of furniture seen before are now in this different room. Main entrance at the rear, side doors left and right.*

When the curtain rises MARCHESE FONGI, *hat and stick in one hand, with the other is holding open the door on the left and addressing* BALDOVINO *offstage.* FABIO *appears to be waiting as if unwilling to be seen or heard.*

FONGI (*into the next room*): Thank you, Baldovino, thank you... you don't imagine I'd miss such a splendid meeting. I'll be back with the other members of the board in half an hour. See you then.

FABIO (*in an anxious whisper*): Yes? You think he really will?

FONGI (*still winking, he answers first with a nod*): He's fallen for it all right!

FABIO: It looks like it. It's taken almost a week!

FONGI (*waving three fingers of one hand*): Three... three hundred... 300,000 lire! What did I say? It couldn't fail! (*Taking* FABIO *by the arm and moving towards the main entrance:*) It'll be quite a showdown. Just you leave it to me. We'll catch him red-handed!

(*They both leave. The stage is empty for a moment, the door on the left opens.* BALDOVINO *and* MAURIZIO *enter.*)

MAURIZIO (*looking around*): You're well set up here, aren't you?

BALDOVINO (*vaguely*): I know. (*With an ambiguous smile:*) All quite above board. (*Pause.*) So tell me... where have you been?

MAURIZIO: A little trip. To get away from it all.

BALDOVINO: Really?

MAURIZIO: Why not? You don't believe me?

BALDOVINO: How far away? You mean you didn't go to Paris or Nice or Cairo – so where did you go?

MAURIZIO: A land of rubber and bananas.

BALDOVINO: The Congo?

MAURIZIO: Yes. The jungle. The real thing, you know.

BALDOVINO: Aha! Did you see any wild things?

MAURIZIO: A few poor tribal natives…

BALDOVINO: Wild beasts, I mean, leopards or tigers?

MAURIZIO: Good Lord no! But they put a sparkle in *your* eyes!

BALDOVINO (*with a bitter smile, cupping his hand to show his nails to* MAURIZIO): You see what we've come to? But we don't cut our nails to appear less aggressive. Just the opposite. Grooming our hands makes us look more civilized: better fitted for a struggle far fiercer than the one our brutal forebears fought, poor wretches, with nothing but their bare nails. That's why I've always envied animals in the wild. And you've been in the jungle, you rogue, and you never even saw a wolf!

MAURIZIO: Forget that! Let's talk about you – well, how's it going?

BALDOVINO: What?

MAURIZIO: With your wife of course… or should I say your good lady?

BALDOVINO: How do you think? It's fine.

MAURIZIO: And… er… you get along all right?

BALDOVINO (*staring at him a moment, then getting up*): What did you expect?

MAURIZIO (*changing his tone, regaining assurance*): I find you in great shape.

BALDOVINO: Yes, I keep busy.

MAURIZIO: I'm sure you do! I hear Fabio has launched a joint stock company.

BALDOVINO: Yes, to give me a finger in the pie. It's doing very well.

MAURIZIO: And you're the managing director?

BALDOVINO: That's why it's so successful.

MAURIZIO: Indeed. That's what I heard. I'd like to get in on it myself, but... they say you're terribly strict.

BALDOVINO: To be sure! And I don't cheat!... (*He goes up to* MAURIZIO *and clasps both his arms.*) Just think! To handle hundreds and thousands of banknotes, see them as so much waste paper and no longer feel any need for them.

MAURIZIO: That must really please you...

BALDOVINO: Divine! And not a single deal that's gone wrong! But it's hard work, you know, very hard. And they all have to follow my example!

MAURIZIO: Yes, I know... that's just it...

BALDOVINO: They're moaning, are they? Tell me. They're squealing? Champing at the bit?

MAURIZIO: They're saying... they say you don't have to be quite so... punctilious, that's all.

BALDOVINO: Don't I know it! I suffocate them all. Anyone who comes near me – but you understand: what alternative do I have? For ten months now I've not been myself, not my own man at all.

MAURIZIO: No?... Who are you then?

BALDOVINO: As I told you – almost a godhead! You should be able to see that! Even physically I only appear to exist. I'm immersed in figures and financial speculation, though only for other people. Not a penny, not a fraction of it for me. And that's the way I want it. Here I am in this beautiful home and it's as if I neither hear nor see not touch anything here. At times I'm astonished even by the sound of my own voice or my own echoing footsteps; by the knowledge that I too need a glass of water or the time to rest – it's a delightful way to live, you know... in the perfect detachment of pure form!

MAURIZIO: You ought to feel some pity for us poor mortals!

BALDOVINO: I do. But I can't behave any other way. I told your cousin the Marchese, I warned him well in advance – I'm only sticking to our agreement.

MAURIZIO: But you get a kick out of it too. A devilish kick.

BALDOVINO: Devilish? Oh no! It's the pleasure enjoyed by the saints in the church frescos, floating in the air, reclining on a cloud.

MAURIZIO: You realize, though, that it can't go on for ever like this.

BALDOVINO (*gloomily, after a pause*): I know all right! It must come to an end soon perhaps... But watch out, it all depends how. (*Staring into his eyes:*) I say this for their sake. Open your cousin's eyes! He's too keen to be rid of me as soon as he can... You're worried? You've heard something?

MAURIZIO: No, nothing, Truly.

BALDOVINO: Come on now, be honest. I'm sorry for them, it's quite natural.

MAURIZIO: I've heard nothing, promise you. I've spoken to Signora Maddalena, but I haven't seen Fabio yet.

BALDOVINO: Oh, I understand. They must both have thought, her mother and your cousin: "We'll marry her off for form's sake. Then after a while on some pretext or other, we'll send him packing." It was the best solution for them. But they can't really expect it! Here too their attitude has been appallingly casual.

MAURIZIO: You suspect this but how do you know?

BALDOVINO: Isn't it true that they made my honesty the whole basis of our agreement?

MAURIZIO: Well, there you are! How can they hope...

BALDOVINO: You're so naive. Reason is one thing, feeling is another. It's easy to work out a logical course of action and hope in one's heart for a different outcome. I could please them both, believe me, and provide a pretext to let them dispose of me. But they can't rely on that. Because, although

I could do it, I won't – in their own interest. I won't because I just don't believe they can genuinely want me to do it.

MAURIZIO: God! What a frightful man you are! You even refuse them the hope they might be able to put you in the wrong.

BALDOVINO: Now look. Supposing I did. At first they'd breathe again. They'd be free of the crushing burden of my presence. They'd appear to retain at least some of the honesty found wanting in me. Agata would still be a married woman separated from a disreputable husband. His disgrace would allow her, young as she is, to seek consolation with an old friend of the family. What was forbidden to a single young woman is excused in a wife no longer bound to fidelity in marriage. All right? Why shouldn't I, the husband, then be dishonest and make myself scarce? Because it wasn't only as a husband I let myself in for this. If that had been all, I would never have done it. There'd have been no real need of *me*. I was needed in so far as this husband was soon to become a father. By soon I mean… at the normal time. What was needed here was a father. And this father – well, it was in Fabio's interest too – simply had to be an honest man! Because, though I as her husband can walk out without wounding my wife – as she can revert to her own maiden name – as a father my dishonest departure couldn't help harming the child, who by law can have no name but mine. And the further I fall, the more the boy will suffer for it… Fabio couldn't possibly wish for that.

MAURIZIO: No, you're right there!

BALDOVINO: So, you see? And you know me. If I did it, I'd sink into iniquity. To take revenge on them for driving me away in disgrace, I'd want the little boy with me. He is legally mine. I'd leave him with them for two or three years to give them time to get attached to him, then I'd prove my wife was living with her lover in adultery. I'd take him away and drag him down with me… right down. You know the horrible beast there is inside me. How I've tried to control him by chaining him to the terms of this agreement. It's in their interest above all that I should observe them. And I fully intend to. Because if I felt no longer bound by them, God knows where I'd end up. (*Suddenly changing his tone.*) Enough of this!... Just tell me: did they want you to see me as soon as you got back? Out with it! What were you meant to ask me? Tell me quickly please! (*He looks at his watch.*) I've given you more time than I should. You know the boy's to be christened this morning? The members of the Board have been invited and I have to fit in a meeting with them before luncheon... Was it your cousin or her mother who sent you?

MAURIZIO: It's true. It's about the baby's baptism – the name you want to inflict on him...

BALDOVINO: I know!

MAURIZIO: I'm sorry... but isn't it...

BALDOVINO: I know, poor little lad. It's such a ponderous name! Enough to squash the life out of him.

MAURIZIO: Si-gis-mon-do!

BALDOVINO: It's a tradition in my family... my father's name and his father's too...

MAURIZIO: Not a reason that appeals to them, you must see!

BALDOVINO: I wouldn't have chosen it either, you know. So it's hardly my fault, is it? It's an ugly, clumsy name, especially for a child... and I confess (*very softly*) that if he had been my own son, really mine, I doubt if I'd have called him that...

MAURIZIO: There you are, you see!

BALDOVINO: What do I see? That it should be clear to you now why I can't give this name up. It's the same old story: it's not for my sake. It's for the façade, on account of the form. You realize that, since he has to have a name, I can give him no other. It's no good, you know, no good at all their persisting. I'm sorry, but you can tell them I won't give way! Why the hell don't they let me get on with my work? All this is a waste of time. I'm sorry, dear friend, to welcome you back like this. Until later then? See you later. (*He hurriedly shakes his hand and goes off left.*)

(MAURIZIO *is left standing, like someone wrong-footed. A moment after,* SIGNORA MADDALENA *and* FABIO *come in sheepishly from the right, one after another, anxious to hear the news.* MAURIZIO *looks at them and scratches his neck. First* MADDALENA, *then* FABIO, *look questioningly at him, without a word, she piteously and he with a frown.* MAURIZIO *responds with a negative shake of his head, half-closing his eyes and spreading out his arms.* MADDALENA *collapses on a chair and sits there helplessly.* FABIO *sits too but is very tense, clenching his fists on his knees.* MAURIZIO *also sits, shaking his head and sighing deeply. None of them has the courage to break the crushing silence.* MAURIZIO's *nasal sighs are answered by* FABIO's *open-mouthed snorting.* MADDALENA *can neither snort nor sigh, but every time the others do she shakes her head disconsolately and the corners of her mouth turn down a little more. The actors must not be afraid of prolonging this dumb show. All at once* FABIO *leaps to his feet and starts pacing fretfully up and down, clenching and unclenching his fists. Shortly after,* MAURIZIO *stands up too, goes to* MADDALENA *and bows, proffering his hand to take her leave.*)

MADDALENA (*quietly and mournfully taking it*): You're going?
FABIO (*instantly turning on them*): Let him go then! I don't know how he had the cheek to show himself. (*To* MAURIZIO:) Don't you dare look me in the face again. (*He resumes his pacing.*)
MAURIZIO (*not daring to protest, hardly turning to look at him and speaking softly to* MADDALENA *whose hand he is still holding*): Agata?
MADDALENA (*quietly and plaintively*): In there with the baby.

MAURIZIO (*softly, still holding her hand*): Say goodbye for me. (*He kisses her hand, then turns and spreads out his arms.*) Ask her... to forgive me.

MADDALENA: Oh, she at least... she has her baby boy now.

FABIO (*still pacing up and down*): Oh yes! And a fine time she'll have with him once he falls under the influence of this monster!

MADDALENA: That's my nightmare!

FABIO (*still pacing*): He's made a good start with that name!

MADDALENA (*to* MAURIZIO): For ten months now, believe me, we hardly dare say a word.

FABIO (*still pacing*): Imagine the way he'll want to bring him up!

MADDALENA: It's awful... he won't even let us see the daily papers.

MAURIZIO: You can't? Why not?

MADDALENA: He's got a thing about the press, you see.

MAURIZIO: But in the house, how is he? Strict? Bad-tempered?

MADDALENA: Not a bit of it! Worse... extremely well-mannered! He says the most painful things to us in such a way... using arguments that are so outlandish, and so unanswerable, that we always feel we must do exactly what he wants. He's a frightful man, Setti, terrifying! I'm almost afraid to breathe.

MAURIZIO: My dear signora, what can I say? I'm quite devastated. I'd never have thought...

FABIO (*exploding again*): Oh, give it a rest! I can't leave here just now because of the christening, but if I could, I would. Nothing's stopping you! Get out! Can't you see I won't hear another word? I can't stand the sight of you!

MAURIZIO: You're right. Yes, I'll go, I'll go...

(*Enter a* SERVANT.)

SERVANT (*opening the rear door, announcing*): From Santa Marta. The parish priest.

MADDALENA: Ah! Show him in.

(*Exit the* SERVANT.)

MAURIZIO: Goodbye, signora.

MADDALENA: You really feel you must go? You won't stay for the christening? Agata would love you to be here. Please come. I'm counting on you.

(MAURIZIO *spreads out his arms again, bows, glances at* FABIO *without daring to address him and goes out at the rear with a nod to the* PRIEST, *who has just entered, introduced by the* SERVANT *who closes the door as he leaves.*)

MADDALENA: Come in, Father. Please sit down.

PRIEST: I hope you're well, signora.

FABIO: Reverend Father!

PRIEST: My dear Marchese! Signora, I've come to discuss our arrangements.

MADDALENA: Thank you, Father. The altar boy you sent is here already.

PRIEST: Excellent!

MADDALENA: Yes, and we've prepared everything in there, including the ornaments he brought from the church. Oh, and there's a cherub, you know? It looks really lovely! Now I'll take you in to see…

PRIEST: And Signora Baldovino?

MADDALENA (*somewhat embarrassed*): Well yes, I'll send for her.

PRIEST: Not if she's busy. I just wanted to know how she was.

MADDALENA: Oh yes, she's fine now, thank you. As you'll understand, she's much taken up with the baby.

PRIEST: So I imagine.

MADDALENA: She can't tear herself away.

PRIEST: And it's you, Signor Marchese, who'll be the godfather?

FABIO: Why… yes…

MADDALENA: And I'm the godmother.

PRIEST: That goes without saying... And... er... the name? Still the one you gave me?

MADDALENA: I'm afraid so... (*With a deep sigh.*)

FABIO (*furiously*): Horribly afraid!

PRIEST: Yet, you know... after all... Sigismondo was a great saint... a king! I'm a humble servant of hagiography...

MADDALENA: Oh, we know what a scholar you are!

PRIEST: No, no... please... don't exaggerate! An enthusiastic amateur perhaps... yes... Saint Sigismondo was a king of Burgundy, whose wife was Amalberga, Theodoric's daughter... But when she died, the widower unfortunately married one of her ladies-in-waiting... a treacherous woman who infamously plotted to make him commit... the most... yes, the most atrocious of crimes... against his own son...

MADDALENA: Heavens above! His own son? What did he do?

PRIEST: Well, he... (*A gesture with both hands.*) He strangled him!

MADDALENA (*to* FABIO, *in a shocked cry*): Did you hear that?

PRIEST (*quickly*): Ah, but he repented of course. Immediately. And in atonement he submitted to the strictest penitence. He withdrew to a monastery and put on sackcloth. His virtuous conduct there, and the punishment he endured with saintly resignation, led to his being honoured as a martyr.

MADDALENA: He was tortured too?

PRIEST (*with half-closed eyes, extending his neck and bowing his head, with one finger indicating decapitation*): In the year 524 if I'm not mistaken.

FABIO: That's choice! A splendid saint! He strangled his own son... and had his head cut off...

PRIEST: The worst sinners, Marchese, often turn into the most respected saints! And believe me, he was a truly learned man. It's to him we owe the famous Lex Gombetta, the Burgundian Codex!... That's only a theory. Strongly contested. But Savigny maintains... and I support him... oh yes... I trust Savigny.

MADDALENA: The only comfort I see, Father, is that I can call him by the shortest form of his name – Dino!

PRIEST: Yes, indeed… Sigismondo… that's wonderful! Dino! A very good name for a child. Suits him perfectly, doesn't it, Marchese?

MADDALENA: Yes, but will he let us use it?

FABIO: That's it, precisely.

PRIEST: Well, after all, if Signor Baldovino is so keen on his father's name… we'll have to be content – so now what time have we fixed on?

MADDALENA: We'll have to let him decide that too, Father… Excuse me. (*She presses a bell on the wall.*) We'll ask him to come at once. If you don't mind waiting a moment. (*The* SERVANT *enters from the rear door.*) Tell Signor Baldovino that the priest is here and ask him to come in… He's in there. (*She points to the door on the left. The* SERVANT *bows, crosses the stage, knocks on the door and goes in.*)

BALDOVINO (*entering hurriedly from the left*): Oh, most Reverend Father, I'm highly honoured. Please don't get up.

PRIEST: The honour is mine. Thank you, signore. We've disturbed you.

BALDOVINO: Oh no! Not at all! I'm delighted to see you here. How can I help you?

PRIEST: I wonder if you'd mind… you see… we wanted to agree a time for the baptism.

BALDOVINO: At your disposal, Father. Whatever suits you. Both the godparents are here, the nurse is in there, I think, I'm ready… and the church is just down the road.

MADDALENA (*amazed*): The church?

FABIO (*barely controlling his anger*): The church?

BALDOVINO (*turning to them in astonishment*): Why, what's wrong?

PRIEST (*quickly*): Well, Signor Baldovino… it was all arranged… don't tell me you didn't know?

MADDALENA: It's all ready in the other room.

BALDOVINO: Ready? What for?

PRIEST: For the baptism. So you can have the ceremony here to make it more meaningful.

FABIO: We've even been sent a few sacred objects from the church.

BALDOVINO: More meaningful? Forgive me, Father, but I never thought I'd hear you say a thing like that.

PRIEST: No, but... what I mean is... it's the custom, you see, for all the best families to have this celebration in their home.

BALDOVINO (*simply, with a smile*): And wouldn't you prefer, Father, that people like us set an example of that Christian humility that in God's eyes sees no distinction between rich and poor?

MADDALENA: No one means to offend God when a christening is kept to the family!

FABIO: Of course not! I'm sorry, but you seem to enjoy spoiling everything. You always object to what others propose. It seems odd to me that you of all people would interfere and preach to us.

BALDOVINO: My dear Marchese, please don't tempt me to raise my voice. Perhaps you'd like to hear the principles I believe in?

FABIO: Oh no! Not that! I won't hear a thing from you!

BALDOVINO: If you take me for a hypocrite...

FABIO: I never said that! Stubborn and prejudiced, that's all!

BALDOVINO: You think you can read my mind? What do you know about it? I can see why you imagine, being aware of my sentiments, that I shouldn't care how you conduct this christening which you have all set your minds on. Well, it goes beyond that. What if it's not for my benefit, but the child's? Like you, I'm totally in favour of this ceremony, but I intend it should be carried out correctly. The boy must be taken to church and baptized at the font. Why should he enjoy a privilege that betrays the whole spirit of this sacrament? I find it strange that you oblige me to say all this in front of the parish priest. He can't fail to acknowledge that a baptism celebrated with great simplicity in the place intended for it is an occasion far more solemn, more devout. Isn't that the case?

PRIEST: Indeed it is, no doubt about it.

BALDOVINO: What's more, I'm not the only interested party. Since it concerns the child, who depends first and foremost on his mother, let us hear what she has to say. (*He rings the bell on the wall twice.*) We'll let our priest do the talking. We won't say a word. (*The* MAID *comes in from the right.*) Ask the signora if she can spare a moment. (*The* MAID *nods and goes.*)

PRIEST: Well, really you know… I'd rather you talked to her, signore, you're so persuasive…

BALDOVINO: Oh dear no! I'd better not be here. You can tell her what I think. (*To* MADDALENA *and* FABIO:) Then you can both give your views. That way the boy's mother is free to choose for herself. And we'll accept her decision. Here she is. (AGATA *enters the room from the right. She is wearing an elegant housecoat. She is pale and tense.* FABIO *and the* PRIEST *stand up.* BALDOVINO *is already standing.*)

AGATA: Oh, good morning, Father.

PRIEST: My congratulations, signora.

FABIO (*bowing*): Signora…

BALDOVINO (*to* AGATA): It's about the baptism. (*To the* PRIEST:) Reverend Father.

PRIEST: My respects, signore. (BALDOVINO *exits left.*)

AGATA: I thought it was all settled. I don't quite know…

MADDALENA: Yes, it's all ready in there… it looks splendid!

FABIO: Now there's a new problem!

PRIEST: Yes, you see… Signor Baldovino…

MADDALENA: He doesn't want the baptism at home!

AGATA: Why's that?

MADDALENA: Why, because he says...

PRIEST: Allow me, signora? He didn't exactly say no. He wants you to decide, signora, because after all... it's up to the mother. So if you want to hold the baptism here...

MADDALENA: Of course! As we agreed!

PRIEST: I really see no harm in it.

FABIO: It's been done in so many homes.

PRIEST: I said that, didn't I? I pointed it out to him myself.

AGATA: So what's left for me to decide?

PRIEST: Ah well, you see... Signor Baldovino maintained – and quite rightly one must admit – with a moral rectitude that does him honour, that a baptism held in a church is bound to be more solemn and devout. Ah! And he put it so beautifully – "without enjoying a privilege," he said, "that betrays the whole spirit of the sacrament." A matter of principle, you see. Of principle.

AGATA: Well, if you would rather...

PRIEST: In principle, dear lady, how can I not agree?

AGATA: Then we'll do as he wants.

MADDALENA: Oh no, Agata! You too?

AGATA: Why, yes, Mamma.

PRIEST: In principle, I said, signora. But on the other hand...

FABIO: You wouldn't mind holding it here?

PRIEST: By no means, why should I?

FABIO: He enjoys upsetting us all!

PRIEST: But if that's what the signora wants...

AGATA: Yes, Father, I do. In church.

PRIEST: That's settled then. It's near at hand. Just let me know when. My respects, signora. (To MADDALENA:) Signora...

MADDALENA: I'll see you out.

PRIEST: Please don't bother... Signor Marchese...

FABIO: My respects, Father.

PRIEST: There's no need, signora.

MADDALENA: But of course... this way please...

(*They both leave by the main door. Looking extremely wan,* AGATA *is about to leave on the right.* FABIO, *in a fury, goes up to her and speaks in a low agitated voice.*)

FABIO: Agata, for God's sake, don't push my patience too far!

AGATA (*gravely indicating, more with her head than her hand, the door on the left*): Not here, please, Fabio!

FABIO: Always… it's what he wants, again!

AGATA: If what he wants is right…

FABIO: To you he's always been right, everything he's said since he was first sent to try us.

AGATA: Not that again! We all agreed, didn't we?

FABIO: But now it's just you. All you needed was to get over the first shock. Then listening to him behind the door was enough to overcome your reluctance – now look at you! You're only too happy to abide by the terms I only first accepted to set your mind at rest. Now it's you, it's because of you… that he knows…

AGATA (*all at once, stiffly*): …What does he know?

FABIO: You see? You see? You're on his side! He knows there's been nothing between us since then.

AGATA: It's for my sake!

FABIO: No, for his sake, for him!

AGATA: It's for me. I can't bear the idea he'd think anything else.

FABIO: Yes, that's it! You want him to respect you! As if he'd had nothing to do with our agreement.

AGATA: Listening to you just reminds me of one thing only: that the shame, if shame there is, is as much ours as his. You want it to be his alone. That makes me ashamed and I won't have it!

FABIO: But I want what belongs to me and ought to be mine again! You, Agata! You, you, you! (*He grabs hold of her frenetically and tries to pull her to him.*)

AGATA (*struggling, with no sign of yielding*): No... no... stop it! Let me go! I told you! Never, never again, till you manage to get rid of him!...

FABIO (*without releasing her, his ardour increasing*): I will! I'll do it today! I'll turn him out like the swindler he is. And I'll do it today!

AGATA (*stunned, no longer able to resist*): A swindler?

FABIO: Yes, yes... a swindler! A criminal! He's done it now! He's been cooking the books!

AGATA: Are you sure?

FABIO: Of course I'm sure. Already he's pocketed more than 300,000 lire. Now we'll send him packing... today... and you'll be mine again, mine, mine, mine...

(*The door on the left opens and* BALDOVINO *appears, wearing a top hat. Finding the couple embracing, he at once stands still in surprise.*)

BALDOVINO: Oh, I beg your pardon... (*Then with a severity tempered by a shrewdly amused smile:*) Well, well! It's only me of course, so it doesn't matter. But it could have been a servant. I suggest you should at least lock the door.

AGATA (*highly indignant*): There was no need for that!

BALDOVINO: Not on my account, signora. I'm reminding the Marchese. For your sake.

AGATA: That's what I was trying to tell him. But now... (*severely*) he has something to say to you.

BALDOVINO: To me? By all means. What about?

AGATA (*scornfully*): You should know!

BALDOVINO: Do I? (*Turning to* FABIO.) What is it?

AGATA (*imperiously to* FABIO): Tell him!

FABIO: No, not now...

AGATA: I want you to tell him now, while I'm still here...

FABIO: It would be better to wait...

BALDOVINO (*quickly, sarcastically*): Perhaps you need witnesses?

FABIO: I don't need anyone. You have embezzled 300,000 lire.

BALDOVINO (*very calmly, with a smile*): No. More, Signor Marchese. Much more! Not three, but five hundred and sixty-three thousand... Wait! (*From his inside pocket he takes out his wallet from which he removes five small cards listing the figures of an officially stamped statement of accounts and from the last one reads out the total sum:*) 563 thousand 728 hundred lire and 60 centimes. More than half a million. Signor Marchese – you greatly underestimate me!

FABIO: The amount is neither here nor there. I don't give a damn. You can keep the lot and get out!

BALDOVINO: Hold on, Marchese... not so fast! You think you have every reason to fly off the handle. Not so. You must realize first that it's all far worse than you think.

FABIO: Not again, Mr Know-all.

BALDOVINO: Know-all? Oh no! (*Turning to* AGATA:) Please come over here and listen carefully. (*Then, when she has moved forwards, frowning coldly:*) If it pleases you both to take me for a thief, we can even agree about that. And the sooner the better. But I beg you above all to consider how unfair you are to me. You see these? (*He holds up accounts spread out fan-wise.*) These entries – you see, Marchese – show that your company is in credit to the tune of more than 500,000 lire from savings and excess profits. But forget that, Agata. We can sort that out. All I had to do was slip them into my pocket... according to them (*pointing to* FABIO *and meaning to include all the members of the Board*), had I fallen into the trap they set for me. That same misshapen individual Marchetto Fongi, who was here again this morning, was meant to trip me up. (*To* FABIO:) Oh I don't deny it was quite skilfully planned! (*To* AGATA:) You don't know about these things, Agata.

But they'd concocted a suspense account for me, showing this surplus profit which I could have quietly laid hands on, sure that no one would be any the wiser. If I *had* been taken in and stolen the money, the inventors of this phoney account would have caught me red-handed. (*To* FABIO:) Wasn't that the idea?

AGATA (*hardly mastering her indignation, staring at* FABIO *who never answers her*): And you did this?

BALDOVINO (*quickly*): No, Agata. You mustn't let it upset you. Scornful as you are when you ask him that question, bear in mind that it is I and not Fabio who would suffer the most – if he is placed in an intolerable situation, mine becomes intolerable too.

AGATA: Why yours?

BALDOVINO (*gazing at her with great intensity, then quickly looking down, disturbed and seemingly bewildered*): Why? Because... if you actually began to look on me as a man, a real human being, I... I could never... oh, Agata... it would have a terrible effect on me: I could never look anyone in the face again. (*He puts his hand to his brow and covers his eyes to control his emotion.*) No... enough of this! It's really time we decide what to do. (*Bitterly:*) I thought I'd enjoy myself today, cutting Marchetto Fongi and the board members down to size. You too, Marchese, who kidded yourself you could catch me out like this, a man like me. But now I come to think of it... you were able to sink so low as to label me a swindler in order to hang on to you (*indicating* AGATA). And you never gave a thought for the shame that would shadow your newborn child when I'd been booted out like a thief in front of five witnesses – I believe the pleasure I take in being honest should have a better outcome. (*He hands* FABIO *the accounts he had shown before.*) These are for you, Marchese.

FABIO: What am I supposed to do with them?

BALDOVINO: Tear them up. They're the only proof of my innocence. The money's all in the safe, down to the last centime. (*He looks him steadily in the eye, then harshly and scornfully:*) But now *you* have to steal it.

FABIO (*as if lashed in the face*): I do?

BALDOVINO: Yes, you. You.

FABIO: Are you mad?

BALDOVINO: You don't want half measures, do you? I told you what would be bound to happen if you agreed to me being honest – that you would be responsible if anything went wrong. You steal the money and I'll play the thief. Then I'll leave, because I really can't stay here any more.

FABIO: But this is madness.

BALDOVINO: No, it's not. I'm using my head. For you and for us all. I don't say you should send me to jail. You couldn't anyway. You'll be stealing the money, but on my behalf. That's all.

FABIO (*confronting him angrily*): What are you saying?

BALDOVINO: Now don't take offence. That's just one way of putting it. You'll come out with clean hands. You'll remove the money from the safe just long enough to prove that I took it. Then you return it naturally, so your associates don't suffer in any way for the trust they had in me out of respect for you. I'll still pass for the thief.

AGATA (*rebelling*): No, no! You can't do it! (*Confrontation of the two men. Then, correcting without contradicting the impression her protest has made:*) And what about the child?

BALDOVINO: It's unavoidable, signora...

AGATA: No, I can't, I won't allow it!

(*A SERVANT appears at the main door to announce:*)

SERVANT: The Board of Directors and Signor Fongi. (*He leaves.*)

FABIO (*quickly, in great consternation*): We'll put all this off till tomorrow.

BALDOVINO (*without hesitation, firmly and defiantly*): I've made up my mind. I'm ready now.

AGATA: I won't have it, I tell you! You understand? I won't let you do it!

BALDOVINO (*utterly resolved*): All the more reason why I should...

FONGI (*entering with the four directors*): May we come in?...

(*At the same moment, from the door on the right, enter* MADDALENA *in a hat and the* NURSE *in her very best clothes with ribbons and bows, carrying the baby in an elaborate cradle draped in a blue veil. Everyone crowds round with various congratulations, exclamations and compliments, while* MADDALENA *cautiously raises the veil to reveal the baby.*)

CURTAIN

Act Three

BALDOVINO's *study. Richly furnished with sober elegance. Door at the rear, side door on the right.* BALDOVINO, *in the same suit he was wearing in Act One, is seated, elbows on knees and his head in his hands, gazing sternly and gloomily at the floor.* MADDALENA *is close to him, talking anxiously.*

MADDALENA: But you must realize you have no right to do this. It's not you that matters now. Or Fabio or even Agata. It's for the baby's sake! For the child!

BALDOVINO (*raising his head and glaring fiercely at her*): And why should I care about the child?

MADDALENA (*alarmed, then quickly recovering*): My God! I suppose not – but remember what you yourself said: about the harm the child would suffer. Precious words that went straight to my daughter's heart. You must realize that now she is a mother, simply a mother, this thought is tearing her apart.

BALDOVINO: Signora, I don't know a thing any more.

MADDALENA: That's not true. After what you said to Fabio yesterday.

BALDOVINO: What was that?

MADDALENA: That he shouldn't have done all this because of the child.

BALDOVINO: I said that?... Oh no, dear lady. I don't care what he's done. I knew he'd do something like this. (*He looks at her with more annoyance than contempt.*) And so, signora, did you.

MADDALENA: No, I swear I didn't!

BALDOVINO: You're right there. To get me out of the house. I'm sure that was the main reason. He hoped, while I was

261

busy elsewhere, to have a free hand here for himself and
your daughter...

MADDALENA (*suddenly interrupting him*): Oh no, not Agata.
That may well have been Fabio's idea... but I assure you
that Agata...

BALDOVINO (*in an outburst, waving his arms*): Good God!
Are you really so blind? How can you say that to me of all
people?

MADDALENA: It's the truth.

BALDOVINO: And that doesn't alarm you? (*Pause.*) Don't you
realize the implications? That it forces me to leave? Instead
of coming to see me, you should be trying to persuade your
daughter that it's best for me to go.

MADDALENA: But how to do it? That's the problem.

BALDOVINO: How's not important. All that matters is that I go.

MADDALENA: No... She'll stop you!

BALDOVINO: Please signora, let me at least keep my wits
about me. Don't rob me of what strength I have left to
foresee the consequences of what others do so blindly.
Blindly, mind, not because they're stupid, but because
when you live, when you're really alive, you can't watch
yourself living. If my vision is clear, it's because I came
here in order *not* to live. Do you insist on bringing me
back to life? Be warned that if life reclaims me I go blind
too... (*Interrupting himself, he strives to control the human
feelings which, whenever they threaten to emerge, make
him seem almost fierce. Then he resumes, calmly if not
coldly:*) Now look... listen... I simply wanted to make the
Marchese aware of the result of his actions, that by trying
to make out an honest man was a thief – not my real self,
you understand, but the man whose honesty he needed
and I consented to represent in order to demonstrate his
own blindness to him – the only way to achieve it would
be to steal the money himself.

MADDALENA: But how can you think he would do that?

BALDOVINO: To pass me off as a criminal.

MADDALENA: But he can't do that! He musn't!

BALDOVINO: He will steal it, I tell you! He'll pretend to. But if he doesn't, I will – do you really want me to take it?

(MAURIZIO *comes in from the right in great consternation. As soon as he sees him* BALDOVINO *bursts out laughing.*)

BALDOVINO: I suppose you've come to beg me as well "not to commit this crazy act"?

MADDALENA (*suddenly to* MAURIZIO): Yes, yes, for God's sake, Setti, persuade him not to!

MAURIZIO: Don't worry, he won't! He knows quite well it's lunacy, not so much for him as for Fabio.

BALDOVINO: Did he urge you to come to the rescue?

MAURIZIO: No, he didn't. It's because you wrote and asked me to come.

BALDOVINO: I know! And of course you've brought me the hundred lire I asked you to lend me?

MAURIZIO: I've brought nothing.

BALDOVINO: Because, being a bright spark, you realized it was all a charade! Bravo! (*He takes hold of the jacket he is wearing.*) However, as you see, I'm dressed for departure – as I told you in my note – in the same suit I came in. All he needs, isn't it, an honest man dressed like this, is the hundred lire I asked the proverbial old school friend to lend me, in order to make a decent exit? (*On a sudden impulse, grasping the others arms with both hands.*) You know how important this charade is to me!

MAURIZIO (*bemused*): What the hell do you mean?

BALDOVINO (*turning to look at* MADDALENA *and laughing again*): This poor lady is staring at me in amazement... (*Friendly and equivocally:*) Now I'll explain, signora... Well, you see, the mistake the Marchese made – a most excusable one, mind, that I understand perfectly – lay simply in believing that I could really fall into a trap. It can all be put right. He will finally realize that as I came here to play a charade I started to enjoy, it has to be played out to the bitter end – oh yes, until the theft takes place. But not a real one, you see? Would I really pocket 300,000 lire as he believed – actually, signora, more than five hundred? Even for this simulated theft, essential as it is, my sole reward is the enjoyment it all brings me. Above all don't worry about the threat I made, merely to impress the Marchese, that I'd come and claim his child in three or four years time. Rubbish. What would I do with a child? Or were you expecting blackmail?

MAURIZIO: Oh, come off it! No one here thinks that!

BALDOVINO: And what if I had considered it?

MAURIZIO: Stop it, I tell you.

BALDOVINO: Blackmail, no. But I meant to keep the game going till I could relish the exquisite pleasure of seeing you all beg me *not* to take the money you'd tried so hard to make me steal.

MAURIZIO: But you haven't taken it!

BALDOVINO: Exactly! Because I want him to take it with his own fair hands! (*As he sees* FABIO *appear at the doorway on the right, very pale, out of breath and in great turmoil:*) And I promise you, he will steal it!

FABIO (*deathly pale and anxious as he goes to* BALDOVINO): I'll steal it?… Me?… But then… Oh my God! Did you leave the safe keys with anyone else?

BALDOVINO: No, why?

FABIO: My God! My God!… But then… Could someone have found out? Could Fongi have told someone?

MAURIZIO: Is the money missing from the safe?

MADDALENA: Heaven forbid!

BALDOVINO: No, Marchese, don't worry. (*He taps his jacket to indicate his inside pocket.*) I have it here.

FABIO: Ah! So you *did* take it?

BALDOVINO: I warned you. No half measures with me.

FABIO: But what are you really after?

BALDOVINO: Never fear. I knew a gentleman like you would be horrified at the thought of removing that money from the safe for a single minute, even as a joke. So last night I went and took it myself.

FABIO: You did, did you? And why was that?

BALDOVINO: Why? To allow you, signore, to make a magnificent gesture... and put it back.

FABIO: You still persist in this madness?

BALDOVINO: I really did steal it, you see. And now, if you don't do as I say, what should still be a charade will become what you first wanted it to be.

FABIO: I did... Don't you realize I've changed my mind now?

BALDOVINO: But *I* haven't.

FABIO: What *do* you want?

BALDOVINO: Precisely the same thing as you. Didn't you tell Agata yesterday that I had money in my pocket? Well, now I have.

FABIO: But you don't have me in your pocket, by God!

BALDOVINO: Yes, I do. You as well. Now I'm off to the board meeting to make my report. You can't stop me. Of course I won't mention the surplus profits Marchetto Fongi so cleverly conjured up for me. And I'll give him the satisfaction of showing me up. Oh, have no fear. I'll give a superb performance as an embarrassed thief caught in the act. Then we'll sort it all out back here.

FABIO: You won't do it!

BALDOVINO: Oh yes, signore, I will.

MAURIZIO: But you can't deliberately pretend to be a thief when you're not one.

BALDOVINO (*firmly, threateningly*): I told you, if you persist in opposing me, I'm determined to walk off with the money.

FABIO: But why? For God's sake why? If I myself ask you to stay?

BALDOVINO (*with sombre, slow gravity, turning to gaze at him*): And how could you really expect me to stay here now?

FABIO: I told you how sorry I was, most sincerely sorry...

BALDOVINO: What for?

FABIO: For what I've done.

BALDOVINO: But it's not what you've done, my dear sir – that was quite natural – but what you haven't done!

FABIO: And what should I have done?

BALDOVINO: What should you have done? After a few months you should have told me that if we both stuck to our agreement – it cost me nothing and it was natural for you – there was someone here more important than either of us, whose integrity and noble spirit – as I often predicted to you – would have prevented her keeping to it. Then at once I would have shown you the absurdity of your proposition: that an honest man could be brought here and persuaded to accept such a role.

FABIO: Yes, you're right. In fact I was cross with him (*indicating* MAURIZIO) for involving someone like you.

BALDOVINO: No, he was absolutely right to choose me. Believe me! Did you really want to take on an honest mediocrity? How could any ordinary man have agreed to such an arrangement, unless he was a scoundrel? I alone could do so, because, as you see, I'm also willing to pass as a thief.

MAURIZIO: But how can you? Why?

FABIO (*at the same time*): What for? You enjoy it?

MAURIZIO: Who's forcing you to do it? No one wants you to!

MADDALENA: No one! We all beg you not to!

BALDOVINO (*to* MAURIZIO): You, as a friend. (*To* MADDALENA:) You, for the child's sake. (*To* FABIO:) And you, why you?

FABIO: The same reason as hers.

BALDOVINO (*looking him straight in the eye*): No reason apart from the child? (FABIO *is silent.*) I'll tell you the true reason. Because now you see what your actions have led to.

(*To* MADDALENA:) Do you think, dear lady, that he really cares about the child's good name? Illusion. (*Indicating* MAURIZIO:) He knows only too well... the sort of life I used to lead... Yes, and my present life... spotless since this baby came into the world... could perhaps wipe out the memory of so much... in my sad and murky past. But he, signora (*indicating* FABIO), had other things on his mind just now than the child. (*Addressing the others too.*) But what about me? Don't I exist? You seem to think I can stay here for ever to lighten your darkness. And that's all? I'm a poor sick human being too! I have blood in my veins, black blood, made bitter by my poisonous past, and I'm afraid it might boil over. Yesterday, in there, this gentleman (*indicating* FABIO), in front of your fine daughter, accused me to my face of this presumed crime. Then, blinder than he is, than all the rest of you, I fell into another still more fearful trap than I did ten months ago. Living here, cheek by jowl with a woman I hardly dared glance at, my feelings were imperceptibly engaged. Your latest childish trick, Marchese, was all I needed to open my eyes to the abyss at my feet. I had intended to keep quiet, you see? Swallow your insult in front of her and confess I was a thief. Then get you on your own, prove to you it wasn't true and compel you privately to hold to our agreement to the end. But I couldn't keep quiet. My senses rebelled. Is any one of you prepared to stop me doing what I have to do? I tell you that to chasten this yearning of my old flesh, as I must, what else can I do but walk off with this memory?

(*They all stare at him in bewildered silence. A pause.* AGATA *comes in from the right, pale and determined. After a few steps, she stops.* BALDOVINO *looks at her. He would like to force himself to stay calm and composed, but in his eyes one can almost glimpse a flash of fear.*)

AGATA (*to her mother,* FABIO *and* MAURIZIO): Leave me to talk to him alone.

BALDOVINO (*almost stammering, with lowered eyes*): No. No, please... You see... I...

AGATA: I must talk to you.

BALDOVINO: It's... it's no good Agata... I've told them... all I had to say...

AGATA: And now you'll hear what I have to say.

BALDOVINO: No, no... for God's sake... it's no good, I tell you... Enough is enough.

AGATA: I insist. (*To the others:*) Leave us alone please. (*The other three go off to the right.*) I didn't come to tell you not to go. I came to say I'll go with you.

BALDOVINO (*another moment of bewilderment. He can hardly stand and speaks in a low tone*): I understand. You don't want to bring up the welfare of the child. A woman like you doesn't accept sacrifices – she makes one herself.

AGATA: I wouldn't call it a sacrifice. It's what I have to do.

BALDOVINO: No, no Agata, you don't. For the baby's sake or yours. I must prevent you at any cost.

AGATA: You can't. I'm your wife. You want to leave? Fair enough. I approve and I'll follow you.

BALDOVINO: Where? What on earth are you saying? Spare yourself and take pity on me... don't make me tell you why... work it out for yourself, because I... face to face... I can't... I don't know how to...

AGATA: No more need for words. What you said the very first day was enough for me. I should have come in at once and offered you my hand.

BALDOVINO: Oh, if only you had! I promise you I hoped... I hoped for a moment that you might... might have come in, I mean... I would never have dared even touch your hand... But it would all have ended there!

AGATA: You would have drawn back?

BALDOVINO: No, Agata. But I was ashamed... just as I am now in front of you.

AGATA: Of what? Of having spoken honestly?

BALDOVINO: That's easy, Agata. It's easy to be honest, you see, when it's just to save appearances. If you'd come in to say that the deception was more than you could bear, I couldn't have stayed a moment longer. Any more than I can now.

AGATA: So you thought I agreed...

BALDOVINO: No, Agata. But I waited when you didn't appear, I spoke as I did to show him that I couldn't *pretend* to be honest – not for my own sake but for yours, all of you. So you must realize that now... now you've changed the conditions, it becomes impossible for me to go on. Not because I don't or won't want to, but because of the sort of man I am, for what I've made of my life till now. Think only of the part I agreed to play...

AGATA: We asked you to do it!

BALDOVINO: Yes, and I accepted.

AGATA: But you warned Fabio in advance what it might lead to, to make him change his mind. And I accepted too.

BALDOVINO: You shouldn't have, should you, Agata? That was your mistake. You never heard my voice here, not my real voice. I only spoke through a grotesque mask – and why was that? Here you were all three of you, poor creatures suffering and relishing the ups and downs of life. A poor unfortunate mother who overcame her scruples and allowed her daughter to engage in an illicit love affair. And you were able to forget that the man you were in love with was regrettably committed to another woman. You all realized you were guilty, didn't you? And at once you tried to find a solution by calling me in. And I came in with my stultifying concept of unnatural fictitious honesty. So in the end you courageously rebelled against it. I was sure that in the long run your mother and the Marchese would never be able to live with the consequences. Their natural feelings were bound to revolt. I was aware they were huffing and puffing. And believe me, I enjoyed watching him hatch this last plot to avert the most serious of the dangers I had warned him about. You, Agata, were the one at risk. If you stuck with it all to the last. And you did. And you could – because becoming a mother, sadly the young girl in love had to die. Now you are a mother. And nothing else. But I, Agata, am not the father of your child – do you know what this means?

AGATA: Ah! It's all on account of the child? You want to leave because you're not the father?

BALDOVINO: No, no! Listen! That's not what I'm saying. The mere fact that you should want to come with me shows that you feel the child is yours and belongs to you alone. And this makes the boy still more precious to me than if he were really mine – a token of your sacrifice and your esteem for me.

AGATA: Well, then?

BALDOVINO: But what I've said is meant to remind you that this is not the real me. Because you can think of nothing but your child. I am only a mask, the mask of a father.

AGATA: Oh no!… I'm talking to the real you, the man behind the mask.

BALDOVINO: And what do you know about the real me? Who am I?

AGATA: This is you. Here and now. (*And as* BALDOVINO, *overwhelmed, bows his head:*) If I dare to look at you, you can raise your eyes to me. Because here we should all bow our heads, as you alone have been ashamed of the faults in your life.

BALDOVINO: I never dreamt Fate would let me hear words like that… (*Violently, as if emerging from a spell:*) No, no, Agata! Enough! Believe me, I don't deserve this. Do you know what I have here… in my pocket? More than 500,000 lire.

AGATA: You'll give that money back and we'll go away.

BALDOVINO: What? I'd be mad! No, Agata! I'll not return it. I-will-not-give-it-back!

AGATA: In that case the baby and I will follow you just the same...

BALDOVINO: You would come with me... even a thief? (*He collapses into a chair, bursts into tears and hides his face in his hands.*)

AGATA (*after staring at him for a moment, she goes to the door on the right and calls out*): Mother!

(*As* MADDALENA *comes in, she sees* BALDOVINO *crying and stops, dumbfounded.*)

AGATA: You can tell those gentlemen there's nothing more for them to do here.

BALDOVINO (*suddenly on his feet*): No, wait!... The money! (*He takes a large wallet from his pocket.*) Not her... it's up to me! (*Trying to hold back his tears and control himself, he searches vainly for his handkerchief.* AGATA *suddenly offers him hers. He interprets this gesture as something that associates them in grief for the first time. He kisses the handkerchief and dabs his eyes, as he holds one hand out to her. With a deep sigh of joy he masters his emotions and says:*) Now I know what I have to tell them.

CURTAIN

THE VICE

La morsa (1910)

Translated by Carlo Ardito

Characters

ANDREA FABBRI
GIULIA, *his wife*
ANTONIO SERRA, *a lawyer*
ANNA, *a servant*

The action takes place in a small provincial town.

A room in the Fabbri household. Upstage, the main entrance.
A side door to the left; two side windows to the right.

   Shortly after the curtain rises, GIULIA, *who has been looking*
out of the window, her back to the audience, starts in surprise.
She puts her crochet work down on a small table and, quickly but
warily, shuts the door on the left, then waits by the main entrance.
   ANTONIO SERRA *enters.*

GIULIA (*hugs him, happy though quietly*): Here already?
ANTONIO (*fends her off nervously*): No. Please.
GIULIA: Are you alone? Did you leave Andrea?
ANTONIO (*his thoughts elsewhere*): I came back first. Last
   night.
GIULIA: Why?
ANTONIO (*irritated by her question*): I made up an excuse.
   Actually, it wasn't really an excuse. I had to be back here
   this morning. On business.
GIULIA: Why not tell me? You could have warned me.

(ANTONIO *looks at her silently.*)

GIULIA: What's happened?
ANTONIO (*in an undertone, tensely, almost angrily*): What's
   happened? I think Andrea suspects us.
GIULIA (*startled with fear in her voice*): Andrea? How do you
   know? Did you give us away?
ANTONIO: No. Maybe we both did.
GIULIA: When? Where?
ANTONIO: Here. When we were coming downstairs. Andrea
   was in front of me, remember? Carrying a suitcase. You

275

were by the door, holding a candle. And as I walked past…
God, how stupid one can be!

GIULIA: He noticed?

ANTONIO: I thought he turned round, as he walked downstairs.

GIULIA: Oh my God! So you've come to tell me… Go on…

ANTONIO: You didn't notice anything?

GIULIA: Not a thing. But where is Andrea? Where?

ANTONIO: Tell me, was I already coming down the stairs when
he called you?

GIULIA: And said goodbye to me! Was that when he turned
on the landing?

ANTONIO: No, it must have been before that.

GIULIA: But if he saw us…

ANTONIO: Caught a glimpse of us, at most. A matter of a
second.

GIULIA: He let you come on ahead? Is this possible? Are you
sure he didn't leave as well?

ANTONIO: Quite sure. There's no train from town before eleven.
(*Consults his watch.*) It's just about due. Meanwhile we're
not sure… the suspense is intolerable. You understand?

GIULIA: Let's calm down. Tell me everything. What did he do?
I must be told everything.

ANTONIO: What can I tell you? In this kind of situation the
most casual remark seems charged with significance: every
look or gesture, or tone of voice…

GIULIA: As I said: let's keep calm.

ANTONIO: That's easy to say. (*After a brief pause, and more
relaxed:*) It was here, do you remember? Before we left we
were discussing the case we had to take care of in town.
He was getting all worked up…

GIULIA: Well?

ANTONIO: The moment we were in the street, Andrea went
quiet and walked with his head down. I looked at him: he
seemed uneasy about something. He was frowning. "He's
found out!" I thought. I was shaking. Then all of a sudden

he said, quite simply and naturally: "Isn't it sad," he said, "travelling at night... leaving home of an evening..."

GIULIA: Just like that?

ANTONIO: Yes. He thought it was sad for those left behind, too. Then he said something that really put me in a cold sweat: "To have to say goodbye, on a staircase, by the light of a candle..."

GIULIA: He said that? *How* did he say it?

ANTONIO: Perfectly naturally. In the same tone. I don't know, maybe he did it on purpose. He mentioned the children, he said he'd left them in bed, asleep, but not in his usual loving, reassuring tone. He mentioned you.

GIULIA: Me?

ANTONIO: Yes. But he was looking at me.

GIULIA: What did he say?

ANTONIO: That he loved your children so much.

GIULIA: Nothing else?

ANTONIO: On the train, he returned to the subject of our legal business. He asked me about Gorri, the lawyer, whether I knew him. Oh yes, he wanted to know among other things whether he was married, and laughed. This, you see, had nothing to do with the matter in hand. Or was it I who—

GIULIA (*quickly*): Be quiet!

ANNA (*from the threshold of the main door*): Excuse me, madam. Shall I go and pick up the children?

GIULIA: Yes. But wait a little.

ANNA: Isn't Mr Fabbri coming home today? The carriages are already on their way to the station.

ANTONIO (*looking at his watch*): It's nearly eleven.

GIULIA: Already? (*To* ANNA:) Wait a few more minutes. I'll tell you when to set out.

ANNA: Very good, madam. I'll finish setting the table while I wait. (*Leaves.*)

ANTONIO: He'll be here presently.

GIULIA: You've nothing to tell me? You couldn't find out anything?

ANTONIO: Yes: that he's good at pretending, if he really does suspect anything.

GIULIA: Andrea, who is so bad at controlling his feelings?

ANTONIO: And yet... could it be I'm so nervous I'm blind to the obvious? Is that possible? Once or twice I thought I saw through his words. But then I reassured myself by thinking I was just plain afraid. I studied him, observed his every move and gesture, the way he looked at me, the way he talked. As a rule he's a man of few words, and yet over the three days we were together you should have heard him! But often he'd relapse into a disquieting silence, only to break it by bringing up the legal business. Could this be why he seems so worried? I asked myself. Or is it due to something else? Maybe he is talking just now merely to allay any suspicions on my part. On another occasion I had the impression he avoided shaking hands with me. And mind you, he was aware I had put out my hand first. He pretended not to notice. The day after we left he was decidedly odd. He started walking away, then he called me back, as if he'd regretted his lack of civility. He's going to apologize, I thought. In fact he said: "Sorry – I forgot to say goodbye. Never mind!" On other occasions he'd talk about you, the house, but it was just small talk. It occurred to me he was avoiding looking me in the eye. At times he'd repeat a sentence three, four times, for no reason at all, as if he was thinking of something else. And when he changed the subject he somehow managed to change tack suddenly and start talking about you and the children. He threw questions at me – was he trying to trick me into an admission? He was laughing, but with an ugly look in his eyes.

GIULIA: And you?

ANTONIO: Oh, I was always on my guard.

GIULIA: He must have noticed you were nervous.

ANTONIO: Did he already have suspicions? Maybe he did.

GIULIA: In that case you confirmed his mistrust. Anything else?

ANTONIO: Yes... The first night, at the hotel – he insisted on taking one room with twin beds – we'd been in bed for some time and he noticed I wasn't asleep, that is... he couldn't have noticed since it was pitch dark! He must have assumed it. Bear in mind that I lay still, in the middle of the night, in the same room with him and afraid he'd find out... can you imagine it? I lay there staring into space... you know... ready to defend myself. All of a sudden he broke the silence and said, and I quote: "You're not asleep."

GIULIA: How did you react?

ANTONIO: I said nothing. I didn't answer. I pretended to be asleep. A little later, he repeated: "You're not asleep." Then I called out: "Did you say something?" And he said: "Yes, I wanted to know whether you were asleep." But he had not been asking me a question, he'd said quite plainly: "You are not asleep" in the sense that I couldn't sleep. At least, that's how it struck me.

GIULIA: Nothing else?

ANTONIO: No. I couldn't sleep for two nights after that.

GIULIA: Afterwards, how was he with you?

ANTONIO: The same as always. No change.

GIULIA: Andrea? Putting on an act? If he'd really seen us...

ANTONIO: And yet he turned round, as we were coming down...

GIULIA: I doubt whether he noticed anything. Could he?

ANTONIO: He may not be completely sure...

GIULIA: You don't know Andrea. Control himself like that, without giving anything away? What do you know? Nothing! Even supposing he'd seen us as you passed by and leant towards me... If he'd had the least suspicion... that you'd kissed me... he'd have walked back upstairs... yes! Just think how we'd both have felt! Listen – no: it just isn't possible. You panicked, that's all. Andrea has no reason to suspect us. You've always been pretty friendly towards me in front of him.

ANTONIO: I grant you that, but suspicion can arise from one minute to the next. Don't you see? A thousand other things acquire a particular significance. The slightest hunch becomes proof positive, doubts turn into certainty: that's what I'm afraid of.

GIULIA: We'll have to be careful.

ANTONIO: Now you tell me. That's what I've always urged.

GIULIA: Are you blaming me now?

ANTONIO: I'm not blaming you. Haven't I asked you a thousand times to be careful?

GIULIA: Yes. You have.

ANTONIO: Why did we have to flaunt ourselves so stupidly... giving ourselves away, just for the sake of a whim... like the other night. You were the one—

GIULIA: That's right, blame me.

ANTONIO: If you hadn't—

GIULIA: Yes... You're afraid, is that it?

ANTONIO: Do you think we've reason to be merry and carefree, you and I? You in particular! (*Pause. He paces up and down.*) Yes, it is fear. Don't you think I worry for you as well? You think I'm afraid, do you? (*Another pause. He resumes walking up and down.*) We were too sure of ourselves, that's it! And now all the stupid risks we took are staring me in the face. I ask myself how could he have failed to suspect us both up till now. How could he? We were making love right here... under his very eyes, you could say. We took advantage of every situation, the least opportunity that offered, whether he left us alone or even when he didn't. We were giving ourselves away with every gesture, with the look in our eyes... It was madness!

GIULIA (*after a long pause*): You blame me now. It's only natural. I have betrayed a man who trusted me even more than he trusted himself. Yes, it is my fault. I am mostly to blame.

ANTONIO (*stopping to stare at her, then resuming his pacing, curtly*): That's not at all what I meant.

GIULIA: Of course you did! I know you did. Look, you may as well add that it was I who decided to run away from home with him. It was I who pushed him into eloping with me, because I loved him – then betrayed him with you. You're right in blaming me now, absolutely right! (*Goes right up to him, and speaks feverishly.*) But I, listen, I ran away with him because I loved him, not in order to settle down to a dull, quiet life… to all this luxury in a new home. I had all that before. I wouldn't have gone off with him… But he, as you know, felt he had to apologize for what he'd done. Andrea: a paragon of respectability! The damage was done. Now it had to be patched up somehow. Quickly. And how? He gave himself up to his work, provided us with a luxurious home and plenty of leisure for me to enjoy it. He worked like a slave, work and nothing but work was all he thought about. All he expected from me was a little praise for his hard work and integrity… and maybe a little gratitude, too! I might have fared worse. He was a good man, he'd have made me rich all over again if need be. Richer, in fact. All this was meant for me. Every night I waited for him impatiently, happy at his return. He'd come back exhausted, satisfied with the day's work, planning tomorrow's tasks. Frankly, in the end, I got tired, too, of having to force this man to love me, and reciprocate my love for him. A husband's esteem, trust and friendship can seem like insults to a wife at times! And you took advantage of the situation, though you now blame me for having loved you and betrayed my husband: now that we're in danger you are afraid, I can see you're afraid! What have *you* got to lose? Nothing. While I… (*She buries her face in her hands.*)

ANTONIO (*after a short pause*): You ask me to keep calm. If I'm afraid at all it's for you… for your children.

GIULIA (*with disdain, hardly stifling a shout*): Don't you dare even mention them! (*Breaks into tears.*) Those poor innocent creatures!

ANTONIO: Tears, now. I'm going.

GIULIA: That's right: go! There's nothing left to detain you!

ANTONIO (*quickly, and in earnest*): That's not fair! I have loved you, just as you have loved me. You know it's true. I warned you to be careful. Was that wrong? More for your sake than for mine. You've said it yourself: if it came to the worst, I'd nothing to lose. (*After a short pause:*) I've never blamed you or reproached you. I had no right to. (*Passes a hand over his eyes, then changes his tone of voice.*) Come on, get hold of yourself! Andrea probably doesn't suspect a thing. That's what you think, isn't it? He didn't notice a thing. So... come on, nothing is finished. We can—

GIULIA: No. No. It's impossible. How could you even think of it? No, we'd better end it now.

ANTONIO: As you wish.

GIULIA: So much for your love.

ANTONIO: You're driving me mad!

GIULIA: No, we'd better end it now, this minute, no matter what happens. It's definitely over between us. What's more I think it would be better for Andrea to know everything.

ANTONIO: Are you mad?

GIULIA: Far, far better. What kind of a life am I leading? Think about it! I've no longer the right to love anyone. Not even my own children. When I kiss them I feel that the shadow of my guilt falls across their faces! No. No. Would he kill me? I'd do it myself if he didn't!

ANTONIO: You're talking nonsense!

GIULIA: Am I? I've always said it: it's too much for me. There's nothing left for me now. (*Attempts to control herself.*) You must leave now. He'd better not find you here.

ANTONIO: You want me to leave? Leave you alone? I came specially... Wouldn't it be better if I...

GIULIA: No. He mustn't find you here. But come back once he's here. That's important. Come back soon, but try to control yourself. Be relaxed, at your ease, not as you are now. Talk to me normally, in front of him. I'll help you.

ANTONIO: Very well.

GIULIA: Yes. Soon. If anything...

ANTONIO: If anything... what?

GIULIA: Nothing. Anyway...

ANTONIO: What is it?

GIULIA: Never mind, I'll say goodbye.

ANTONIO: Giulia!

GIULIA: Go!

ANTONIO: I'll see you later. (*Leaves.*)

GIULIA (*stands still in the middle of the room, her eyes staring into space, lost in gloomy thoughts. She lifts her head with a desolate, weary sigh and presses her hands to her face. But she does not succeed in ridding herself of her obsession. She paces up and down the room, stops in front of a cheval mirror, next to the main door, and is briefly distracted by her own reflection in the mirror. She walks away, and eventually sits by the small table on the right. She buries her head in her arms and, after sustaining this attitude for a little while, lifts her head, deep in thought*): Might he not have gone back up the stairs? Made an excuse... He'd have found me there, behind the window, looking out... (*Pause.*) If only Antonio weren't so afraid! (*She shakes her head, in an attitude of contempt and disgust. A pause, then she gets up, paces up and down for a while and returns to the coffee table, undecided. She rings the bell twice.*)

ANNA (*enters*): You rang?

GIULIA (*still deep in thought*): Yes, everything must be ready. You'll make sure, won't you Anna?

ANNA: Everything is ready, madam.

GIULIA: The table is set?

ANNA: It is.

GIULIA: The master's room?

ANNA: It's ready.

GIULIA: Go and get the children.

ANNA: Immediately. (*Begins to leave.*)

GIULIA: Anna!

ANNA: Madam?

GIULIA (*still undecided after some thought*): Let them be a while longer. You can pick them up when my husband is back.

ANNA: That'll be better. He should be here any moment. In fact, if you'd like me to wait downstairs for the carriage to come back from the station I could help with the luggage.

GIULIA: No. Wait. Not yet.

ANNA: The children are so happy their daddy's coming back today. He promised them presents, you know: a horse this high for Carluccio... Ninetto would like one as well. They were squabbling this morning, in front of their granny: "Daddy loves me better than you!" said Carluccio. And Ninetto said to him: "Yes, but Mummy loves me better. So there!"

GIULIA: The darling!

ANNA: And he can barely talk!

GIULIA: Go and fetch them!

ANNA (*listening*): Wait – I can hear the carriage... (*She leans out of the window.*) It's back. Shall I go down and help?

GIULIA: Yes. Do.

(ANNA *leaves.*)

GIULIA (*extremely nervous now, she resumes pacing the room; she stops, listens, goes back to the small table and mechanically picks up her crochet work*): I'll know straight away. (*She listens again, then starts crocheting with feverish movements, unaware of what she's doing. Suddenly she stops and listens again.*)

ANNA (*off*): The master is here! (*She enters, carrying a suitcase which she places on a chair near the entrance.*)

(GIULIA *rises with her crocheting things, affecting indifference, and walks towards the entrance.* ANDREA *enters.*)

GIULIA (*holds out her hand*): I've been expecting you. (*To* ANNA:) Go and get the children.
ANNA (*hesitatingly*): The master said…
ANDREA: They're at my mother's? Let them stay awhile. I'll unpack first. Then they'll find their presents when they get back.
GIULIA: As you wish.

(ANNA *leaves.*)

ANDREA: I'm exhausted. And I've a splitting headache.
GIULIA: Did you open the windows on the train?
ANDREA: No. I kept them shut. But the noise… I couldn't sleep a wink.
GIULIA: Was the train full?
ANDREA: Yes it was.
GIULIA: And my little feather pillow?
ANDREA: Bother! Isn't it here? I must have left it on the train. No doubt about it. Pity. Still… You're well? The children?
GIULIA: Everybody's fine.
ANDREA: You said you were expecting me? Serra must have told you.
GIULIA: Yes. He dropped in a little while ago. You didn't write to me. Not even once.
ANDREA: True, but I was only away three days. Serra came back last night…
GIULIA: He mentioned it. Said he'd call later.
ANDREA: Good. I'm glad you sent the children to my mother. She dotes on them. Did you go and see her?

GIULIA: No. You know I only go there with you.

ANDREA: I know, but by now, surely…

GIULIA (*changing the subject*): How did your case work out?

ANDREA: Didn't Serra tell you?

GIULIA: Hardly… briefly, at any rate. He didn't stay long.

ANDREA: We're making good progress. Though Antonio left me in the lurch… By the way, Gorri, the lawyer, praised him to the skies! Yes – a clever chap, your partner! He handled the case very well. As far as that goes… (*He breaks off and changes his tone of voice.*) If everything works out as I hope it does, guess what? I'll wind everything up here – and wham! Off we go. No more headaches for me, no more work! We'll up and move into town! What do you say to that?

GIULIA: Live in town?

ANDREA: Look at you – aren't you keen?

GIULIA: It isn't that.

ANDREA: Ah! The city! The city! I'd like to live it up, now! Enjoy myself!

GIULIA: What made you decide?

ANDREA: I haven't quite decided yet. But if it's at all possible… Listen: I'm not going to rot away in this place. I've had it up to here! After all they've done to me! And in any case it's for your sake too.

GIULIA: As far as I'm concerned, anywhere would do…

ANDREA: Come on, come on! In town you'd have diversions you couldn't possibly dream of in the country. You need a change too. If only to breathe in the atmosphere of a city, the hustle and bustle of it all. Then again, here, there's my mother, and you and she—

GIULIA: I hope it isn't because of her that you want to move.

ANDREA: No. That wouldn't be the main reason.

GIULIA: You know only too well that it's your mother who doesn't like me…

ANDREA: I know, I know, and this would be an additional reason. But there are others. (*A short pause.*) You know, in town I bumped twice into your brothers, and every time—

GIULIA: What did they do?

ANDREA: Do? Nothing. What could they do? I'd like to see them try. Nothing. As usual, they pretended not to have seen me. Oh yes! (*Hums a tune.*) It's no use – they just can't get over it! What pride! And anger, too, now. You see, I'm no longer the nonentity I used to be! That robbed them of the satisfaction of seeing you suffer, sorry you'd left their roof to join me. They can't get over it! And I – that's it – am determined to settle down in town just to spite them. I bet they'll enjoy it! Even Serra would come along with us, I believe. What's to keep him here?

GIULIA: His practice?

ANDREA: Oh yes: big deal! Business proper is dealt with in town. What's here? A herd of sheep, once we've left. Incidentally, we'll have to think of some way to reward him. Of course I've done him a number of good turns, but this doesn't really count.

GIULIA: He might think otherwise.

ANDREA: Nonsense. Business is business, and good turns don't come into it. Friendships are bought in business. He deserves something, anyway. If only you knew how well he backed up my claims! With perfect fairness, of course. Sometimes they even try to deny I've done this place some good. Not so much gratitude as – never mind! I'm not saying I've enriched the place – and I could easily say I have – but they could acknowledge, if nothing else, that I've managed to get rid of malaria and a few other things. Why deny me that much credit?

GIULIA: They don't understand.

ANDREA: Quite so. When it's a question of showing gratitude, no one ever understands. It was a swamp they turned over to me; you remember what it was like, when we came here. You remember, don't you, we'd run away from town. All that land produced was weeds which even the sheep wouldn't graze on. I risked all my capital, that is… yours, to drain it, fertilize it, cultivate it. I turned that land into the richest in the area. Very well. My lease comes up for renewal and what happens? Not only do they try to dispossess me but they even deny I've given the place a new lease of life! "You made money out of it!" Thank you very much! Who was it that took risks? Risked everything? Come on! Besides, it was your money.

GIULIA: What's that got to do with it?

ANDREA: It was your money. And if I'm a rich man now, it's due to you.

GIULIA: I didn't do the work.

ANDREA: I did the work. I'll grant you that. And I took my chances. I looked around me on the train. They were all full of admiration for the work I've done. But in the old days they all thought I was mad. A swamp! Yes, that's what they thought it was. To me it was the land of plenty! I'd been obsessed with the idea ever since I was a lad. Think about it: people used to die like flies from malaria. Old Mantegna was in my compartment; you know him, don't you? Two of his daughters died of it. He told us about it with tears in his eyes. His wife also died of it.

GIULIA (*has resumed her crocheting*): They didn't live together by then.

ANDREA: I should think not! Especially after what… (*Laughs.*) But he missed her more than his daughters. We all had a good laugh over that. Poor man, he's gone gaga. They poke fun at him now. Did you know they beat him up?

GIULIA: Really?

ANDREA: Yes. A long time ago. His wife's lover beat him up – Mantegna himself told us all about it, in great detail, on the train. Can you imagine how we laughed? "Put yourself in my shoes," he said. Then he turned to Sportini (he was there too, sitting next to me, the customs officer, you know?) "Ah

Sportini," he said, "You of all people should feel sorry for me!" Pandemonium followed. Luckily a young fellow was with us, you know, a worldly young chap... full of modern ideas. Are you listening?

GIULIA: Yes, I wanted to ask you...

ANDREA: To go in to dinner? Is it ready? Let's go then. Now listen: this young chap started to talk. "You wanted to catch them at it?" he said. "Good Lord, that's prehistoric stuff. What's the point? The gentleman here got beaten up. The usual sudden trip... the wrong train... silly stunts employed by elderly husbands who pretend they've lost their railway timetable, when in fact they've lost their wits. There's no psy-cho-lo-gy to it! Let me explain. You have your suspicions, and you want proof? Why on earth should you want to catch them at it? What a ridiculous idea! Why bother two people who are having a perfectly agreeable time together?" – Witty young fellow, don't you think? – "If I," he said, "had a wife, and – God forbid! – and I suspected her" (I thought he was pulling old Mantegna's leg at this point) "I'd pretend not to have noticed anything at all. I wouldn't look for proof, I wouldn't upset her prematurely. I'd see to it – and here's the test – that she herself, and I mean all of her, should give herself away to me, that she herself became the living, shining proof of her own misdeeds!" Interesting, don't you think? (*He pulls the chair closer to her.*) Listen to what he went on to say. "At the psychologically right moment I'd turn to my wife, ask her to sit down and then, casually, I'd tell her a story about these fashionable affairs which nevertheless touched on her guilt, and gradually I'd screw the vice even tighter until..." (*He takes a small mirror from* GIULIA's *work basket and puts it in front of her face.*) Presto! You place a hand mirror under her nose and ask her, quite politely: "But my dear, why have you gone so pale?" (*Laughs a trifle strangely.*) Ha ha ha! Isn't it perfect? "As you can see... I know everything!"

GIULIA (*pushes the mirror away with her hand, forces herself to smile and rises, pretending to be unaffected by his words*): Nonsense!

ANDREA: Have I upset you? Tell me the truth. Weren't you interested?

GIULIA: Why should I be interested... in Mantegna's wife? (*Begins to leave for the dining room.*)

ANDREA: Well then, Serra...

(GIULIA *turns slightly, very pale, to look at him over her shoulder.*)

ANDREA (*controlling himself, changing his tone of voice*): Yes, I'll say to him: listen, chum, I don't quite know what to do about you. Let's not stand on ceremony, we are friends. Tell me what I should give you and I'll give it to you. What do you think?

GIULIA: Do as you think best.

ANDREA: The thing is, I'm afraid, if I put it to him like that...

GIULIA: He'll refuse?

ANDREA (*rising with a sigh*): Conscience, my dear, spawns strange scruples! Having seduced my wife, he'll refuse my money.

GIULIA: What are you saying?

ANDREA (*frowning, but still in control of himself, as if on the verge of laughter*): Isn't it the truth?

GIULIA: Are you quite mad?

ANDREA: You're telling me it isn't true? Well well! She denies it!

GIULIA: You are mad.

ANDREA: Me? Mad? So it isn't true?

GIULIA: You think you can frighten me? How can you say such a thing? What right have you to insult me like this?

ANDREA (*grabs hold of her*): Me... insult you? You're trembling!

GIULIA: It isn't true! What proof—

ANDREA: Proof? Right? Do you think I'm an idiot? A madman? And you... an innocent victim? I saw it with my own eyes. I did, I did, do you understand? I saw it all.

GIULIA: It isn't true. You're imagining things.

ANDREA: Really? You think I'm stupid into the bargain? I saw it all with my own eyes, and you dare deny it? You have no shame. You started shaking the moment you heard me... like him... like him... over there... I tortured him for three days! He ran away in the end... he couldn't stand it any more. He came to tell you, didn't he? He came to tell you. I let him come ahead of me. Why didn't you go off with him? Deny it, deny if you dare!

GIULIA: Andrea... Andrea...

ANDREA: You're coming clean, now...

GIULIA: Have pity!

ANDREA: Pity?

GIULIA: Kill me. Do what you like with me.

ANDREA (*grabs her again, in a towering rage*): You'd deserve to die, you wretch! That's what you deserve. Yes, yes, I don't know what's stopping me. No, no – look – (*releases her*) I don't want to soil my hands... for my children's sake. Did you give them any thought? Of course you didn't, you coward! (*Seizes her again and pushes her violently towards the door.*) Go! Get out of my house! This instant! Get out!

GIULIA (*desperate*): Where do you want me to go?

ANDREA: You dare ask me? Go to your lover! You even betrayed your brothers to come with me, to run away with me! It'd serve you right if they shut the door in your face! Go to your lover... I'll give you everything, everything... Take your money with you... Do you think I want to hang on to your money? It'd soil my hands now! I'll start all over again, for the sake of my children! Get out!

GIULIA: Andrea, please! Kill me, rather! Don't talk to me like that. I ask you to forgive me, for their sake. I promise you I'll never look you in the face again. For their sake...

ANDREA: No.

GIULIA: Let me stay, for them...

ANDREA: No!

GIULIA: I'll do anything. I beg you!

ANDREA: No!

GIULIA: Please, Andrea!

ANDREA: No, no, no! You'll never see them again.

GIULIA: Do anything you want with me...

ANDREA: No!

GIULIA: They're my children, too!

ANDREA: Now you think about that? Now?

GIULIA: I wasn't myself. I was insane...

ANDREA: And so was I!

GIULIA: I wasn't myself! It was my fault, I've no excuses, I know. I accuse myself and no one else. It was a moment of madness, believe me. I loved you, yes! I felt you were neglecting me... But I'm not blaming anybody. I'm the only guilty one. I know, I know, I'd run away with you... But, don't you see... I loved you?

ANDREA: Loved me? So you could betray me? Was I the first man in your life? You'd have done the same with anyone.

GIULIA: Never! But I'm not trying to find excuses...

ANDREA: Get out then!

GIULIA: Wait! I don't know what I can say any more... I'm to blame, I know... as far as the children are concerned... yes, yes it's true... But if there's no way you'll put up with me, allow me to make amends for them... You can't deny that! Don't take them away from me!

ANDREA: So I'm taking them away from you? Come, come! I can't listen to that rubbish! You'll never see them again!

GIULIA: No! No! Andrea! I'm asking you for the last time, I beg you, on my knees, look... (*Kneels before him.*)

ANDREA (*violently*): No! I say no! That's all! I don't want to hear your voice or see you any more! The children are mine and stay with me. Get out!

GIULIA: If that's the case, then kill me!

ANDREA (*shrugs his shoulders, unconcerned*): You do that. (*Goes up to the window and gazes out.*)

(GIULIA, *as if crushed by circumstance, slowly bows her head, her eyes fill with tears and then she sobs convulsively.* ANDREA *turns to look at her, then looks out of the window again motionless.*)

GIULIA (*gradually stops sobbing, and after a short interval rises, pale and sobbing intermittently; she approaches her husband*): Now... listen...

(ANDREA *turns to look at her again.* GIULIA *bursts into tears again.*)

ANDREA (*his back turned*): You're just pretending again!

GIULIA: No. Listen. If I'm never to see them again... not even for the last time... Now... I beg you! Please!

ANDREA: No. I've said no!

GIULIA: For the last time... just time to kiss them... to hold them in my arms... and... nothing more!

ANDREA: No!

GIULIA: You are very cruel. Very well. At least... promise me that... when they come home... later... you'll never... speak badly of me... promise me! They're not to know, ever! And when...

ANDREA (*in a strange tone of voice, turns to* GIULIA *and beckons her with a gesture*): Come... come... here...

GIULIA (*hesitating, terrified*): Why? (*Then, with a start:*) Ah! They're here!

ANDREA (*grabs her and pushes her towards the window*): No, no... look... look... over there... do you see him?

GIULIA (*clutching him*): Andrea! Andrea! Have pity!

ANDREA (*pushes her in the direction of the door on the left*): Go in there. What are you afraid of?

GIULIA: Please, Andrea! Don't!

ANDREA: In there, I said! Are you afraid for him?

GIULIA: No! No! He's a coward.

ANDREA: Wait for him in there. You're two of a kind.

GIULIA (*her back against the door*): No! No! Goodbye, Andrea! Goodbye! (*Kisses him quickly and rushes into the next room, slamming the door.*)

(ANDREA, *stunned, surprised, facing the closed door, puts his hands to his face.* ANTONIO SERRA *enters. On noticing* ANDREA *he lingers on the threshold. A shot is heard from the next room.* ANTONIO *cries out.*)

ANDREA (*turns suddenly towards* ANTONIO): Murderer!

THE CURTAIN FALLS

A DREAM – OR IS IT?

Sogno (ma forse no) (1929)

Translated by Carlo Ardito

Characters

THE YOUNG WOMAN
THE MAN IN EVENING CLOTHES
A WAITER

A room – or is it? A sitting room perhaps. There is certainly a young woman lying on a bed: or is there? Maybe it isn't a bed, but a sofa, the back of which has been lowered.

In any case to begin with nothing much is clearly visible, since the room is barely lit by an unnatural light which issues from a lamp placed on the lawn-green rug in front of the sofa. The light seems likely to disappear from one moment to the next at the slightest stirring of the sleeping woman.

The lamp is in fact part of the young woman's dream, just as the dream has turned the sitting room into a bedroom, and the couch into a bed.

Upstage is a closed door. On the right wall is a large mirror on a small console artistically worked to resemble a gilt casket. The console just now is not visible, and for the time being the mirror looks like a window.

The reason for this deception is simple: the mirror reflects the window opposite, on the left wall, and naturally, in the young woman's dream, the window is where the mirror reflects it. The dream window will, in fact, be opened later by the man, who has yet to appear.

Below the mirror a drape is drawn across the shelf of the console. The drape is of the same material as the wall coverings, and cannot therefore be picked out from the rest. Thus lowered, it serves to conceal down to ground level the void into which the dream has made the console vanish. It will reappear, with the drape on it, the moment the dream is over, and the mirror has once more become a mirror. From the ceiling hangs a chandelier, now unlit, with three rose-coloured globes of frosted glass.

At a given point, in the semi-darkness of the room barely lit by the dream lamp, there emerges from under the couch *now acting as a bed a hand – an enormous hand – which gradually lifts the hitherto lowered side of the sofa. And as the back of the sofa gradually lifts into place, so does a man's head, outsized also, behind it. Its expression is troubled, the hair tousled, the forehead wrinkled into a frown, the eyes frozen into a hard stare laden with menace.*

It is a spectral mask out of a nightmare.

It continues to rise until the trunk is revealed of a man in a dinner jacket under a black cape and a white silk scarf. He hovers over the young woman who has opened her eyes and is now protecting her face with her hands in fear, shrinking away from the apparition.

The lamp over the rug on the ground dims, and the head disappears behind the back of the couch. It is the matter of an instant. The three globes of the chandelier are now lit and from them there issues a soft roseate light: we now see standing upright by the sofa the man in evening clothes, no longer a spectral figure out of a nightmare but of normal proportions. This does not mean that he appears as real, but as someone out of a dream, with the same menacing expression, though altogether more normal than a little earlier.

The ensuing scene, changeable and as it were suspended within the inconsistency of a dream, will be continuously punctuated by pauses of varying length, and also with sudden interruption in the action. The man will from time to time abruptly stop moving and become completely expressionless, like a puppet at rest. He will recover from these sudden stoppages and each time will assume attitudes in marked contrast with previous ones, in accordance with whatever new impressions the young woman forms of him in the erratic imagery of her dream.

THE YOUNG WOMAN: You here? How did you get in?

(THE MAN IN EVENING CLOTHES *stands still at first: then barely turns to look at her. He takes a shiny door key out of his waistcoat pocket and shows it to her, then replaces it in the pocket.*)

THE WOMAN: Ah, you found it again. Just as I suspected. Remember when I asked you to give it back, after your last indiscretion?

(THE MAN *smiles.*)

THE WOMAN: Why are you smiling?

(THE MAN *stops smiling and looks at her darkly, as if to convey to her that it is useless to lie to him or to expect him to believe that the key had been taken from him owing "to his last indiscretion".*)

THE WOMAN (*attempting to control the fear caused by his gaze*): That's the only reason I asked you for it. I wasn't that concerned about having it back. I just slipped it into my pocket and forgot about it. It must have dropped to the carpet when I rose to go into the other room.

(*The moment she turns her head to indicate the other room, with all the speed of a pickpocket* THE MAN *performs the deed she imagined: he bends down as if to pick up a key from the floor and slips it into his waistcoat pocket. As he performs this action, his eyes light up with malice and his lips twist into a malevolent grin. But the moment he stands up again he resumes his former posture, as if he had never moved.*)

THE WOMAN (*after waiting for him to say something*): What's the matter with you? Why are you looking at me like that?

THE MAN: Nothing's the matter. How am I supposed to be looking at you? (*As he is speaking these words he approaches her, bends over her, placing one knee on the edge of the sofa, one hand on the back of it and the other, with great delicacy, on her forearm.*) I can't keep away from you. I don't feel I'm alive, as I am now, unless you're next to me, just like this – unless I'm inhaling the perfume of your hair – the ecstasy of it! – the smoothness of your skin… the scent of your flawless being. You're my whole life.

(THE WOMAN *jumps to her feet and moves away, brushing past him as she does so. She is showing him that she finds it intolerable to hear him repeating his usual endearments. It was her, in fact, who made him repeat those words, by remembering for a moment that he – in love with her – has appeared to her so often with that same disquieting expression which now, in her dream, is filling her with fear. She at once regrets her sudden gesture, which might give him the impression she no longer loves him: will he now pretend he's spoken those words merely to taunt her? Consequently she turns towards him with some unease.*

THE MAN *having lingered in suspense, like an automaton, in his amorous attitude, bent over her or rather the place where she had been lying, the moment she turns towards him collapses unceremoniously onto the sofa, his legs and arms spread out, throws back his head and bursts into a long scornful laugh. As he laughs, the back of the sofa gives way under pressure until it is level with the seat. At the same time the chandelier gradually dims until he lies flat on the bed, still laughing. During the fleeting period of darkness between the extinction of the chandelier and the relighting of the lamp on the floor, he will have turned on his side on the sofa which has again turned into a bed, leaning on an elbow, his head supported by his hand. It is as if he had been lying there for some time, talking quietly, a sad smile on his lips, addressing the young woman who is now sitting on the bed at his feet.)*

THE MAN: Naturally a woman can't force a man, or a man a woman, to return a love he no longer feels. But then one should have the honesty to come straight out with it: "I don't love you any more."

THE WOMAN: One often doesn't say it out of pity, not because one's not sufficiently honest. It's often convenient to be honest.

THE MAN: Just as it's convenient for a woman to convince herself she's keeping quiet out of pity. When a woman says her silence is due to pity she's already deceived the man.

THE WOMAN: Not true!

THE MAN: Yes it is. And she's deceiving herself. Concealed within this pity of hers you'll always find some other reason.

THE WOMAN (*rising*): Thank you for making your opinion of women so clear.

THE MAN: But even if there were no concealed reasons, don't you see that the pity would be a sham?

THE WOMAN: I've always known that deception can be tempered with pity.

THE MAN: How so? By making someone believe you still love him when you no longer do? A futile deception. Anyone who's really in love immediately notices the absence of love in a partner. And Heaven help him if he pretends not to notice: that'd signal an invitation to betrayal. True pity, devoid of ulterior motive, can only be just that to those who feel it – pity, no longer love. To pretend otherwise is a corruption of pity. And this will give way to contempt, which in turn will lead to and induce betrayal. In any case the original betrayal was caused by neglecting to admit the deception.

THE WOMAN (*sits down again as before*): You think one should admit it?

THE MAN (*unruffled*): Yes. With frankness.

THE WOMAN: You think deception, even when tempered with pity, amounts to betrayal?

THE MAN: Yes. When it is accepted, as a beggar accepts alms. (*Pause.*) I'd like to know how you'd deal with a beggar who kisses you full on the mouth to show gratitude at your charity.

THE WOMAN (*with a vague smile*): If the charity handed out to him in the first place was love, a kiss is the least the beggar could ask for.

THE MAN (*rises suddenly and angrily pulls up the back of the couch*): I was forgetting I was talking to a woman. (*He walks excitedly up and down the room.*) Loyalty – now loyalty is a debt, the most sacred debt we owe to ourselves. Betrayal is horrible. Horrible.

THE WOMAN: I can't make out why you're talking to me like this tonight. Or why you're getting so excited into the bargain.

THE MAN: It's not so much what *I* said: it's what *you* said. I'm speaking in the abstract.

THE WOMAN: And so am I, my dear. How can you possibly doubt me?

THE MAN: You know perfectly well I'm always doubting you and have every reason to do so. (*He moves deliberately and opens the dream window, letting in an outsized moonbeam and a soft sea murmur.*) Don't you remember? (*He stands by the open dream window, looking out.*)

THE WOMAN (*gazing straight ahead, sitting down, searching her memory*): Yes, it's true. Last summer... by the sea...

THE MAN (*still by the window, as if lost in contemplation of the sea*): ...Shimmering in the moonlight...

THE WOMAN: Yes, yes; it was sheer madness...

THE MAN: I said to you: we are challenging the sea by feeling so safe and snug in this frail dinghy. A wave could sink us from one moment to the next.

THE WOMAN: …And you tried to frighten me by rocking the boat…

THE MAN: Do you remember what else I said?

THE WOMAN: Yes. Something unpleasant.

THE MAN: I wanted you to feel the fear I experienced by entrusting myself to your love. You took it amiss. Then I tried to make you understand that just as we were both trying, that night, to challenge the sea by feeling so safe in that little boat which the merest wave could sink, so was I challenging you by placing my entire trust in your love, however slight it might have been.

THE WOMAN: You dared to think it slight? Even then?

THE MAN: But of course! From the start, my dear! Necessarily so. Not so much because you wanted it. In fact you thought you'd given me every assurance. But it didn't amount to much, since you yourself, my dear, could never be sure that tomorrow, or the day after, you'd still love me. There was even a time when you felt you loved me, as you did not earlier. There will come a time when you'll feel you no longer love me. Perhaps that time has come… Look at me!… Are you afraid to look at me?

THE WOMAN: I am not afraid. I know you're a reasonable man. You said yourself just now that no one can force anyone to return a love he no longer feels.

THE MAN: I dare say I was being reasonable. But Heaven help you, Heaven help you if you should stop loving me while I'm still in love with you, with every fibre of my being!

THE WOMAN: You simply must be reasonable.

THE MAN: Oh yes, yes, I'm going to try to be reasonable. I'll be as reasonable as you like, just to please you. And so that you won't feel afraid any more, shall I show you how reasonable I can be? Here goes: I shall be very understanding as long as the flame burns bright only up here – (*he touches his forehead*) I understand full well, as you know, that your love, which began quite suddenly, can die just as suddenly for any reason at all, due to something unforeseen, unforeseeable. What more can I say? I'll say this: at the crossroads, through a chance meeting, a sudden blinding combination of circumstances, an unexpected, irresistible stimulation of the senses...

THE WOMAN: Oh, come to that...

THE MAN: Well, it could happen... Why not?

THE WOMAN: Because we are reasonable beings. Reason pulls us back.

THE MAN: Back? Back to what? Duty?

THE WOMAN: It stops us being overwhelmed...

THE MAN: But that's just what life does to us. It overwhelms us, it always has done! Why should I be the one to tell you, as if you didn't know it? God help us if the flame should burn here... (*touches his breast*) and you turn your heart to ashes! You've no idea what ghastly smoke can rise from a burning heart, from blood... bubbling blood... what a dreadful night the smoke causes in your brain – a veritable tempest that darkens and blots out your reason! Do you think you're up to preventing this storm from hurling lightning... setting fire to your house and killing you? (*As he speaks these words his countenance undergoes a terrible change: no sooner has he mentioned a storm than the growing distant rumble of thunder is heard beyond the open window, and the ray of moonlight turns into a sinister flash of lightning.*)

(THE WOMAN, *terrified, hides her face in her hands.*

THE MAN, *immediately when she hides her face, stops in mid-gesture, his face expressionless, like a robot. The sound of thunder and flashes of lightning also cease suddenly, replaced by a soft moonbeam as before. Everything is now mysteriously still and will remain so as long as the young woman hides her face in her hands.*

THE WOMAN, *her hands still hiding her face, rises and moves a few steps towards the window as if to shut it.*

THE MAN, *though remaining still as if in suspended animation, barely turns his head and arms in her direction, as though moving towards the window she had caused his slight movement.*

THE WOMAN *takes her hands from her face and gazes out of the window, amazed by the stillness and serenity of the moonlight. In her astonishment she smiles, remembering "the moment" when she fell in love with the man – it happened in fact in a living room, by a window through which the moonlight was flooding in. She turns to him, smiling.)*

THE MAN (*immediately assumes the expression of that "moment", that is of a man in a living room who has noticed from the corner of his eye the woman he is in love with move towards a window; pretending he needs a breath of fresh air, he shows surprise at finding her by the window*): Oh, excuse me. You here? It's unbearably hot, isn't it? Far too hot to dance. Perhaps we should all go into the garden – look at that moon! We could leave the orchestra behind, indoors. They could go on playing... think how nice it would be to listen to the music from a distance, in the coolness of the garden, dancing in the clearing by that fountain! (*From a distance, muffled, as if from above, the sound of a piano.*)

THE WOMAN: I thought the sight of the garden and the moonlight wouldn't encourage you to go out there with a crowd... but only with that beautiful lady in the pink dress... the one you've been dancing with all evening.

THE MAN: How can you say that? It was you who—

THE WOMAN (*cutting in*): Quiet! They can hear you.

THE MAN (*lowers his voice*): ...It was you who said I shouldn't dance with you too often, so as not to make it obvious... now you reproach me...

THE WOMAN (*in hushed tones, after signalling him to be quiet*): Go into the garden, but don't let anyone see you. I'll join you in a little while, the moment I can.

THE MAN (*delighted, after a quick look around to make sure no one is looking, furtively takes her hand and kisses it*): I'm going. I'll wait for you. Hurry! (*He leaves the window, and moves cautiously through the living room in the direction of the closed door. Once there, he turns round for a final look before opening the door. He opens the door and leaves.*)

(THE WOMAN *stands, as if in hiding, by the window, bathed in moonlight. Gradually the moonbeam fades, as well as the light from the lamp on the floor, and the sound of the piano music grows fainter and more distant, since the vision of that "moment" is fading within her. When it has faded completely, all the lights are extinguished and the piano music has ceased, in the instant of darkness which will precede the relighting of the three pink globes, the window will be closed, and the young woman will again be sitting on the sofa.*

THE MAN *stands by the sofa, scowling as before.*)

THE WOMAN (*after waiting for him to say something, stamps her foot*): Come on, are you or are you not going to say something? Don't tell me you're going to stand there in front of me all night looking like that! (*In an attempt to control her mounting rage she is on the verge of tears.*)

THE MAN: The way I'm looking is not my fault: you've put that frown on my face. You know I'm still in love with you, that if I were to turn and look at myself in the mirror, with this expression on my face, I wouldn't recognize myself. The mirror would be telling the truth, showing an image of myself unknown to me, an image you've imposed on me. For that very reason you've made the mirror vanish and made me open it as though it were a window.

THE WOMAN (*almost shouting*): No, no, it is a window. It's a window! I swear it's a window! Don't even bother to turn and look!

THE MAN: Don't worry, I won't look. Yes, it's a window all right. Of course it's a window, since I've gone and opened it! And is there not a garden over there, where our mouths met for the first time in an endless kiss? And in front of the garden is the sea, which we challenged together one moonlit night this summer? Nothing frightens an uneasy conscience more than a mirror. And you know that for other reasons, all due to you, when I think of what I've done for you and am actually doing – why I daren't look in a mirror. Now, at this very moment, looking as I am, standing here, you know full well where I am – you came there once – in that yellow gambling room at my club – and I'm cheating, cheating for your sake – nobody luckily caught me in the act – but I'm cheating, I'm cheating all right, in order to make you a present of that pearl necklace...

THE WOMAN: No, no, I don't want it any more! I don't want it! I know I told you once I'd like to have it, but just to—

THE MAN: ...To humiliate me.

THE WOMAN: No. To make you realize that I expected too much from you.

THE MAN: You're lying still! You weren't trying to convince me your demands were excessive – no. You wanted me to realize you were made for a rich lover, someone who could easily satisfy your expensive tastes.

THE WOMAN: Oh my God, you should have worked that out right from the beginning, knowing who I was, the kind of life I was used to leading!

THE MAN: You too knew who I was when we started off. I've never had much money. I did my best to find the means to keep up with your lifestyle, so you wouldn't miss much or make too many sacrifices. And if you were honest about it, you'd guess that everything I've done—

THE WOMAN (*cutting in*): I did guess.

THE MAN: I got up to all sorts of tricks...

THE WOMAN: I guessed... and admired the way you managed to hide any embarrassment you might have experienced...

THE MAN: Because it was nothing to me... it was the least I could do to reward you for allowing me to love you.

THE WOMAN: But you did expect me to—

THE MAN: ...To what?

THE WOMAN: Need you ask? You've appealed to my honesty! You expected me to take into account what it was costing you...

THE MAN: I told you: it cost me nothing. Just as I hoped it would cost you nothing to give up your most expensive tastes.

THE WOMAN: And I did! So as not to force you to spend money I knew you couldn't afford. Oh yes, I did give up a lot, an awful lot. You can't imagine how much!

THE MAN: On the contrary. I can well imagine it.

THE WOMAN: And you call that natural?

THE MAN: Yes... if you loved me, that is.

THE WOMAN: It made me furious!

THE MAN: That I thought it natural?

THE WOMAN: Yes. That simply because I loved you I should stop wanting things! That's why that evening, on purpose, as I walked past the jeweller's window – on purpose I tell you, I did it on purpose just to be cruel!

THE MAN: You believe I didn't realize it?

THE WOMAN: Did you think me cruel?

THE MAN: No. Just a woman.

THE WOMAN (*striking her fist on her knees, then rising*): That again! Can't you understand it's your fault, you men, if women behave as we do, because of the idiotic idea you have of us? It's your fault if we're cruel. It's your fault if we deceive you. It's your fault if we betray you.

THE MAN: Gently, gently now… Why are you getting so worked up? Do you think I'm not aware of the fact you're trying to justify yourself?

THE WOMAN (*turns to him, astonished*): Me?

THE MAN (*steadily*): Yes – you. What's so surprising about that?

THE WOMAN (*embarrassed*): Justify myself? What for?

THE MAN: You know perfectly well what for – I said "just a woman" to balance your word "cruel". I thought it fair, not cruel, that on that particular night as you walked past the jeweller's window you should, in jest and yet seriously make a mouth-watering grimace… (*Imitates a child in the act of eyeing a favourite sweetmeat, at the same time rubbing his hand over his chest.*) "Ooh, how I'd love to have that pearl necklace!"

(*She laughs and, suddenly as she laughs, the set is plunged into darkness. A shaft of light picks out the panels of the gilt casket or cabinet beside the upstage door, which slide open to reveal a lavish jeweller's shop window, displaying many unnatural-looking pieces. Among them, eye-catchingly in the centre and beautifully laid-out on a bed of velvet, is the pearl necklace, which also looks somewhat unnatural. At the very moment the shop window is lit up, like a sudden mirage, the woman will stop laughing. The vision will last for some time and utter silence will prevail. The spotlight on the shop window will render the actors invisible, just as the rest of the room will be plunged in darkness. In any case, the two have turned their backs to the casket. The vision of the jeweller's shop window is intended for the audience only. At a given point two male hands, slender and very white, will be seen parting the curtains within the shop window and then picking up the necklace with great care. Without causing the vision of the jeweller's shop window to disappear, the three pink globes of the chandelier will fade up slowly, revealing the man in evening clothes and the young*) *woman, standing still, entranced by the vision behind them, which causes them to speak stiffly, in an undertone, staring straight ahead.)*

THE MAN: Would you like me to steal them?

THE WOMAN: No. No. It was just a passing thought on my part. I don't want them, not from you! I've already told you that I said I asked for them out of cruelty! You couldn't possibly give them to me unless you stole them!

THE MAN: Or by stealing from others so I could buy them for you! Which is what I am doing! While – didn't you notice? – hands other than mine removed the pearls from the window – for you – and you know it – you know it – *(at this point he relinquishes his rigid manner and turns on her menacingly)* and you dare tell me you don't want them from me any more? Of course you don't want them from me! Someone else will give them to you! You've already betrayed me, you wretch! *(He grabs her by the arms, since she has got up in a fright trying to get away from him.)* And I know who it is! Bitch! *(He shakes her.)* You've gone back to your first lover, haven't you? He's just come back from Java! I saw him! I saw him! He's trying to hide, but I've seen him!

THE WOMAN *(has been struggling with him and now succeeds in breaking free)*: It's not true! It's not true! Let me go!

THE MAN *(seizes her again, throws her onto the sofa and puts his hands round her throat, as if to strangle her)*: Not true? I tell you I've seen him, the loathsome creature! You're expecting him to give you those pearls, while I'm soiling my hands cheating my friends at the club! You're only happy when you can satisfy your cruelty!

(He is on her and about to strangle her. She is already yielding under his savage attack. The lights flicker, then suddenly go out, since she is dreaming she is being strangled by him. Absolute darkness, which is to last only a moment or two.

*During the period of darkness, loud, heavy, surreal knocks
on the door are heard, as though they were reverberating
within the dream. Meanwhile the panels on the console
shaped like a casket will slide shut, and a drape will again
cover it; the mirror will again become a mirror proper, no
longer reflecting the window which, on the left wall, is now
open, admitting the light of the setting sun. The man in
evening clothes has vanished, and the room is lit by soft,
clear daylight. As this light comes up, the hitherto heavy
and loud knocking at the door turns into normal, discreet
knocks – three in fact. At the same time the young woman
will wake up from her dream and raises her hands towards
her throat, a reminder that she had recently been choking.
She takes several deep breaths, which clearly cause her discomfort, and express the fear she experienced in her dream.
She is still surprised by the nature of her dream, and looks
around like someone unsure of the reality of her present
surroundings. She attempts to rise from the couch, but falls
back, her legs too weak to support her. She hides her face
in her hands and sustains this posture for some time. Again
we hear three discreet knocks at the door.)*

THE WOMAN (*stands up and listens for a while before answering*): Come in. (*She steps towards the open window, straight-
ening her hair. A waiter enters, carrying a salver bearing a
jewel case wrapped in the finest tissue paper and tied with a
silver ribbon. He begins to approach her but she stops him.*)
Leave it over there. (*She points to the console. The waiter
leaves the packet as instructed, bows and exits, shutting the
door. She stands still, as if uncertain. In the jewel case is the
precious gift she was expecting. But her joy at receiving it
is countered by the recent nightmare and the menace of its
message. What if the lover she has just seen in her dream in
the act of strangling her should suspect her betrayal, proof
of which is staring at her on the console? She furtively goes*

up to the console, intending to hide the jewel case. She picks it up and looks suspiciously for some time at the entrance door. However, unable to resist the temptation to take a peep, she nervously unwraps the packet, then opens the jewel case. She first takes out a visiting card and reads the words written below the name. Finally, she takes out the pearl necklace, looks at it, admires it and smiles. She clutches it with both hands to her breast and closes her eyes. She tries it on in front of the mirror, but without securing the clasp on the nape of her neck. More knocking at the door. She quickly removes the necklace, picks up the visiting card from the console, opens the small drawer below it, stuffs everything in it and shuts it. She turns to the door.) Who is it? – Come in. *(The waiter enters and hands her a visiting card.)* Show him in. *(Ushered in by the waiter, the man who in the dream was in evening clothes enters. He is now wearing a lounge suit, and is to all appearances calm and collected.)* Darling! Come in, come in. *(The waiter bows and exits, shutting the door.)*

THE MAN *(after kissing her hand at some length)*: Am I late?

THE WOMAN *(affecting the utmost indifference)*: No, no... *(She sits on the sofa.)* Can you tell I've been asleep?

THE MAN *(looks at her carefully)*: Not really. *(In an undertone.)* Just a nap? *(He sits down on a chair.)*

THE WOMAN: Yes. Just now. I suddenly felt very sleepy. Strange...

THE MAN: Any dreams?

THE WOMAN: No. No. The proverbial forty winks, that was all. I don't know... I must have been lying in a cramped position. *(She strokes her neck with her hand.)* I... I suddenly felt I couldn't breathe. *(She smiles.)* Ring the bell, please. Let's have some tea.

(He rises and presses the bell button by the mirror. He sits down again.)

THE MAN: I was afraid I was late. I had a disappointing experience. I'll tell you about it later. (*The waiter knocks at the door and enters.*)

THE WOMAN: We'll have tea now, please. (*The waiter bows and leaves.*) A disappointing experience?

THE MAN: I was planning to surprise you.

THE WOMAN: You? Wanted to surprise me? (*Laughs.*)

THE MAN (*crestfallen*): Why are you laughing?

THE WOMAN: Surprise me? You?

THE MAN: You don't think I can surprise you any more?

THE WOMAN: Of course you can, darling. Anything is possible. But you know how it is. If you've known someone too long, surprises… well – anyway, you sounded so depressed – (*imitating him*) "I wanted to surprise you…" (*Laughs again.*)

THE MAN: I sounded depressed because I was genuinely disappointed.

THE WOMAN: I bet I can guess why.

THE MAN: Guess? What?

THE WOMAN: Wait a moment. Were you disappointed on my behalf, or sorry for yourself?

THE MAN: For you, of course, and me too since I couldn't surprise you.

THE WOMAN: Then I've guessed. And I'll show you you can't surprise me any more. (*Goes behind the chair he is sitting on, puts her arms on his shoulders, without embracing him, but locking her hands together in front, and leans her face on his cheek.*) You really wanted to give me that pearl necklace?

THE MAN: I went into the jewellers to buy it. (*In sudden astonishment:*) Then you knew it had been sold?

THE WOMAN: Yes, darling. That's how I guessed.

THE MAN: How did you know it was sold?

THE WOMAN: Simple! How, you ask? Last night I went past the shop and noticed it was gone.

THE MAN: It was there till four in the afternoon. I saw it myself.

THE WOMAN: Impossible. I was there at about seven: it wasn't there.

THE MAN: That's odd. They told me they sold it this morning.

THE WOMAN: You went and asked?

THE MAN: I went in to buy it. And they said it was sold this morning.

THE WOMAN (*feigning indifference*): Who did they sell it to? Did they say?

THE MAN (*without a trace of suspicion, thus not attaching any importance to her question*): Yes. They sold it to some man. (*Pulls her round in front of him.*) Forgive me, but – since you knew of my disappointment – and guessed immediately it had to do with the necklace – surely that's a sign you'd given it some thought.

THE WOMAN: Not at all.

THE MAN: What do you mean... no? It shows you were expecting me to give you the necklace.

THE WOMAN: Well, I knew you'd been gambling heavily every night at the club, and were on a winning streak...

THE MAN: Quite so. And do you know why? I'm sure of it in fact: because I was so obsessed with your desire to own that necklace – and that obsession somehow helped my game: as a result I kept winning.

THE WOMAN: Have you won a great deal?

THE MAN: Yes. (*With spontaneous warmth:*) And now you'll help me pick some other beautiful pieces for you. Something you really want!

THE WOMAN: No! No!

THE MAN: Please say yes! If only to do away with my disappointment for failing to give you what you coveted!

THE WOMAN: No, darling. I never seriously wanted that pearl necklace, or that you should be the one to provide it. It was all due to a sudden whim, that evening, walking past the shop window... No. I'm going to be good from now on.

THE MAN: I know. I know you're good – so good… to me. All my winnings of the past few nights are yours… all yours. I can assure you of that. I owe it all to you.

THE WOMAN: So much the better! I'm even happier now – that I've brought you luck… and even that you couldn't find the pearls. Let's not talk about it any more, please. (*A knock at the door, and the waiter enters with a groaning tea tray.*) Here's our tea. (*The waiter puts down the tray on a lacquered table by the console and moves it next to the sofa. Just as he starts serving, the woman stops him.*) That's all right, leave it. I'll do it. (*The waiter bows and leaves.*)

THE MAN (*with forced indifference, for the sake of saying something*): Incidentally, I meant to tell you… Guess who is back from Java?

THE WOMAN (*pouring tea*): Yes, yes, I know…

THE MAN: Oh, somebody told you?

THE WOMAN: Yes, the other night… I forget who it was.

THE MAN: They say he's made heaps of money.

THE WOMAN: Milk or lemon?

THE MAN: Milk – thank you.

CURTAIN